Covid-19
Conspiracy Theories

Covid-19
Conspiracy Theories

*QAnon, 5G, the New World Order
and Other Viral Ideas*

JOHN BODNER, WENDY WELCH,
IAN BRODIE, ANNA MULDOON,
DONALD LEECH *AND* ASHLEY MARSHALL

Foreword by Anna Merlan

McFarland & Company, Inc., Publishers
Jefferson, North Carolina

ALSO OF INTEREST BY WENDY WELCH
AND FROM MCFARLAND

*From the Front Lines of the Appalachian Addiction Crisis:
Healthcare Providers Discuss Opioids, Meth and Recovery* (2020)

*Public Health in Appalachia:
Essays from the Clinic and the Field* (2014)

LIBRARY OF CONGRESS CATALOGUING-IN-PUBLICATION DATA

Names: Bodner, John, author.
Title: Covid-19 conspiracy theories : QAnon, 5G, the New World Order and other viral ideas / John Bodner [and five others] ; foreword by Anna Merlan.
Description: Jefferson, North Carolina : McFarland & Company, Inc., Publishers, 2021 | Includes bibliographical references and index.
Identifiers: LCCN 2020047273 | ISBN 9781476684673 (paperback : acid free paper) ∞
ISBN 9781476643212 (ebook)
Subjects: LCSH: COVID-19 (Disease) | Medical misconceptions. | Conspiracy theories.
Classification: LCC RA644.C67 B63 2021 | DDC 362.1962/414—dc23
LC record available at https://lccn.loc.gov/2020047273

BRITISH LIBRARY CATALOGUING DATA ARE AVAILABLE

ISBN (print) 978-1-4766-8467-3
ISBN (ebook) 978-1-4766-4321-2

Printed in the United States of America

*McFarland & Company, Inc., Publishers
Box 611, Jefferson, North Carolina 28640
www.mcfarlandpub.com*

To our long-suffering spouses, partners,
and friends who have patiently supported us
through the frustrations and victories
and obsessions of the writing process—
and who never want to hear about another
conspiracy theory as long as they live

"What *I* know I *know*, what you know you only *believe*...."
—David Hufford

Table of Contents

Foreword by Anna Merlan 1

Introduction 5

ONE. Conspiracy Theory 101: A Primer 9

Two. The "Wuhan Virus": A Cautionary Tale of Origin Conspiracy Theories 29

THREE. Recycling White Power Rumors After the Black Death 59

FOUR. "But My Cousin Said": Covid-19 and Black Communities 73

FIVE. Harmful Additives: Pre- and Pandemic Anti-Vaccination Thinking 95

SIX. Apocalypse Now, or Later? End Times and the New World Order 117

SEVEN. QAnon, Pizzagate and the Pandemic 143

EIGHT. Waves of the Future or Waves of Oppression? 5G Fears 164

NINE. Drawing Lines in Shifting Sand: The Covid-19 Cartoons of Ben Garrison 180

TEN. When All Is Said—or Done: Examining Ourselves, Talking to Others 204

Acknowledgments 218

Author Biographies 219

Chapter Notes 221

References Cited 229

Index 253

Foreword
by Anna Merlan

The Covid-19 pandemic hovered over New York City for months before descending with a sudden, sickening crash in the second week of March. As the caseload ticked up—42 people, then 95, then a dawning, dizzying realization it wasn't going to slow down any time soon—the mayor declared a state of emergency. The governor placed a ban on gatherings over 500 people. The quiet, edgy sense of rising panic could be felt in the streets, the grocery stores, the suddenly anxiety-provoking subway.

And then the fake text messages started to flood in, forwarded from people supposedly in the know.

"A friend just alerted me," one read, "that her friend who works in the emergency management team at the NYPD plans to put containment actions in place this weekend." The text went on to claim that the subways would be partially shut down, all non-emergency vehicles would be banned from the road, and that everyone needed to stock up on cash and food: "Groceries and ATM machines will have limited ability to be refilled." Another widely circulated, entirely fake missive claimed to be from a personal friend of the former mayor's daughter—a wealthy, connected person, the subtext went—who was said to also be preparing for a coming emergency shutdown of the city.

More messages started to circulate nationally: the Department of Homeland Security (DHS) would institute a nationwide lockdown. "Friends of friends" who worked at the CIA and the renowned Cleveland Clinic made similarly dire warnings.

"They will announce this as soon as they have troops in place to help prevent looters and rioters," one message read, supposedly from a friend working at DHS. "He said he got the call last night and was told to pack and be prepared for the call today with his dispatch orders."

The texts were all fake, of course, and their most dire predictions were untrue, but they worked. They sowed panic, and they were spread by people

1

in September 2020 of a coming thaw, my hope is that you read this book in a better and calmer time. Ideally, with the benefit of hindsight, you'll be able to more clearly see the forms that conspiracy theories took in this era, and resolve—as we've resolved so many times before—to greet frightening events with knowledge instead of fear, and with facts instead of conspiracy theories. It's no exaggeration to say that our future depends on it.

Anna Merlan is a journalist based in the United States and the author of Republic of Lies: American Conspiracy Theorists and Their Surprising Rise to Power.

Introduction

Conspiracy thinking might have always been part of our lives, but in times of great uncertainty, it manifests everywhere. The first pandemic of the social media era meant that theories spread faster than, well, a virus. The Flu Pandemic of 1918 (often referred to as "Spanish Flu") encouraged its own conspiracy thinking, but at that time a rumor's spread relied on word of mouth and sensationalized journalism, bolstered by anti-immigrant sentiment. All these were in abundant supply, but nothing fans these sparks into a fire nowadays like the Internet's swift and far-reaching presence. The disease associated with the Severe Acute Respiratory Syndrome Coronavirus 2 (SARS CoV-2) emerged when, in political and a few other contexts, conspiracy was already almost the default way of understanding the world.

This work draws heavily on social media examples throughout the early months of the pandemic, including but not limited to YouTube, Instagram, Twitter, 4chan, and Facebook. Names were changed or removed from these public posts, and the authors practiced their respective discipline's ethical fieldwork guidelines in collecting. Individual authors also held conversations with colleagues via social media or other communication forms; these are identified separately from public posts as private Zoom meetings, phone calls, etc.

We wrote from March through July of 2020, which means George Floyd's murder by police occurred mid-writing; as we worked, we watched societies change. Subsequent protests transformed aspects of the pandemic and introduced a host of traditional and novel rumors and conspiracy theories. While our analysis is informed by these, we could not cover subsequent events with the scholarly rigor and cultural sensitivity they deserve. Others will write those important books later.

You will see several ways of approaching conspiracy theory in this work, given that the team of writers includes public health policy specialists, folklorists, nonprofit directors working in marginalized communities, a medievalist, a speech and communications instructor, and a journalist;

atheists, Christians, and a Jew; people of color and people of European descent; Americans, Canadians, and an ex-pat Brit. We wanted to bring a well-rounded experience to the discussion. We had a grand time introducing one another to our takes on conspiracy theory (and life) while dicing up how we would cover the various topics. You may see occasional differentiation among the voices of those writing because there were six authors. This divergence of voices is perhaps a meta-narration of one of the major themes running through this book: consider the source. That advice has become one of the foundational rules to assessing news and information from any medium. Who said it, when, and why? Our six authors are all academics, each individual bringing a piece to the whole, each speaking in their own authentic voice with unique lived experiences behind their interpretation of facts. Such is life. Would that such ideas were a little less divisive these days. Perhaps we should teach children to discuss hot topics with cool heads in the same way that we teach how to share scissors rather than run with them.

That brings us to a second recurring theme throughout this book, dealt with specifically in the concluding chapter: how to talk to those who disagree with our stance on a particular conspiracy theory. As in, "that's not a conspiracy theory; it's true!" How do we respectfully defend our position with those we love who may wholeheartedly embrace, for instance, QAnon and the Qult (as they spell it) that it has become?

More than ever these days, we need to understand the ways in which conspiracy theories have entered mainstream politics through astroturfing, amplification, and political weaponization—all terms you will find in the first chapter. This book was written for three types of reader: those interested in the pandemic's societal effects; scholars of conspiracy theory, journalism and public relations, rhetoric, speech communication, storytelling, etc.; and university students required to read in depth about any of those topics. This book is also a record of the crisis for future generations, who we fervently hope will lack firsthand experience of what living through a global pandemic was like.

We spend considerable time in the first chapter outlining the structural composition and popular uses of conspiracy theories, in preparation for explaining where the pandemic's CTs (as we occasionally call them for brevity) followed expected patterns, and where they flew far afield or even created new conspiracy theories. (Among other concepts you will discover as you read is that CTs tend to recycle and update rather than spring newly formed from a novel crisis.) If you want to skip all the backgrounding theory and dive into the more intense elements of Covid-19 conspiracy theories, jump over to Chapter Two, but keep in mind that several concepts referenced later are explained in the first chapter. Also, if you are the student mentioned above and you skip Chapter One, you might not ace your final. Just saying.

In Chapter Two, which is about origins, you will find background information on contamination, dirty others, and the double-edged sword of why people want stories to tell about beginnings—plus why science needs those tales to be accurate. Next, we dive into the long, twisted roots of how nothing new, even a novel coronavirus, ever moves that far from the ancient origins of anti–Semitism and the desire of any given group to dominate another. From there we isolate legends that appeared in communities of color, and also show you how historic trauma and earned mistrust factor into differentiating true conspiracies from conspiracy thinking and theory. A long history of health disparity in communities of color has bloomed into a prickly bush of "here we go again" vigilance regarding medical safety and public health. There is also a section on militias, explaining how they fit into and manipulate CTs for their gain.

Chapter Five then moves into anti-vaccination thinking—and trust us when we say, Covid-19 proved a boon to the anti-vaxxers. This group is one of the most educated and motivated in conspiracy-land; we have tried to avoid mischaracterizing their positions by differentiating between their stances against childhood diseases, and a novel global health threat. That chapter paves the way for specific concerns among global End Times adherents, people who believe that a Mark of the Beast (plus all that goes with it) have been accelerated by Covid-19's bursting into the world, which again pulls in militias and the boogaloo movement.

From there we hop into how ostension (the acting out of legend and related narratives like conspiracy theories) factored into QAnon and the Deep State, a prevailing conspiracy theory that has become a lucrative business for some which is approaching near cult status. QAnon hit public awareness during the early months of the pandemic because of Eduardo Moreno, the train engineer charged with one count of train wrecking. No one was injured after Moreno tried to ram the USNS *Mercy* hospital ship docked in Los Angeles's harbor with his train. He jumped the tracks because he believed the ship was there to transport child slaves (Flynn 2020). As old as Armageddon and child abduction based CTs like QAnon are, one new kid on the block appeared in the top conspiracy theories related to Covid-19: 5G technology and their towers. We take you on a tour through the fears, the science, and the scuttlebutt of this novel conspiracy theory for a novel coronavirus.

Finally, as a kind of summation of the wild tour through Covid-19 conspiracies, we offer a pictograph retrospective examining the cartoons of Ben Garrison, whose work you will know even if you don't immediately recognize the name. Some of his cartoons, perhaps most famously "Masks,"

Who believes conspiracy theories, and why?

And not just history; CTs are increasingly defining our future. All too often, conspiracy theories turn murky, even dangerous; historically they have led to wars and toppled governments. When they enter politics and public health, conspiracy theories inflict serious damage.

A 2014 University of Chicago poll found that fully half of all Americans believed at least one conspiracy theory, ranging from 9/11 being an inside job to President Barack Obama not having an American birth certificate (Vedantam 2014). A 2020 podcast series sponsored by *The Conversation* put the number of people who believe at least one conspiracy theory as high as 80 percent (Bligh 2020). LiveScience.com posted in September 2019 that 29 percent of Americans reported belief in a "Deep State" conspiracy trying to take down U.S. President Donald Trump (Vittert 2019); QAnon, as this group was known, gained fertile ground during the pandemic.[4] Specific to Covid-19, the Pew Research Center conducted a survey from March 10–16, 2020, and found that three in ten Americans believed the virus was purposely created in a laboratory. A May 4–11 survey in the United Kingdom said one in five people believed the virus was bio-engineered, with 19 percent of that group agreeing that "Jews have created the virus to collapse the economy for financial gain" (Freeman et al. 2020).

Conspiracy theories are widespread in modern society, and studied across a wide range of fields: political science, folklore, psychology, history, religion, and media studies examine CTs, with perhaps less cross-pollination of the wisdom each field has collected than the world currently needs. A great deal of history, sociology and psychology lies embedded in the actions of those who believe CTs, but key differences remain between what we could call mainstream academic disciplines and those conspiracy theorists. Of course, "conspiracy" is the key to any definition that distinguishes a mainstream theorist from the conspiracy theorist—and you will also see the word "elites" used to describe and silence mainstreams who contest CTs. And per Knight and Hofstadter, the existence of real conspiracies in history, such as the Tuskegee Study we will be discussing in a few chapters, provide indisputable facts that sometimes unthinkable things happen because small, powerful groups implement a secret plan. The problem of differentiating between actual and fantastic conspiracies lies in defining facts, plausibility and bias. However you define the practice it is a growing problem.

Types and categories

Conspiracy theory is a label that outsiders (like your authors) put on the kind of story people tell when trying to interpret events that seem threatening to them—personally or within their community. People active in conspiracy theory communities call themselves researchers, truthers, and woke, not conspiracy theorists; any person assigning the CT label doesn't share that sense of threat. Although this makes its use insulting to some, conspiracy theory is a troublesome label we are stuck with. In this and other ways, conspiracy theories are similar to myths.

"Myth" is a difficult term because it has the common understanding of being a mere falsehood or, as in the case of things like the Greek myths, an ancient story. Anthropologists and folklorists use myth to refer to foundational narratives that fundamentally inform a group about who they are. They often deal with creation: how the world, humans, and/or this particular group came into existence; their events are typically extraordinary, supernatural, often religious. Myths are not metaphorical to the group from which they originate, although they can later be taken as such, and often are by sympathetic outsiders who like the story but don't believe it in a literal way. The extraordinariness in the myth is part of the belief system for the culture that created it: God *did* enter history by sending his son to bring good news; Prometheus *literally* brought fire to humanity. To believe the story is to be a member; to not believe, even in sympathetic dismissal, is to be not a member. Myths are intellectual and moral certainties that inform how the entire universe is to be understood from a shared platform of values. That binary of belief and belonging informs and orients an individual's worldview, if not defining it outright.

A myth can also be about events that are externally verifiable rather than supported only by the consensus of the group. We can therefore refer to the myth of the American Founding Fathers without being insulting. The remarkable intellectual activity, personal risk, and military skill that occasioned American independence is shaped and reshaped over time from the actions of admirable yet flawed people into a narrative that is virtually sacred, as the concept of "civil religion" suggests (Bellah 1967)—which helps explain why recent debates against the removal of historic monuments sometimes employed a sacrilege analogy.

Like myths, CTs would very much benefit from being considered holy texts, or at least earnest and intense efforts at communicating how the conspiracy should shape your life, because it is important that you know how the world works. As such, in whatever form they take, CTs communicate, strengthen, justify, and reaffirm their core theme while inviting others into the belief. On their surface lie the communicative means to get that deep meaning into our acceptance zone, past our defenses if we aren't already sympathetic to the core theme—words, pictures, humor; underneath the form of the CT bubbles a need for us to understand something vital to our safety.

As diverse as the expression of a CT can be, the content still tends to have predictable parts. Where a rumor might be vague—foreigners brought a disease, e.g.—CTs will identify a specific group; competent conspiracy theorists avoid vagueness across all their myriad expressive forms because the urgency of the message demands detail.

Political scientist Michael Barkun (2013) lays out three types of CTs: event conspiracies around a specific, limited set of events (e.g., the Kennedy Assassination or the moon landing); systemic conspiracies focusing on a group taking over a specific system (e.g., Freemasons, Deep State); and super-conspiracies that connect multiple conspiracy beliefs across systems and actors (e.g., QAnon). In each form, a group will be blamed for our current crisis, and suggestions for how to remove them will be made. The differences between Barkun's conspiracy types are how large, invisible, and potentially nefarious the set of actors may be. Barkun also suggests categorizing CTs five ways, based on *where* the enemy is located: outside enemies (in the pandemic, Wuhan); enemies within society (militias or Satanists); enemies above (powerful people as specific as Jewish bankers or imprecise as "elites"); enemies below (marginalized communities); and benevolent conspirators (secret forces for good, Trump vs. the Deep State).[5]

In conspiracy theory real people are transformed into archetypal characters to fill a role. Various Deep State conspiracies you will see later in this book transform Donald Trump into the perfect hero, a veritable holy warrior, while Hillary Clinton becomes the monster, the villain who smells of sulfur—if Alex Jones is to be believed in his October 10, 2016, broadcast. Other stock characters include the dupe, accomplice, coconspirator, deep cover source, whistleblower, etc.

Conspiracy theories almost always open with a bid for authority. The writer will outline their vast research, or self-identify as a doctor, government whistleblower or other appropriate insider figure you should believe (although they often are not who they claim, surprise, surprise); or the information is marked as coming from an institution or media source trusted by the conspiracy community. Such theories are often couched as happening to a friend-of-a-friend; "FOAFtale" was coined as a nickname for contemporary/urban legends, and it often appears in their close cousin conspiracy theories as well (Dale 1978). The person sharing the story or meme will assert a relationship to the victim or hero, but when pressed will have multiple, perhaps untraceable, degrees of separation.

Two kinds of knowledge authority permeate conspiracy theories, recognizable by anyone who has ever taught a speech class on persuasion: scientific or other mainstream academic experience, and personal experience, often called lived experience. Conspiracy narratives based on experience skip scientific authenticity and appeal using personal relationships.

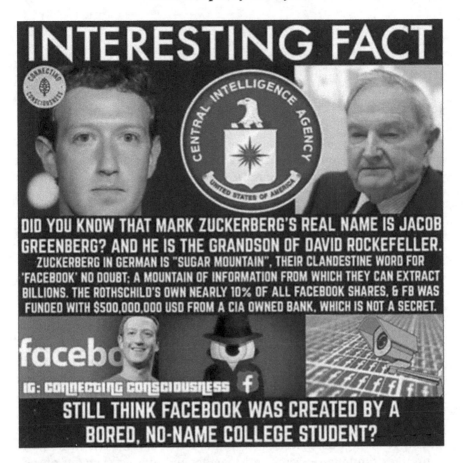

Figure 1.1. An image macro (since deleted) from Instagram user @connecting_ consciousness, broadly circulating.

Both appeals attempt to command authority and withstand surface scrutiny using obfuscation or outright lies laid over facts, while the whole story or meme is laced with emotional appeal. Emotional appeal is a big factor in the success of CTs; if the theory can make you angry or frightened, you will be less likely to sift past the first layer of evidence to the point where the theory breaks down. Disinformation runs on emotion (Jankowitz 2020). In fact, CTs often use emotion to zip past logical checkpoints.

In this meme (Figure 1.1) even casual skepticism would reason that, given how long Facebook has been around, if Zuckerberg were descended from the Rockefellers, this information would have been plastered everywhere years ago. The meme (ironically shared widely on Facebook) tries to get past that breakdown point with a bid for authority (a fake CIA crest). CTs generally use a kernel of truth to wrap false information in credibility.

In this example, the German translation of Zuckerberg really is Sugar Mountain.

Academic authority bids, as Figure 1.1 shows, prove a bit trickier. It is hard to muster authority from nothing, and communities like anti-vaccination parents or New World Order anti-globalists[6] also tend to reject standard sources such as mainstream media, universities, and governmental departments. This radical distrust is one of the reasons why conspiracy thinking values whistleblowers so highly. Conspiracy theorists need the information contained in various institutions but do not trust the officials therein, so only an apostate who has converted to the Truth can bring them actual data.

Conspiracy thinking seems at first glance to be separate from belief in those things one might call superstitions or the supernatural, as they involve contemporary concerns and "real" actors (however much the CT about Bill Gates versus the real man may diverge). Traditional beliefs commingle effortlessly with conspiracy thinking, yet supernatural influences and narratives are often hidden behind a curtain of mundane human agents and their actions. The Satanic Panic CTs of the 1980s,[7] anti-vaccination CTs throughout history, and various Covid-19 CTs often espouse a narrative that a New World Order is accelerating the onset of Armageddon, but only the first acknowledges the existence of demons. To say Bill Gates is part of a One World Government cabal getting The Final Battle started is one thing; to acknowledge that this concept is, in Christian and Muslim belief, a final battle between demonic and heavenly forces means one has to place Gates on a supernatural chessboard. This makes for unexamined dichotomies leading to strange alliances. Different (and even seemingly antagonistic) conspiracy communities can come together and support elements of each other's worldview if they don't look too closely at every element. For example, Boogaloo Bois (whom you will meet in a later chapter) also believe in a coming showdown between good and evil, but cast it as a second American Civil War more than an Armageddonesque angels-against-demons fight, but the basic shapes of the stories are similar, down to a perfect ethnostate as the Boogaloo heaven.

Covid-19 has broken down normally siloed CT communities that would not have interacted yet nevertheless share worldviews and deep stories. Deep stories is Arlie Hochschild's term to describe the various underlying narratives that partially explain how different communities (right or left; working class or wealthy; rural or urban) perceive and interpret the world around them. They are similar to secular myths and act as "the paradigms through which we viscerally experience everyday life. We feel our way into deep stories" and those feelings will form the core of how we frame our worldviews (quoted in Phillips and Milner 2020).

During the pandemic new affiliations and group configurations are rising as groups converge around shared deep stories of individual freedom and its dark, fearful inversion: One World Government. As one example, anti-lockdown Facebook pages throughout spring 2020 brought together liberal anti-vaxxers and conservative militias in an unlikely affinity, a pragmatic the-enemy-of-my-enemy-is-my-friend alliance because of a shared deep story about the nature of individualism and freedom (Hume 2020).

Finally, we have to recognize that conspiracy theory is a group project, a kind of snowball storytelling. In the same way that you roll snow into increasingly large spheres to form snowmen (or start an avalanche), studying groups online reveals the slow accumulation of datasets, interpretations and arguments, preserved in all their chaotic glory and added (when applicable) to the ever-growing narrative. Borrowing observations from fandom studies shows how this process works. Camille Bacon-Smith, an early scholar on fan communities, said no one person could manage the wealth of information for any given fan source texts (book or movie series, for example). The collective work of many people sharing information on fan sites is necessary to help fans navigate the vast amount of information which also provides one type of meaningful engagement with the source text and creates a community of fellow fans (1992). The Internet has made such lovefests easier, but it also created even greater amounts of information. In that ocean of info one needs a collective to avoid missing insights or opportunities. With conspiracy theories, groups like QAnon takes collective creation, preservation and distribution to a higher level than previously seen in CT communities. On the more chaotic anti-lockdown Facebook groups, CT construction is also shaped by multiple opinions. Emojis and silence, among other interactions, signal approval or disapproval; subsequent posters build on what gained praise and drop what was criticized or ignored. Over time and through literally thousands of repetitions, a consensus as to what kind of theory the community will support shapes the online narratives.[8]

Such narratives will also be told orally for proselytizing and socializing; a way of looking at this snowball form of storytelling comes from folklorist Margaret Yocum (1997). She studied family sagas, a saga being a story made up of a multitude of smaller stories. No one person can know all the family stories that make up the saga, so at gatherings participants contribute various stories that they know but others may not, each contribution a thread to the cloth-like saga the family will never finish weaving. In doing so, they preserve and perpetuate the stories; the stories need the family, and the family need the stories. In the same way, communities that form via conspiracy theories tell discrete pieces of a larger snowballing story that adapts over time, and also responds to hostile debunking forces that surround the communities.

Psychology

Family matters often lead eloquently into mental and behavioral health. In this realm, examinations of CTs tend to take the approach shared by Jan-Willem van Prooijen, associate professor of psychology at Vrije Universiteit Amsterdam in the Netherlands. He suggested that humans are "hardwired" toward CT belief because of pattern recognition. The predisposition is in essence a holdover from when we were hunter-gatherers. Pattern recognition is a survival mechanism ranging from simple (distinguishing the markings of a predator from the background foliage pattern) to complex (anticipating negative outcomes from individual or group actions). Misinterpreting independent and unconnected phenomena as forming a pattern is a key feature of conspiracy thinking. Working alongside faux pattern recognition to make CTs persuasive and convincing is a feature associated with risk assessment: what are the consequences of a false negative versus a false positive. Essentially this means the fallout from being right or wrong about a threat. Assume a cloth mask worn correctly will reduce your likelihood of coronavirus infection, and if it doesn't, you have inconvenienced yourself but no harm is done. But if you decide not to wear a mask, and they do help prevent infection, you harmed yourself and others. The risk assessment hardware in our brains urges us to give greater weight to negative consequences. Or, for those who prefer the academic language version, "people possess a functionally integrated mental system to detect conspiracies that in all likelihood has been shaped in an ancestral human environment in which hostile coalitions—that is, conspiracies that truly existed—were a frequent cause of misery, death, and reproductive loss" (van Prooijen and van Vugt 2018:776). Those well-versed in economic theory may hear echoes of the term "risk-adverse."

One further conspiracy thinking trait examined in psychology overlaps with folklore: people will simultaneously believe in two contradictory theories, even when it is pointed out to them. In a study conducted at the University of Kent, psychologists showed that participants who believed Osama bin Laden was already dead when American Special Forces raided his compound, also believed he still lives and has been granted safe passage to a neutral country. Mutually exclusive ideas held simultaneously point to conspiracy thinking as enabling a monological belief regarding whomever is our conspiracy theory's villain; we can believe anything bad about them, even contradictory things. Be it Bill Gates, the government of one's country, or the super-rich secretive society that meets annually in Davos, Switzerland, the villain of the conspiracy theory is horrible. That's the important part to the theorist. Conspiracy theories may play fast and loose with facts, but are brutally consistent in trajectory. If we believe that Gates wants to make Black people sterile and will give away the vaccine for free so all the Black people get it, we can also believe that he wants to make everyone pay big money to take his vaccine in annual doses for the rest of our lives. If he can't do both things at the same time, he is still capable of being bad enough to do both, so it doesn't matter if we repeat both kernel narratives about him. Believing both is a product of conspiracy thinking that prioritizes the goal of exposing the bad actor: within conspiracy thinking, truth can be a casualty so long as Truth remains (Wood, Douglas and Sutton 2012).

It will greatly help your understanding of Covid-19 conspiracies if you look less for logical adherence to a single theory than theories grouped in colluding or even conflicting circles around the same bad actors. People are not monogamous in conspiracy theory love affairs.

Politics

Least of all in politics. Conspiracy theories have long been useful to encourage or quash grass-roots mobilization for or against powerful political figures. Any nation's leader will be the subject of dozens of CTs during his or her reign. Yet such rumors die when their term ends; that Bush spearheaded 9/11 or that Obama was born in Kenya raged during their presidencies and dissipated when they left office. According to political scientists Joseph Uscinski and Joseph Parent, people stop caring when the target of their concern loses power over them (2014). Also, Uscinski was firm on the point that liberals and conservative alike hold CTs, in almost equal measure. He defended this idea in a May 14, 2020, podcast for fivethirtyeight (Druke and Koerth 2020). A differentiation and predisposition to feel that CTs form more on the right than the left stems from media engagement and current political actors, Uscinski said. This idea is unpleasant to contemplate for people of all political persuasions; we each want to believe that it is "the other side" that holds silly theories, while we, to echo David Hufford, *know* what we know.

Unique to the era preceding and entering the pandemic, say political scientists who study conspiracy theory, is the rise of world leaders willing to promulgate and capitalize on CTs. While conspiracy theory has never left politics, it had seen a rise with the concomitant global rise in populism. As Covid-19 took hold, world leaders began a blame game that uses conspiracy theories like nefarious origins of the virus, the Deep State, and/

for the veracity of the data/fact. Second, they will argue a relationship exists between sets of data/facts. Third, they will provide as an overarching interpretation of the first two points that a conspiracy to do harm is afoot and that the conspirators need to be identified. Sometimes, as in Cunial's case, the data are stripped of their original context to better work with the CT she wishes to promulgate: that Gates is a genocidal pandemic profiteer. In all of his public speeches it is clear that Gates doesn't want to kill people; he wants to lessen high birth rates that are a natural consequence of high infant mortality rates. But someone who reads "fewer births" as synonymous with "anti-life" (such as those whose faith prohibits abortion or, at least, encourages one to be fruitful and multiply) can hear the same information as a Gates supporter and conclude a separate meaning. His pro-birth-control stance would uphold Cunial's belief that Gates is evil. So the Italian politician added words Gates did not actually say to make her meaning certain, a clarification she perhaps considered in keeping with the Truth that needed to be told. Or perhaps Cunial believed Gates said "genocide," having not fact-checked that quote from whoever sourced it to her. The added sentence confirmed her bias against Gates, so she went with her gut. This is common in that snowball effect of conspiracy theory storytelling: additives happen. Capital "T" Truth is not allowed to be a casualty in legitimate persuasion, another marker for discerning whether a person is engaged in fact-finding and fact-sharing, or conspiracy-spreading.

Confirmation bias

Cunial would have been influenced by her confirmation bias; population reduction is not likely to go over well in a Catholic country. We all hold confirmation bias, a concept easy to point out in accusation, yet difficult to describe in dispassionate terms. Everyone, including the authors of this book, its readers, and those who confirm or refute the theories discussed herein, has confirmation bias.

The term was coined by English Psychologist Peter Wason in 1960. Popular terms synonymous or aligned with confirmation bias include myside bias, denial, fake news or fake news syndrome, cherry picking, and echo chambers and filter bubbles (those last two particularly relevant in social media). Confirmation bias is a tendency (resulting from several smaller cognitive operations) to favor, remember, and recall information that aligns with your preexisting beliefs.

In essence, confirmation bias intertwines lived experience with ethnocentrism, as well as cultural upbringing (Plous 1993). Ethnocentrism is evaluating other cultures in relation to our own as the highest standard, a kind of unexamined assumption that developing nations in Africa, for example, want to "evolve" to become like Canada or the United States. Our backgrounds, surroundings and personal experiences shape our beliefs. It is not "wrong" to have confirmation bias or ethnocentrism; these are innate. But it is unwise to ignore their influence on how we process and create information. Self-awareness of our own biases is a powerful learning tool.

An example: statistically you have a far better chance of surviving a car wreck while wearing a seatbelt, although in more than half of all such fatalities, the person wore a belt. In rare instances, seatbelts contribute to rather than prevent death. Were a family member to be in such an incident and survive because they didn't wear their seat belt, they may never wear one again and, perhaps, neither will you. At first this will be understood as based solely on lived experience but, turning back to the statistics, if over half of fatalities were wearing a belt, are they any safer? Lived experience contributes to confirmation bias and wars with scientific evidence; seatbelts have been proven to reduce fatalities by 45 percent.[11] We look first for what confirms our experiences and/or beliefs, and the lived experience of a close family member outstrips the lived experience of the many, because the many show up as mere statistics. They don't look like lived experience, but "scientific proof," or "empirical evidence." Depending on your natural bias toward such sources and your relationship to your loved one, they may be more trustworthy in your mind. Because of this confirmation bias, you are statistically at a higher risk of dying in a car crash.

Resistance to seat belt laws in the 1980s echoed Covid-19 mask mandates beginning in May 2020. A 1984 Gallup poll found 65 percent of Americans opposed laws making the belts mandatory (Ackerman 2020). The rhetoric against both is similar; in a hard-biting *Chicago Tribune* editorial in February of 1987, William J. Holdorf wrote, "In this country, saving freedom is more important than trying to regulate lives through legislation," and concluded his editorial with "Safety imposed is freedom lost." Ralph Nadar, the consumer safety expert who campaigned for seat belts, was interviewed some 30 years later about the parallels between the two protests. He thought mask protestors were more likely displaying "an ornery personality trait" than following a political agenda (Ackerman 2020).

Mask wearing has proven to be one of the most wrought issues of the pandemic as spring gave way to the heat of summer. Like earlier debates about seat belts, it reflected a giant fracture in social values. On one side were those emphasizing civic duty—considering their responsibility to help and protect others in their community, versus those emphasizing personal liberty—the desire for full autonomy with no legal restrictions or responsibilities (Rozsa et al. 2020). The latter group found their biases confirmed in dubious studies that claimed mask wearing was dangerous; these posts rapidly spread across anti-lockdown groups. Memes about masks evincing fear or cowardice also confirmed individual positive self-identities of anti-lockdown protesters as brave patriots. New World Order–One World Government tyranny creep conspiracy theories abounded around masks—"tyranny creep" is a type of slippery slope or "boiling frog" theory where our loss of freedoms goes largely unnoticed because of its slow erosion through small incremental anti-freedom acts and policies. Masks, tyranny creep, and boiling frogs abounded on social media throughout the long hot summer of 2020. No amount of debunking through sharing conflicting scientific studies did much to change the conversation in anti-lockdown Facebook groups monitored by one of our authors. This division based largely on confirmation bias and shared deep stories sometimes turned to violence. As businesses tried to enforce mask wearing, employees found themselves subjected to threats, assault, and on several occasions, shot and killed (Kornfield 2020; MacFarquhar 2020).

The use or threat or force to protect one's "freedom" escalated to such a level that American militia members carried military style semi-automatic rifles, ammo vests, and other paramilitary gear in March–May 2020 as they attended lock-down protests at state capitals. The mask issue, and related debates, seem to follow along the lines of Hofstadter's *The Paranoid Style in American Politics* rather than any specific CT: summarized, the protestors felt that following requirements for public health and safety equated to socialism, and were therefore destructive of American values (Morse 2020). Later, after the killing of George Floyd brought out supporters of the Black Lives Matter movement in separate protests, similar heavily armed figures appeared saying they were there to assist police in keeping order against "rioters" and the issue of masks grew entangled with BLM protestors complying or not, and being accused of spreading Covid-19 by the original protestors who refused to wear masks in the first place. Yes, that is as convoluted as it sounds.

One final point should be made: confirmation bias not only influences how we read scientific evidence and statistics, it also encourages us to forget what does not fit our personal belief and remember what does. If you tell the story of your family member's car accident at a party and three people think it anomalous but one person says, "Oh, that happened to my cousin!" you may later retell the cousin story, but you will most likely dismiss and forget the other remarks. You may not even realize that you've heard stories at a 3:1 ratio against your belief. Lived experience confirmation outweighs empirical evidence refutation in memory, just as it did at the point where you decided seat belts were unsafe. This relates back to the convolution of anti-mask militiamen grousing on Facebook that BLM protestors don't wear masks. We can believe conflicting information at the same time, without examining that we believe it. Those we despise will spread Covid-19 by not wearing masks; we can refuse a mask and everything will be fine. What's the cognitive problem?

Conspiracy theories tend to rely on confirmation bias to gain entry to our minds. As you will see in the QAnon chapter, we might consider someone whose politics we don't like corrupt anyway. When we hear they are running a child sex abuse ring in the basement of a pizza shop (even if said shop doesn't have a basement) we will grab hold of that theory, store it in our brains, and add it to other negative information about those politicians. Persuasion theory (out of communication studies) confirms what confirmation bias teaches us: that people who did not believe the politician was bad in the first place would dismiss the pizza child trafficking ring from their minds with nary a second thought.

Somewhere in the middle, in the territory of an open mind seeking facts, a person could hear about Pizzagate, go look at a picture of the pizzeria to confirm it lacks the requisite basement, examine who was pushing the CT, and decide, "Much as I would like Pizzagate to be true because I don't like that politician, this is bad intel." That person exhibited no predisposition based on bias, or perhaps overcame it because they had trained themselves to ask productive question of themselves and information. That person might not exist in America these days, first because it is such a divided country, and secondly because they took time to investigate beyond reading article headlines.

Amplification and astroturfing

Now is a good time to mention two terms that relate to fact-checking and critical thinking. Whole books have been written about each concept, so we just want to provide you with a working definition here, because they relate to the ability to research conspiracy theories effectively. Amplification is when platform gatekeepers (such as news shows) give conspiracy theorists (or their ideas) an opportunity to speak, often in an effort to publish a fair and balanced viewpoint. On July 26, Sinclair Broadcast Group was criticized for giving Dr. Judy Mikovits (of *Plandemic*) a media platform.[12] Mikovits attempted to discredit pandemic response scientists in the interview (Aleem 2020). A growing concern exists in free market media that ascertaining who has factual information as a criterion for news platform access has become less important than not seeming biased. This makes journalistic decisions about who to cover, and in what way, difficult.

To give a conspiracy theory air time is to feed it; sadly, to try and squelch one by refusing it air time is to reinforce the belief that the theory is correct, and therefore dangerous to "elites" who control airwaves and professional platform time.

Astroturfing is a pun on grass-roots; where the latter term refers to spontaneous action from concerned citizens, astroturfing references hidden agents who deliberately cultivate concerns. In its literal Merriam-Webster definition, it is "organized activity that is intended to create a false impression of a widespread, spontaneously arising, grassroots movement in support of or in opposition to something (such as a political policy) but that is in reality initiated and controlled by a concealed group or organization (such as a corporation)." As an example, domains using the word reopen proliferated beginning in March 2020; the firm KrebsonSecurity researched the domain codes and found several funded by gun advocacy groups (2020).

Cause and effect

Conspiracy theories offer a sense of control. As we noted early in this chapter, they offer a way of understanding change and causality. Everything happens for a reason; no such thing as accidents exist; negative events are the result of human intervention acting out in secret; and these actors and their plots are discoverable. You'll note that this idea of causality imagines the world as a set of interpersonal relationships with a direct, almost mechanical relationship between the results plotters desire and the actions necessary to bring them about. Think of the Wizard furiously pulling levers and cranks as Toto draws back the curtain to an incredulous Dorothy. In this worldview, structures, institutions, technology and systemic ideological constructs cannot perpetuate horrible things like deindustrialization, ecological racism and its negative health outcomes, or the intergenerational trauma of BIPOC (Black, Indigenous, People of Color) communities.[13] That's because in CTs nothing happens independent of any specific human act or desire. Because CTs reject and do not contain "systemic" explanations, they prove remarkably democratic. Anyone can become a researcher with the hope of exposing the villains. And because of the promise that the plots are knowable and the solution to an ill is exposing the villains, the task seems attainable by people with a wide variety of skill sets.

Consequently, someone who participates in conspiracy research becomes an actor rather than a passive victim. They *know* things. They are not one of the sheeple[14] but an awakened observer who can discern actions that will free us from the entangling snare of (pick one): One World Government; the Illuminati; or 5G technology towers. Using their skills and creativity helps conspiracy thinkers understand the world and "wake" a wider community of researchers. Where these communities gain a place on the Internet, like QAnon on a bulletin board like 8kun, individuals can take on roles within the community, garnering praise and some elevated social status within the group. Thus, participating in conspiracy theories can be thought of as a therapeutic response to personal and social contexts of tensions and crises. Problem is, participation cannot solve the underlying issues the individual faces because CTs identify the wrong causes and solutions.

Conspiracy theories have the unfortunate side effect of isolating people, even those who want to be agents for change and to address the underlying problem. An experiment exposing people to made-up conspiracy theories showed an immediate suppressing effect on their sense of control and autonomy, making them less inclined to take actions such as voting or engaging in mainstream politics; instead they isolate into self-containment or ally themselves solely with the group researching and transmitting the CT (Douglas and Leite 2017; Jolley and Douglas 2014a, 2014b). In part because of the isolationist tendencies they promulgate, conspiracy theories confirm cohesion within specific like-minded groups. Cohesiveness is a powerful draw in uncertain or lonely times.

Besides its role in group solidarity, conspiracy theories offer certainty when science can't keep up—like during a pandemic during which information on best health practice changes almost daily. Just as nature abhors a vacuum, the human appetite for explanations cannot abide there being none forthcoming. If one is not available through empirical evidence—or not available fast enough—a conspiracy theory will rush in to fill the void. Most Covid-19 CTs recycle older ideas, revamped and energized for this crisis, with one exception. As we will see in the chapter devoted to them, 5G found novel placement in relation to Covid-19. For the rest, the pandemic has been both a crisis and an opportunity. Making room within the logic of the conspiracy to contain and explain the pandemic caused difficulties among New World Order conspiracy theorists, among others, when President Trump began wearing a mask in July 2020 and said it was patriotic to do so; contact tracing (which he also semi-approved in summer speeches) and masks could suddenly no longer be cast as creeping totalitarianism to a portion of conspiracy adherents who support the President while for others these pronouncements could be explained away and the basic shape of conspiracy thinking retained. Attracting new adherents and expanding networked ecosystems came easily to other groups like militias, anti-vaxxers, and Qult members during the pandemic. Within the ancient frameworks of scapegoating outsiders, blaming the devil or his earthly minions, and denigrating non-whites, we find the uncomfortable roots of such stories as QAnon, the New World Order, and virus origins.

Hence, the world in which we find ourselves today. Let's now dive into the stories of several Covid-19 conspiracy theories.

Two

The "Wuhan Virus"

A Cautionary Tale
of Origin Conspiracy Theories

"Once there was, and twice there wasn't"—traditional Turkish
story opening

If you haven't read the introduction, be warned that several terms
explained there go flying by here at lightning speed. We are about to
dive into the conspiracy theories around the origins of the coronavirus
pandemic.

Conspiracy theories often play into the dangerous human instinct
to fixate on finding the origins of a disease, and it is here that CTs closely
mimic academic history, and make bids for scientific authenticity. Theories
of where the virus came from follow an age-old instinct to identify scapegoats, as we will see in this chapter and the one comparing the Black Death
era to Covid-19.

Paradox of origins

Let us start with the more ironic elements of seeking "how did we get
here" stories with which to comfort (or perhaps enflame) ourselves and
those around us. In her study on HIV/AIDS and contemporary legend,
folklorist Diane Goldstein says the following about the human desire for
and use of origins, AKA etiological, stories: "[Origin tales] speculate about
how we came to our current state of being, how the things that we take to be
normative developed or appeared where once they were not. AIDS narratives are no different. A significant part of AIDS legendary tradition betrays
our obsession with origins" [2004:77].

The natural desire to explain the present through narratives that
appear to be about the past is universal—and leads to the paradox of origins

in a pandemic. On the one hand, scientists, epidemiologists, and public health specialists need origin information to plan health interventions: where did the virus start; what was its original genetic structure; when did a new cluster of cases begin? All these questions provide vital data to understand and control the virus. However, when lay people begin the same quest, it often turns into a blame game, more symbolic and explanatory than utilitarian. Curiosity is one thing; seeking a scapegoat is another. Lay inquiry turns dangerous when it seeks someone to blame for our current predicament, rather than baseline understanding for how to get out of it. As Goldstein has noted:

> The question of origins is by definition a question of the transgression of alien substances (the virus) across categorical boundaries into the familiar; in other words, it is necessarily about contamination. The events are extraordinary, controversial, and they invite debate. They threaten cultural norms and encourage the expression of opinions, variants, and negotiated facts [2004:79].

Folklorist Jon D. Lee noted that research on pre-revolutionary France's surviving records of plagues and cholera outbreaks produced stories of "voluntary spreaders of the illness, poisoners of fountains, greasers of door knobs, perverse doctors, nurses … [and] killing vaccines" (2014:60). All of these elements appeared as key features in the unfolding global pandemic.

Citing Margaret Humphreys (2002), Lee likewise observes that "panic over diseases with foreign origins begets racism and xenophobia, since those diseases are blamed upon the people who inhabit the country of the disease's origin" (61). The racialized character of the disease forms the backbone of various competing and evolving dialogue and conspiracy theories surrounding Covid-19.

The World Health Organization is very aware of this. In order to limit the tendency to stigmatize geographic regions or countries and associate them with multiple negative connotations of "contagion," since 2015 WHO has suggested labeling diseases based on (among others) the type of pathogen or the symptom. Thus the "Wuhan Virus" is known officially as SARS-CoV-2 when referring to the specific coronavirus and Covid-19 for the disease (named on February 11, 2020).

Despite what WHO recommended, and perhaps offering an object lesson for why they changed the rules in the first place, closely associating the disease with China and Wuhan produced an avalanche of stereotypes, racist names, memes and eventually the scapegoating of China and ethnically Chinese peoples in various countries. Bloomberg published an opinion piece on February 16 under the headline "OPEC Underestimates China Virus"—five days after the official WHO statement (Lee 2020). The *Washington Post* republished it with the same headline later that day. The American president rewrote a prepared speech on March 19, 2020, scratching out the official name of the disease to insert "China." This was widely criticized; as several historians and a survey piece in the *Washington Post* noted (Shafer 2020), blaming others by naming the flu after their country (along with many conspiracy theories) influenced how the Spanish flu pandemic (1918–1920) was perceived. Critics and healthcare organizations worldwide characterized the President's edit as attempting to shift public attention away from the Federal government's failure to assist in pandemic preparation, such as through procuring healthcare equipment like personal protective gear and ventilators.

Food

The President's renaming may or may not have influenced others, but on and off the Internet, naming the plague took various forms. Most played with its origin (Wuflu) or featured racist and cultural stereotypes, like "kung flu," a term the U.S. President used at a rally in Tulsa in late June (Khalil 2020). It was almost predictable that identifying the Chinese city of Wuhan, one of its wet markets, and bats as the origin of the virus would be accompanied by depictions in the West of "bat soup" alongside other stigmatized food items. Photographs and videos of dogs being butchered and consumed, along with insects and various wild animals, were widely shared across all social media once the origin of the virus became publicly known in January 2020. In a January 29 cartoon titled "Chinese Takeout," political cartoonist Ben Garrison depicted a Chinese dragon in gastronomic discomfort, eating from a plate piled high with animals foreign to Western and Northern food traditions. The cartoon was Garrison's first reference to the coming pandemic, but also nodded to the persistent and racist contemporary legend of dogs going missing from neighborhoods where Chinese restaurants open, by depicting an empty collar with the tag "Fido" clearly visible on the dragon's table (see Bennett and Smith 1993).

The use of food in contagion folklore is powerful for two reasons. First, food is central to how we build personal, social and cultural identities, so social categories of what is and what is not "food" (chickens and cows as opposed to bats and horses) help distinguish borders between groups. Second, food is linked to contamination because it literally enters our bodies to become part of us. As Goldstein noted, being infected with a virus because of alien foodways has the ability to invoke visceral disgust. Such a reaction supports the need to tell legends and conspiracy theories in order to work through a social crisis, but disgust is also part of the pleasure in hearing and sharing contamination legends. The twin emotions of disgust and outrage keep narratives circulating, transmitting their symbolic pay-load to the next listener, reader, or viewer (84).[1]

"Bat soup" or simply bat wings attached to incongruous images, have thus become a motif in several digital folk art expressions, including the 4chan mascot "Corona-chan," an anime-style illustration of "a young Asian woman dressed in a red qipao dress, holding a Chinese flag and a bottle of Corona beer in her hands," while sporting bat wings (Philipp 2020). The hundreds of graphics vary from public health oriented content, kawaii-influenced depictions, to overtly racist, sexist and pornographic drawings. All of these reference the geographic origin of the pandemic, pinpointing Ground Zero for the viral load.

Patient Zero

A second type of origin is the popular notion of a Patient Zero, known as an "index case" in medical terms.[2] Some well-known patient zeros of yore include Mary Malone, an Irish immigrant who earned fame via the catch-phrase "Typhoid Mary," and Gaëten Dugas, a flight attendant once thought to be the North American index patient for HIV/AIDS. The film *93 Days* (Gukas 2016) gives the Hollywood treatment to the actual index patient for Nigeria's Ebola outbreak, a Liberian-American finance minis-try official named Patrick Sawyer. Sawyer used his official capacity to leave Lagos for an "important" conference despite knowing he had been exposed to Ebola. Medical folklorist and legend scholar Andrea Kitta noted in her book *Kiss of Death* (2019) that patient zero is inevitably a central feature in outbreak narratives, a now-traditional story used to organize, anticipate, and explain epidemics.

Such tales were everywhere in early 2020. Patient zero took several roles in these pandemic stories. The most popular role was an irrespon-sible and dangerous super spreader, which is how Covid-19 carrier Dr. Jean-Robert Ngola was initially depicted when he returned to Campbell-ton, New Brunswick, from a trip to Quebec. Dr. Ngola did not quarantine and subsequently exposed more than 150 people to Covid-19, effectively closing down the emergency room where he worked (MacKinnon 2020). Sawyer in the Ebola epidemic and Ngola in the coronavirus pandemic were depicted in media reports and interpersonal storytelling less as malicious than over-burdened with a sense of their own importance, coupled with disdain or disinterest toward the highly contagious nature of their illnesses.

Yet patient zero can also be a malicious person intentionally spread-ing the disease, often as part of a stigmatized minority: Dugas was a homo-sexual man in a career often caricatured as feminine, while Malone was the cook for a wealthy family. The power of this patient zero malevolence trope was exploited in an overtly racist 4chan thread discussing the Covid-19 crisis in Italy. On March 25, 2020, a Chinese language tweet was translated and turned into an image macro, which began circulating on message boards. It included a photograph of a middle-aged female of Chinese ethnic origin and name and exclaimed: "Patient 0 in Italy. The murderer who blamed Italy, found it! Her name is [H] [Y].... Killing lives and killing Italy, the couple toured the Italian provinces and spread the virus" (TCitizenExpress 2020). The same graphic also appeared March 25 in a comment on a *New York Times* Twitter story with slightly altered text: "This woman [H] [Y], fled (with her husband) from Wuhan the day before the lockdown to Italy and becomes Case 0 of Italy! She's a communist party member!" Both the tweet and the 4chan meme presage a story appearing in *The Epoch Times*[3] on April 3 and are likely part of the general anti–China misinformation campaign of this publication; more examples will follow. The disinformation campaign gained its power through fear of the pandemic expressed as fear of outsiders.

Immigrant Chinese communities have long been cast as sources of disease in North America, with these older tropes reappearing during Covid-19. In the late 1800s, outbreaks of plague originating in China spread to Hawaii and then California, leading to politicians targeting Chinese communities in both places. In Hawaii, this rhetoric led locals to burn Chinatown to the ground on New Year's Eve 1904, creating an entire community of refugees. In San Francisco, escalating anti–Chinese measures led to the full blockade and quarantine of Chinatown, an incident so infamous that it became the origin of many anti-geographic quarantine sentiments within public health professions (Randall 2019; Trauner 1979).[4] During the 2003 SARS outbreak in Toronto, anti–Chinese sentiment led many to avoid Chinatown, prompted media attacks on Chinese residents, and both exacerbated and initiated long-lasting divisions between Chinese communities and the rest of the city (Keil and Ali 2018). In both cases, as in Covid-19, the origin of disease led to the exclusion of Chinese communities, and rumors that the disease was spread intentionally.

Patient zero could also be someone taking risks considered only mildly deviant to their culture or community, such as those who "travel, eat foods unknown to them, and meet strangers" (Kitta 2019:30). Contemporary legends frequently build on such conservative taboo violations: "Welcome to the World of AIDS," about accidental HIV protraction, and "The Kidney Heist," about waking up to find one's kidney has been stolen, are typically staged in "big cities" where the business traveler fails to exercise discretion and suffers the consequences.

Those stories circulated long before we had Covid-19's American retirees featured in a February 2020 news reports pertaining to the unfortunate cruise ship *Diamond Princess* which was held in quarantine off the coast of Yokohama in one of the earliest global stories of infection (Rich and Dooley 2020). One need only examine the accounts of some of the *Princess* evacuees (or any passengers from the 40+ cruise ships that saw Covid-19 cases) to see how they fared on returning to their neighborhoods, let alone the plight of stranded crew members unable to return home for fear of being killed (Clark 2020). This consequence is what Kitta likens to a symbolic crisis; the familiar and safe is suddenly transformed into a monstrous hybrid. These are not dangerous and identifiable outsiders, but parents and friends, neighbors horribly transformed and no longer trustworthy, yet just like us. They are not a dangerous other; they become a dangerous community member. Patients who have recovered are told they should permanently self-identify as a Covid case; these patients may suffer neighborhood exclusion, societal stigma, and personal or imposed guilt over infecting their families. Doctors fear for their patients' abilities to return to a normal life and what the long-term social consequences will be given the growing size of the recovered population (Millstein 2020). Among cruise ship crew, suicides were reported as employees slowly realized they literally could not go home (Yingst 2020).

Coronavirus origins

By April 2020, the scientific consensus for Covid-19's origins had solidified in public perception. A naturally occurring coronavirus from a bat, perhaps passing through an intermediary species like a pangolin (a creature similar to an American armadillo), infected a human in a wet market in Wuhan, China. Researchers expressed confidence in this theory largely because it was consistent with historic animal-to-human, or zoonotic, transmission and the analysis of viral RNA. Evidence of a handful of earlier infections raised questions about this origin. Long-term debate about the origin of new diseases is common, sometimes taking years to trace back through DNA evidence and careful investigation of medical and death records. This uncertainty in scientific literature leaves space for CTs to flourish around newly encountered diseases.

Despite the clear scientific consensus, several competing conspiracy theories emerged to suggest some element of human intent and agency for the outbreak. The first cluster of CTs have survived the longest, all focused on the Level 4 microbiology laboratory in Wuhan.[5] The Wuhan Lab conspiracy theories began churning across the Internet once people learned of the lab's existence. They appeared in online communities, alternative news media, and Fox News; they also came from the mouths of various European and North American politicians. Several variations developed, some of which worked together; others contradicted their sister narratives. Keep in mind the point made earlier: narratives that cannot logically be simultaneously true may still be held as equally true (or equally plausible) if they focus on the same villain.

In the first version of the story, the lab accidentally released the virus through unsafe practices. After an April 14 article in the *Washington Post* reported that American officials inspecting the lab had warned of problems with safety and procedures (Rogan 2020), this CT gained additional traction. However, conspiracy theories about the lab as Ground Zero long predate Rogan's report.

Conspiracy theories are often less about explaining an ambiguous event than using an event to confirm beliefs already held. The accidental release theory has two complementary appeals. First, it confirms prejudices about "Third World" countries and their incompetence with advanced technologies, as well as "justifying" outright racist antagonism to domestic ethnic Chinese communities or to Chinese nationals. These attitudes were widely expressed through avoiding traditional Chinese neighborhoods and restaurants, and the earlier narrative about [H] [Y] being Patient Zero for northern Italy's outbreak. Both symbolize anti-immigration and anti-tourism sentiment toward Asian people displayed long before the coronavirus came.

The accidental release story also plays into the racist caricature of the bungling and incompetent Chinese that has historically been a feature of North American popular entertainment and the long history of stereotyping across the West (Hong 2019; Phruksachart 2017). Furthermore, at a time of already heightened bilateral tension between China and North America, the story reinforces Western "rightful" dominance in biomedical and advanced technologies—a position which has come increasingly into question as China moves to supplant America as the dominant world power. Narratives discussing dire warnings regarding America's dependence on China for medical supplies exploded after the pandemic began; prior to then they seem to have been confined to shelved reports from mid-level bureaucrats, at least to public perception (Stevenson, Kulish and Gelles 2020).

As we have seen, conspiracy theories, along with their siblings rumor and legend, gain much of their credibility through association with or transmission by people who wield power and authority. The Wuhan lab origin theory was first boosted by Senator Tom Cotton's (R-ARK) Fox News interview (Feb. 16) where he reproduced parts of the theory, representing a significant turn in the development of the narrative:

This virus did not originate in the Wuhan animal market. Epidemiologists who are widely respected from China who published a study ... have demonstrated that several of the original cases did not have any contact with that food market. The virus went into that food market before it came out. We also know that just a few miles away from that food market is China's only biosafety level 4 super laboratory that researches human infectious diseases. Now we don't have evidence that this disease originated there, but because of China's duplicity and dishonesty from the beginning we need to at least ask the question [quoted in Fordham 2020].

The second version of the Wuhan lab theory, co-existing with its mutually exclusive predecessor, is more insidious: the lab was the site of bioweapons research. As with many narratives of this type, purposeful obfuscation mixes with general public unawareness—what could be termed ignorance if the word did not carry pejorative contexts. The speculation amplified and gained wider traction after being picked up in publications like the United Kingdom's *Daily Mail* (Jan. 23) and the *Washington Times* (Jan. 26) and *New York Post* (Feb. 22) (Rahhal 2020; Gertz 2020; Mosher 2020). At the time of this writing there is no specific evidence that the lab researched or produced bioweapons. The *New York Post*'s story by Steven W. Mosher trying to state the opposite provides a good example of using a common writing trick. When one cannot prove a relationship between two facts, a skilled writer can create the impression of a relationship by presenting two parallel pieces of data so the reader may imply a connection between them:

That's right. China's only Level 4 microbiology lab that is equipped to handle deadly coronaviruses, called the National Biosafety Laboratory, is part of the Wuhan Institute of Virology.

What's more, the People's Liberation Army's top expert in biological warfare, a Maj. Gen. Chen Wei, was dispatched to Wuhan at the end of January to help with the effort to contain the outbreak [Mosher 2020].

Senator Cotton's comments, both at the time he made them and in subsequent media reports, were linked to this bioweapon and the prior accidental release theory; both could not be true at the same time, yet alongside Cotton's assertions of the accidental release, the bioweapon theory floated comfortably through online and professional media. These conflicting Wuhan lab narratives slowly moved into the mainstream, advanced by Trump (Singh, Davidson and Borger 2020) and Secretary of State Mike Pompeo (Borger 2020). Evidence was not provided, although online perpetrators pointed to significant names in pandemic awareness—such as Dr. Anthony Fauci, director of the National Institute of Allergy and Infectious Disease, and the scientific face of the President's coronavirus task force— and asserted (incorrect) dates of Chinese trips and affiliations with research entities. The American administration mentioned the Wuhan lab origin conspiracy theories in mainstream outlets; how much this has to do with the online narrative turning darker and more ominous in various online communities will never be provable.

Conspiracy theorists do not believe in accidents, viewing history as a succession of planned events by specific bad actors to advance a knowable goal. Below is a good example of the collective and competitive storytelling that builds conspiracy theories, as well as a fairly representative selection of propositions regarding the virus release as of March 27[6]:

Fake news coverup, MSN and CNN [original poster]
According to the shills of MSN.com, they have "alleged proof" that the Corona Virus is not a genetically altered bio weapon. So we are supposed to ignore suspicious nature on how this Genetic Genocide appeared in China? Or the very clear and political motive China had to destroy its own people due to threats of rebellion.
[Links to "Sorry, conspiracy theorists. Study concludes Covid-19 'is not a laboratory construct'" on MSN (orig. Holland 2020) and to the China page from CNN] (27 March 2020 10:33:59)
Reply 1 "Aaron" to original poster
it's a bioweapon and real journalism is dead. (27 March 2020 13:02:14)
Reply 2 "Abraham" to original poster
hey, anon, i doubt it was a bioweapon, american or chinese. First of all, even china wouldnt release a bioweapon on their own soil second of all, if it were an american bioweapon it wouldnt have been released in the middle of buttfuck nowhere, china. It would have been released in Beijing or Shenzhen for maximum effect. So yeah, its not a bioweapon (27 March 2020 13:05:51)
Reply 3 "Frank" to original poster
US/Israel had a clear political motive to release it in China. It's so obvious the Covid-19 is a US/Israel bio weapon that killed two birds with one stone. To weaken China, increase anti–Chinese sentiment for conflict with China, increase control over the general population, and to induce massive "bailouts" for our corporate masters. (27 March 2020 14:10:24)
Reply 3.1 "George" to "Frank"
no, your retarded. why would they release a bioweapon in chinas equivalent of wyoming instead of a major financial or tech center? (27 March 2020 14:18:38)
Reply 3.1.1 "Henry" to "George"
Because it would be too obvious, harm our own economy too much, they intended it to spread indirecty, starting in Wuhan may have been a mistake, etc. Use your imagination retard. There's numerous possible reasons. (27 March 2020 14:40:11)
Reply 3.1.1.1 "Isabell" to "Henry"
ok so its a bioweapon that accidentally got deployed in the middle of nowhere literally try reading any medical journal not published by the CCP[7] 27 (March 2020 14:44:36)
Reply 4 "Matthew" to Original poster
Or the very clear and political motive China had to destroy its own people due to threats of rebellion.
Not sure if you're trolling or just super retarded. (27 March 2020 14:49:19)
Reply 3.1.1.1.1 "Jennifer" to "Isabell"
The bioweapon scenario that would make the most sense is China fucked up and

accidentally released some unfinished version on its own people. I think it was just a normal fuckup like SARS but it's a fun scenario to discuss. (27 March 2020 14:51:08)

Reply 3.1.1.1.2 "Karen" to "Isabell"

That's one possible scenario. But not necessarily a bioweapon developed by the west and then deployed in China though. The Chinese could have just been conducting normal research and their Wuhan lab was sabotaged. Then you could just claim they had an accidental contamination. (27 March 2020 15:04:33)

Crosstalk 1 "Nicholas" to "Oliver"

I think the bats constructed this virus in their little cave labs. (27 March 2020 15:27:03)

Crosstalk 1.1 "Oliver" to "Nicholas"

Isn't it odd how quickly animals are reclaiming the land and seas as soon as we retreat into our homes? Is this the start if the animal rebellion? (27 March 2020 15:30:37)

Crosstalk 2 "Quentin" to "Roger"

look into the connection between 5g and the corona virus. Wuhan was the start point for 5g and was turned on there first. The Hertz produced by 5g cause a reaction in the Oxygen molecule that essentially makes it to where we cant absorb the hemo-globin in the Oxygen molecule, which will lead to death by suffocation. (27 March 2020 15:35:56)

Crosstalk 2.1 "Roger" to "Quentin"

You might be onto something. Japan just rolled out 5g and they've been seeing a spike in cases. (27 March 2020 15:41:09)

Reply 3.1.2 "Stephen" to "George"

"Wuhan is the largest city in Hubei and the most populous city in Central China, with a population of over 11 million, the ninth most populous Chinese city, and one of the nine National Central Cities of China." there aren't even 1 million people living in Wyoming right now, lol (27 March 2020 15:45:32)

Reply 2.1 "Beth" to "Abraham"

I dont think the US would totally exclude a target such as Wuhan.

If it were in Beijing or Shenzen, the travel to and from there would be so unpre-dictable that it could no doubt spread to anywhere and potentially threaten the United States. Taking it to a smaller more isolated population center allows containment efforts to slow how long it would take until it reached the US.

If this were a weapon, its become so out of control that I cant imagine whoever's virus it was accepting the possibility of their own leader getting sick as well. (27 March 2020 17:42:27)

Reply 3.1.1.1.1.1 "Leona" to "Jennifer"

It is really, really convenient for the Chinese government to be able handle this dis-ease with their full and unthrottled authority instead of the constant protests and civil disobedience they were dealing with just before. I wonder if China had some kind of plan or ultimatum in case the country was threatened by an eventual revolt. If they had to choose between a viral pandemic or a whole out pre-civil war scenario, they'd pick the disease. (27 March 2020 17:48:53)

Reply 2.2 "Carl" to "Abraham"

"china wouldnt release a bioweapon on their own soil." The year 2001 called and whispers in your ear: anthrax. (27 March 2020 20:16:00)

Reply 2.3 "Dave" to "Abraham"

"i doubt it was a bioweapon, american or chinese."

this, but it doesn't have to be a bioweapon to have escaped from a chinese lab. (28 March 2020 11:26:23)

Reply 3.1.1.1.3 "Dave" to "Isabell"

"that accidentally got deployed in the middle of nowhere" conveniently the epicenter is right beside the wuhan institute of virology. Conveneinly the chinese government has been creating modified corona viruses specifically designed to target people instead of animals for more than 15 years! (28 March 2020 11:26:23)

Reply 3.1.1.1.1.2 "Dave" to "Jennifer"

"I think it was just a normal fuckup like SARS"

good on you for remembering that the chinese people have a long history of researchers getting sick from viruses they are working on and causing outbreaks in china. There were two sars outbreaks in one year in 2004 for this reason. (28 March 2020 11:26:23)

Reply 3.1.1.1.3.1 "Ulysses" to "Dave"

"Conveneinly the chinese government has been creating modified corona viruses specifically designed to target people instead of animals for more than 15 years!"

"In this study, we investigated the receptor usage of the [coronaviruses] by ... by inserting different sequences into the SL-CoV S backbone ... a minimal insert region (amino acids 310 to 518) was found to be sufficient to convert the SL-CoV S from non–ACE2 binding to human ACE2 binding"

Source: Wuhan Institute of Virology, 2007

source for sars escaping the beijing institute of virology twice can search "SARS escaped Beijing lab twice" for article. (28 March 2020 11:37:00)

Reply 2.4 "Elijah" to "Abraham"

"First of all, even china wouldnt release a bioweapon on their own soil" wanna bet? China typically counts it populace as expendable. You think they cared about the builders of the great wall? Why did Mao let farmers work themselves to death? The ccp does not care about its citizens wellbeing, only their loyalty. They're not mutually exclusive (28 March 2020 13:02:32)

Crosstalk 3 "Victor" to "William"

if it's intentional, the goal doesn't seem to be killing everyone but infecting everyone ... maybe so we're more willing to accept being chipped in return for a vaccine (when they announce it's existence) (28 March 2020 14:47:45)

Crosstalk 3.1 "William" to "Victor"

the virus makes men infertile. China very recently had a one-child policy because of overpopulation, and the excess of men vs women. (28 March 2020 15:51:32)

Reply 4 "Xerxes" to original poster

"Genetic Genocide"

If China had engineered it, the virus would be exactly that. We've had the capacity to tailor viruses to specific races since the late 60's, and these days, every modern hospital lab on the planet tailors them to individuals as part of retroviral cancer treatment. Plus every developed nation is fully capable of rigging a virus to lay asymptomatically contagious for years, as HIV does, or simply build some smallpox from scratch.

Nevermind that every other lab on the planet has sequenced this thing, many set in nations hostile to China, with tens of thousands of folks looking over the data. So every other bio intern on the planet would have to be in on the cover up (You know Trump couldn't stay quiet about that.) [29 March 2020 17:52:03].

While the example above may be bewildering in its variety, to the casual consumer of conspiracy theories it is reproduced in full to display the variety and collective (and competitive) process of creating and refining CTs. The following themes can be seen in the exchange. There are three (one ambiguous) assertions that the virus is a bioweapon. Four posters (one ambiguous) assert that the virus' real purpose is to allow for increasing government control over domestic populations. Two posters support the anti–Semitic laced theory that American and Israeli agents released the virus in China. Then there is one instance each of an anti–Chinese racist post and the theory that China released the virus to institute a global pandemic. Four favor the accident theory. Two people make jokes. Two others insert the competing theory of 5G radiation. One lone poster inserts the notion of microchipped vaccines and three people reject or merely argue with the proposition. On the whole, the example displays the variety, vitality and dynamism of CTs in their early stages.

This example ranges from what we might think of as plausible explanations (an accident) to theories that require fantastical biology and technology (5G and race-based bioweapons). In most cases, China and the CCP/CPC are understood as a bad actor, the dangerous outside force that doesn't care about its domestic population and threatens "our" people. In subsequent chapters, the connection between Freemasonry and the Illuminati connected to One World Government conspiracy theories will become clearer; suffice it to say that they stick their heads over the parapet here.

The following example appeared a week later, on Facebook (where this was first found by the authors) and on other multiple sites. Note where parts of it echo competing claims from the previous example, and how the disparate statements above, comprising mostly kernel narratives, have now formed into a full-blown theory[8]:

The coronavirus traveled all over the world from Wuhan China, but it did not reach Beijing or Shanghai or other major cities in China. Can anyone explain how is that possible?

There are so many questions, after all, where it all started, in China, the Chinese stock market did not collapse, but the American and European markets did, and when those markets collapsed, the Chinese bought a lot.

All roads lead back to China

1. They created a virus for which they already had an antidote.

2. They purposely spread the virus for financial gain.

3. There is a clear demonstration of efficiency to such an extent that they built hospitals in a few days. To build so many hospitals they had to be prepared with organized projects, for example, with the ordering of equipment, the hiring of labor, the water and sewerage network, the prefabricated building materials and the storage in an impressive volume. Everything happened so fast that everyone was speechless.

4. They caused chaos in the world, beginning with Europe and the rest of the western worlds.

5. Quickly decimating the economies of dozens of countries.

6. Stop production and manufacturing lines in factories and primary production in dozens of countries.

7. Causing the stock markets to crash and then they bought stocks, bonds and companies at bargain prices.

8. They then quickly gained control of the epidemic in their country. After all, they were ready and he [it] was never really out of control.

9. In all this, they managed to lower the price of basic products, including the price of oil.

10. Now they are going back to mass production while the rest of the world is stopped.

Also note how quickly Chinese unions activated to "hoard" purchases of bus cargo to regional shopping centers across Australia, stripping our shelves of toilet paper and staple foods.

It happened before most of us knew what was happening, even before we knew what the Coronavirus was ["Makana," *Facebook*, 6 April 2020].

The specifics of each point appear tied into a self-supporting argumentative frame, but are actually linked to discrete propositions and events which have their own clustering of narratives and related conspiracy theories. Nevertheless, the example provides a seamless narrative explanation for that time in the pandemic.

A much more simplified version, reiterating that the coronavirus is an economic warfare weapon, is shown in Figure 2.1, a screen shot from a 4chan thread that included this picture as support for their statement. The theory part, or the extra data that appear to buttress the argument, is the inclusion of the false claim that Russia and North Korea were warned and consequently had no cases. Here again we are moving from present

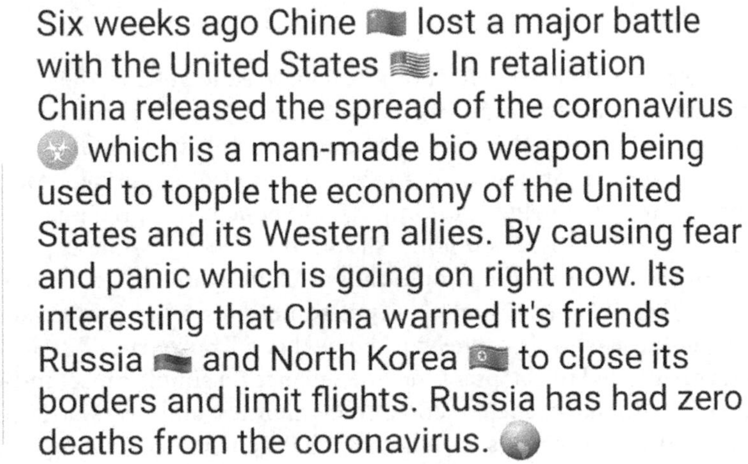

Six weeks ago Chine 🇨🇳 lost a major battle with the United States 🇺🇸. In retaliation China released the spread of the coronavirus ☣ which is a man-made bio weapon being used to topple the economy of the United States and its Western allies. By causing fear and panic which is going on right now. Its interesting that China warned it's friends Russia 🇷🇺 and North Korea 🇰🇵 to close its borders and limit flights. Russia has had zero deaths from the coronavirus. 🌐

Figure 2.1. A screenshot from a 4chan thread.

knowledge backwards towards unknowable information. When the graphic was collected on March 29 it was still possible to claim Russia had no cases; by May it was not, and the graphic did not reappear in our sampling. Nevertheless, as discussed in the introduction, no single proven inconsistency threatens a conspiracy's actuality to its adherents, because the narrative is not held together solely by facts but from a shared worldview.

The last (unnumbered) point in Makana's narrative above references a cluster of Australian contemporary legends based on real events in March. The local subsidiaries of various Chinese property companies such as the Greenland Group purchased bulk medical supplies and shipped them to Wuhan (Bevege 2020). These events produced a short burst of legends and conspiracies surrounding this practice. For instance, the creator of Figure 2.2 took a tweet from the Chinese Ambassador to Austria celebrating the pending arrival of Chinese supplies to Vienna from Xiamen and flipped the cities, adding a cryptic proverbial expression (Li 2020). And because texts like the above manipulated tweet are easily stripped of their original contexts by being copied and pasted ("quoted") into other platforms, as we can see in Figure 2.3, they freely (and sometimes inaccurately) weave into other propositions and emergent stories. These propositions are rooted in that ubiquitous anti–China impulse and thus could become a stable part of a larger conspiracy theory. Or, like this example, they may not be adopted by enough people into a specific story, or get incorporated into a more complex theory bundle, and thus just disappear.

When origins are too tidy: problem-reaction-solution in action

Conspiracy theories reflect our human need to get a whole picture of an ambiguous phenomenon, to feel control over nebulous circumstances. The self-inflicted virus theme is an example; it explains how China proved so enviably effective at slowing the spread, while also explaining how China (an export manufacturing economy) would benefit from the global chaos caused by a pandemic. Each point should provide a possible explanation and be organized around a simple causal relationship: if X occurs then Y happens. This organizational clarity is sometimes more important than veracity to those who share the worldview this CT purports.

As mentioned in Chapter One, the reliance on simple cause-and-effect is part of the social science of conspiracy theories, and bears little resemblance to the messy ways in which global geo-political changes actually occur. One does not need facts or a plethora of data based on years of research, fluency in several languages, and access to sensitive government

Figure 2.2. A photomanipulation of a tweet (Li 2020), posted to 4chan.

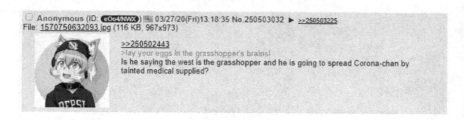

Anonymous (ID: eOo4/NWX) 🏴 03/27/20(Fri)13:18:36 No.250503032 ► >>250503225
File: 1570750632093.jpg (116 KB, 967x973)

>>250502443
>lay your eggs in the grasshopper's brains!
Is he saying the west is the grasshopper and he is going to spread Corona-chan by
tainted medical supplied?

Figure 2.3. Screenshot of a comment from the same 4chan thread as Figure 2.2.

information; instead one can move backward from phenomena that are occurring (China is buying commodity X in a pandemic) to a causal agent (they are the ones who devalued stocks related to commodity X), within an overall logic of anti–China sentiment.[9] Of course the Chinese would do such a thing, theorists say; no further proof is needed because "we all know what they're like."

Researchers on conspiracy theory have labeled this presumptive association and the causal relationship between phenomenon "problem-reaction-solution" (PRS), after the interpretive technique of the popular truther David Icke (famous for claiming that the British Royal Family were lizards from space):

> PRS involves three discrete, but interrelated phases…. Initially, dominant individuals, groups, and/or organizations covertly engineer or exploit a problem to legitimize the enactment of laws, rules, and restrictions. Then, via an unquestioning media, the issue is broadcast, amplified, and popularized. Bringing the problem to the forefront of public attention arouses a strong social demand for action (reaction), which advances acceptance of a "predetermined" solution [Drinkwater et al. 2018:1].

The shutdown of businesses, enforcement of mask wearing, and other Covid-19-related events fit nicely into this idea for many theorists. In the conspiracy world, these predetermined solutions were engineered by "elites," that is, those with power to make laws or issue orders. These elites have a predetermined agenda and will take advantage of the problem of the historical moment (a pandemic) to enact it. If the historical moment does not arise, they will directly initiate the problem (perhaps set loose a pandemic) for the same end. Problem-reaction-solution thinking means that the question of origins and causes need not be answered: keep your eye on the solution offered by those in power instead. For example, in the wake of the attacks of September 11, 2001, the Patriot Act was quickly passed, granting the Federal government greater powers of digital surveillance. Since digital surveillance is clearly advantageous for a totalitarian state to have, could it not be possible (PRS reasoning would have us think), that the attacks were initiated by that state in order to pass the Patriot Act? No 9/11, no Act: therefore they had to make one (Olmstead 2019). PRS is based, loosely, on Friedrich Hegel's model of thesis-antithesis-synthesis, which informs not only the nature of intellectual argument but, he (and subsequently Marx) argued, changes in history.[10]

PRS-type thinking, whether it goes by that name or not, is widely adopted as a rhetorical persuasion device across the political spectrum, forming the basis of respected writers and researchers like Noam Chomsky (2002) and Naomi Klein (2007) as well as the idea behind most American militia groups. The problem, as psychologists like Drinkwater have pointed out, is that when combined with other factors common to conspiracy thinking (like prioritizing emotional reactions over observations or experiences, or privileging pattern over coincidence) and an elastic use of data and expertise to back up one's arguments, PRS will more times than not put two and two together to get five.

A Covid-19 example of PRS, combined with classic clandestine malevolent actor conspiracy theory, is found in a common origin story that retains the Chinese laboratory model but repatriates the conspiracy from China to the United States (moving from enemy outsiders to enemy within). In this telling Fauci shifts from his role in other CTs circulating at this time as an agent of the Deep State to a malevolent actor in league with Bill Gates and a One World Government conspiracy. This shift occurred throughout April 2020, predated by increasing public information on the Wuhan laboratory and its connection to American funders. The information that would form the raw materials of the conspiracy became entangled with Donald Trump's cancelling of the global virus monitoring and research program "Predict," funded by the United States Agency for International Development (USAID) (McNeil 2019).

Begun in 2009 following the H1N1 outbreak (2005) the program was part of a worldwide surveillance and research initiative into novel viruses; it helped train researchers and set up laboratories across the global south and Asia. The cancellation raised little interest until the arrival of the pandemic in America, which renewed reporting on the program's cancellation starting April 2, 2020 (Baumgartner and Rainey 2020). That is also when the general public became aware that America helped fund the Wuhan level four laboratory. Coincidentally, April 2 was also the day Dr. Fauci reportedly began receiving security protection because of death threats. Subsequent conspiracy theories would be shaped by the release of *The Epoch Times* documentary "Tracking Down the Origins of the Wuhan Coronavirus" on April 7 (J. Philipp 2020). The video proposed a vast Chinese military plan to harm the United States through biological warfare associated with the lab's accidental release of the virus, as well as the regime's co-opting of the World Health Organization (among many other charges).

Despite the popularity of the video, its motifs did not stick to most of the CTs continuing into the summer. On April 11 the British tab-loid *The Daily Mail* reported on National Institute of Health funding for Wuhan Laboratory (Owen 2020). The next day, Donald Trump retweeted "fire Fauci," a tweet originally sent from failed Republican House candi-date DeAnna Lorraine. She suggested that Fauci be replaced by Dr. Shiva Ayyadurai, whose comments brought to wider attention the emergent con-spiracy theories surrounding Fauci: "And [Ayyadurai] claims Fauci is a deep-state plant hellbent on 'forced and mandatory vaccines' to support 'Big Pharma'—a claim for which there is no evidence" (Nguyen 2020).

One last element appeared in *Newsweek* on April 27, 2020. As part of its investigation into the Wuhan laboratory controversy, *Newsweek* reported on the history of "gain-of-function" research in the United States (Guterl, Jamali and O'Connor 2020). Briefly, gain-of-function is the bio-engineered acceleration of a virus' ability to move between species, as a way of testing its range of mutation and most likely transmission vec-tors in the wild. Such research has been controversial in America and was briefly suspended from 2014 to 2017.[11] NIH funding for the Wuhan labo-ratory's research into naturally-occurring bat viruses overlapped with the ban on gain-of-function research in the United States, resulting in wide speculation that Fauci was "farming out" prohibited research to the Wuhan facility. Out of this constellation of facts and implications, two varieties of Fauci-centered conspiracy theories emerged.

Below is a series of exchanges from a Facebook thread that ran from April 29 to May 6. Here we can see statements, proto-narratives (a sim-ple statement reflective of what is happening at a specific time, such as "I am reading about origin conspiracy theories") and stories shared mostly without comment or conflict. Participants sharing small and subjective parts of what they know collectively make a body of material from which larger conspiracy theories build: a kind of malignant "Stone Soup." Theories below are grouped under shared themes rather than chronological order within the posting:

Transition between hoax narratives and emergent conspiracy

DAV: From the 1984 onward in the mad science programs Dr. Fauci pursued with our taxpayer money there appears an end game goal of worldwide vaccinations; guess who stands ready to patent and benefit from all our taxpayer research-while I can't point at one individual, there are foundations with whom Dr Fauci is known to have close contacts. All through the years he has failed, isn't that the lack of job accomplishment that applies, in developing government preparedness for viral infectious incidents with training and stocks of medical commodities . He has done enough damage And through arrogant predictions and persistent dire warnings selfrefuted statistically has removed any credibility of his stance. He has to go under the most severe state of rejection from government performance standards

Big Pharma

GRAMMA: this "new drug" is extremely expensive. Clear to me who Failci is working for.

Illegal or Suspect Research

JAN: studied HIV and SARS in 2007 or 8. We started development of Covid and stopped as it violated codes of decency. Then it went to Wuhan and Fauci was still involved....

SHERYL: he was the boss of something and moved part of his budget to Wuhan Lab. The research that he backed in US had a moratorium put on it so he illegally moved it to Wuhan, that's what I read.

BOE: 3.8 million to be exact. Fauci tried to get the research done here, but the law prevented it. So he took it to China. Fauci is an enemy of the state.

Vaccination, Bill Gates, Soros, New World Order

BETTY: ...And why has the Fauci been in contact with the Soros for years, on the Gates Foundation Board and gave how many millions to the Wuhan Lab?!?! Who knows!?!!

DONNA: Part of the globalist agenda—goal—collapse US economy, vaccinate and ID all people globally, one world economy/money, one world government.... BUDS WITH Clinton's, Gates, elitists, Soros ... do lots of research. The virus is real—the questions for me are: 1. How and why is it here? 2. How and why has it been allowed to spread? 3. Why are we allowing those with a conflict of interest (want to see the economy crash) have any say in how decisions are made about opening the country?

PAMELA: I agree Evil man ... and he was also paid millions several years ago by a certain billionaire with a foundation ... purpose of both of these ... eugenics.

CINDY: I knew he was a bad guy just looking at him talking!! Then back in April I saw him give the devil sign with his fingers to the camera w a sinister smile! That was the cherry on top that he was Not on Trumps side ... which means Not on our side! Bill Gates is his leader.

JEN: I've stating he's dirty! Just checking into his background and who's he's been in bed with for years.

Check out his sidekick, the female dr. She worked for Soros! That should make everyone understand why they're pushing the death totals up, including heart attacks, the pneumonia victims, and other none related symptoms. It's the money sham.

It is somewhat surprising how little the motif of blaming the CCP informs the trajectory of this discussion. The focus is clearly on the various crimes and maleficence Fauci has allegedly committed. A similar but shorter-lived effort to affiliate Justin Trudeau with the Wuhan lab appeared on Canadian Facebook pages on April 16 and 17, linking to YouTube stories. They began, "EXCLUSIVE: Trudeau gave 830K for COVID-19 research to WUHAN LAB suspected of kicking off...." The posts gained little attention.

The conjoining of domestic and foreign elite interests, depicting American senior officials working with China, was common enough during the pandemic's early months. Less typical is the reconciling of 5G with the more traditional New World Order (NWO) and "totalitarian creep" hypothesis upon which most of these theories are built.

The next example links Fauci with Bill Gates in a reconciliation of several themes, including vaccination, economic exploitation, individual profit, government and NWO control. Graphs are common on these sites; a picture is worth a thousand words. An individual can lay out their bids for authoritative presentation without having to be a persuasive writer.

The history of racist Chinese tropes highlighted advantageous conditions for the American president's scapegoating of China in the pandemic's early months.[12] Nor is there any indication that the Wuhan Lab theory, or its companion, the Fauci-as-malevolent-actor theory, will fade any time soon. It is also clear that the two theories pit an external scapegoat in China

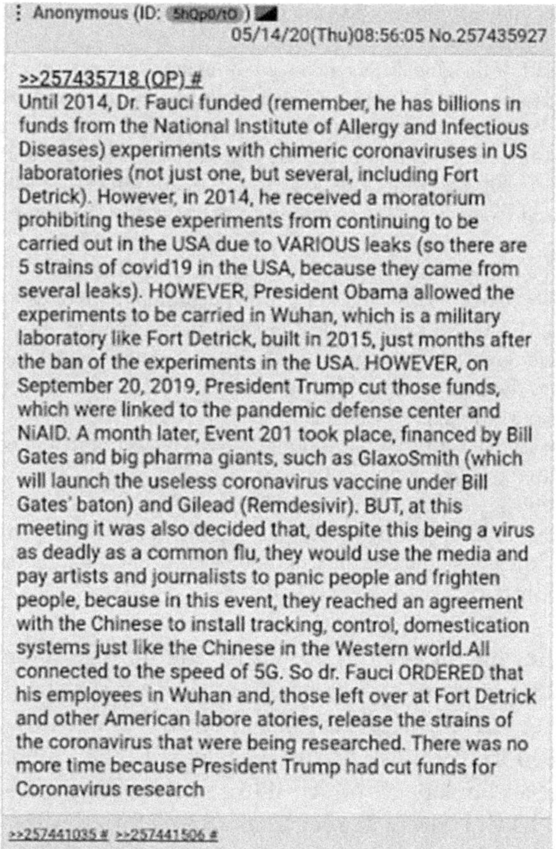

> Anonymous (ID: 5hQp0/tO)
>   05/14/20(Thu)08:56:05 No.257435927
>
> >>257435718 (OP) #
> Until 2014, Dr. Fauci funded (remember, he has billions in funds from the National Institute of Allergy and Infectious Diseases) experiments with chimeric coronaviruses in US laboratories (not just one, but several, including Fort Detrick). However, in 2014, he received a moratorium prohibiting these experiments from continuing to be carried out in the USA due to VARIOUS leaks (so there are 5 strains of covid19 in the USA, because they came from several leaks). HOWEVER, President Obama allowed the experiments to be carried in Wuhan, which is a military laboratory like Fort Detrick, built in 2015, just months after the ban of the experiments in the USA. HOWEVER, on September 20, 2019, President Trump cut those funds, which were linked to the pandemic defense center and NiAID. A month later, Event 201 took place, financed by Bill Gates and big pharma giants, such as GlaxoSmith (which will launch the useless coronavirus vaccine under Bill Gates' baton) and Gilead (Remdesivir). BUT, at this meeting it was also decided that, despite this being a virus as deadly as a common flu, they would use the media and pay artists and journalists to panic people and frighten people, because in this event, they reached an agreement with the Chinese to install tracking, control, domestication systems just like the Chinese in the Western world.All connected to the speed of 5G. So dr. Fauci ORDERED that his employees in Wuhan and, those left over at Fort Detrick and other American labore atories, release the strains of the coronavirus that were being researched. There was no more time because President Trump had cut funds for Coronavirus research
>
> >>257441035 # >>257441506 #

Figure 2.4. Macro posted to a 4chan thread about competing theories on the origin of the virus on 05/14/20.

against dangerous internal elites for the United States. Enemy without or enemy within; either way, someone is available to blame. Such an idea can make us feel better; we are not at the mercy of a non-sentient, uncontrollable world that naturally does things like transfer novel zoonotic coronaviruses, or churn up occasional killer storms. We can eliminate this knowable enemy and get our lives back to normal.

What's interesting is where that last paragraph above resembles or deviates from the scientific approach, as through a mirror, darkly: a non-sentient but knowable enemy has, with no malice or intentional plan, done what it does: mutated and crossed species. But if something from nature attacks humans, it is not because we are important enough to be considered a target; it just happened because nature does that. Such a narrative does not sit well with our need to be the center of our own universe. We want to feel important enough to be targeted.

Finally, the scientific narrative says that we must study and know this disinterested virus in order to conquer it. But that takes longer, and the West already "knows" China is a bad actor. Perhaps an old enemy is better than a new one when we need to self-comfort ourselves with a defeatable villain.

Counter-conspiracy

Several conspiracy theories have emerged from China as pushback against being labelled and blamed for the virus origins. At a February 27 press conference, respiratory doctor Zhong Nanshan reportedly cautioned, "Though the COVID-19 was first discovered in China, it does not mean that it originated from China…. We need greater international cooperation. This is a human disease, not a national disease" (Huaxia 2020). Nanshan's cautious skepticism can be explained as deference to the Chinese state, but his stance also echoed guidelines from WHO, deemphasizing place of origin in naming diseases in order to mitigate stigma. Dr. Nanshan's caution was shortly displaced by an explosive tweet from Zhao Lijian, the spokesperson of China's Ministry of Foreign Affairs, on March 12: "When did patient zero begin in US? How many people are infected? What are the names of the hospitals? It might be US army who brought the epidemic to Wuhan. Be transparent! Make public your data! US owe us an explanation!"

Lijian would go on to link to a post from *Global Research*, a Canadian conspiracy theory website, claiming that the virus originated in the United States; since deleted, the post was preserved by the Internet Archive and cited extensively in reporting of the time (Boxwell 2020). It claimed, among other things:

[T]he CDC totally shut down the US Military's main bio-lab at Fort Detrick, Maryland, due to an absence of safeguards against pathogen leakages, issuing a complete "cease and desist" order to the military. It was immediately after this event that the "e-cigarette" epidemic arose.

We also had the Japanese citizens infected in September of 2019, in Hawaii, people who had never been to China, these infections occurring on US soil long before the outbreak in Wuhan but only shortly after the locking down of Fort Detrick.

Then, on Chinese social media, another article appeared presenting further details. It stated in part that five "foreign" athletes or other personnel visiting Wuhan for the World Military Games (October 18–27, 2019) were hospitalized in Wuhan for an undetermined infection.

As *The Atlantic* originally reported on April 11, the Fort Detrick angle harkens back to a CT that AIDS was manufactured at that American chemical and bio-weapon base (DiResta 2020). In fact, the basic variations and permutations of biomedical conspiracy theories about Covid-19 seem modeled on previous AIDS conspiracy theories, most notably that neither could be zoonotic. Back in 1984, Russians placed an article in a sympathetic Indian newspaper, *New Delhi Patriot,* claiming AIDS was created at Fort Detrick, thus setting in motion a targeted Soviet disinformation campaign. Fanned by Russian scientific papers in subsequent years, this CT became widely known globally (Knight 2003). The earlier conspiracy theory, like Covid-19's today, also involves stories of tampering with the virus to make it more dangerous and deadly, an angle advanced in the work of Dr. Robert Strecker and Jakob Segal. Both men eventually found their work amplified in English tabloids, again similar to the media landscape of the current pandemic. The prolific conspiracy theorist Dr. Alan Cantwell advanced a complex narrative in which the WHO and the CDC colluded to spread AIDS on behalf of a genocidal operation by the military industrial complex which would bring about the New World Order, a CT echoed in 2020 from several sources.[13] Knight's survey of the AIDS conspiracy theories also outlines competing biomedical theories that align with early (but now largely sidelined) theories about Covid-19, the biggest one being that there never was a virus, just a natural imbalance or misdiagnosis blown into a useful hoax.

Finally, the conspiracy theory that the CIA purposefully infected Black communities in America with AIDS morphed with Covid-19 to explain its severe and disproportionate mortality and enduring harm among Black people, marking fault-lines of distrust within historically oppressed and marginalized communities. Given that Black communities disproportionately suffer from the pandemic, the legend's recycling came as no surprise (Villarosa 2020).[14]

The Chinese government's technique of turning the tables by pointing to a U.S. bioweapons facility also suggests familiar echoes. The story would have no resonance if hundreds of conspiracy theories and legends hadn't already existed about Fort Detrick. The bioweapon research facility motif in conspiracy theories and its specific location in Fort Detrick also supports a completely separate purpose and claims-making exercise. The anti-vaccination proponent Dr. Judy Mikovits, in her since-removed YouTube video *Plandemic* (uploaded May 4, 2020) mentioned this location: "Interviewer: And do you have any ideas of where this [virus] occurred? Mikovits: Oh yeah, I'm sure it occurred between the North Carolina laboratories, Fort Detrick, the U.S. Army Medical Research Institute of Infectious Diseases, and the Wuhan laboratory."

For Mikovits to weave the coronavirus into a vast conspiracy that involves forcing vaccinations onto an unwilling public requires that Covid-19 be manufactured by humans; since government institutions are fundamentally untrustworthy, they would clearly be involved in a mass murder plot.

On April 29, in an article on the Veterans Today website shared across several conspiracy theorist Facebook groups, the Fort Detrick genesis of the virus is pushed back to 2006: "Documents below will show that research to create Covid 19 began in the United States in 2006 and culminated in a successful bio-weapon in 2015, with work done at the University of North Carolina and at Harvard and at the Food and Drug Administration's lab in Arkansas" (Duff 2020).

Partially based on a report from the Russian newspaper *Pravda* on American experiments with SARS virus, the *Veterans Today* writer linked various institutions through coauthors of a scientific paper on SARS (which they reproduce in full as "proof"). Furthermore, they pointed to an editorial correction from the journal (also reproduced as proof) that the paper left out a funder, the USAID. "It is suspected, deeply so, that USAID is a front for American biowarfare research such as that done in Tbilisi, Georgia, and elsewhere, much documented." The link to USAID is important here as it is cited in historic conspiracy theories around AIDS, forced sterilization, vaccination deaths, and various narratives of African genocide by Americans.

Ignoring the expansion of scope regarding the CT in the *Veterans Today* article, the fact that the Chinese narrative and the American anti-vaxx party line can coexist is likely the product of different communities not so much cooperating as ignoring each other's agendas save for where they overlap—although we did see unusual alliances later in the pandemic. At this early stage, *Veterans Today* probably co-opted from, rather than colluded with, anti-vaxx sites, based on a Russian disinformation campaign. However, that pesky completeness imperative associated with conspiracy theories/theorists often leaves competing theories in tandem; better to be whole and confusing than partial. When theorists want true holistic credibility as opposed to just aiming vaguely at bad actors, synthesis appears.

Below we see a synthesis example from 4chan (May 14) that tried to reconcile all of the various current theories—but especially the main anti-vaxx points, the two laboratories and the competing national interests of the USA and China:

> Until 2014, Dr. Fauci funded (remember, he has billions in funds from the National Institute of Allergy and Infectious Diseases) experiments with chimeric coronaviruses in US laboratories (not just one, but several, including Fort Detrick). However, in 2014, he received a moratorium prohibiting these experiments from continuing to be carried out in the USA due to VARIOUS leaks (so there are 5 strains of COVID-19 in the USA, because they came from several leaks). HOWEVER, President Obama allowed the experiments to be carried in Wuhan, which is a military laboratory like Fort Detrick, built in 2015, just months after the ban of the experiments in the USA. HOWEVER, on September 20, 2019, President Trump cut those funds, which were linked to the pandemic defense center and NiAID. A month later, Event 201 took place, financed by Bill Gates and big pharma giants, such as GlaxoSmith (which will launch the useless coronavirus vaccine under Bill Gates' baton) and Gilead (Remdesivir). BUT, at this meeting it was also decided that, despite this being a virus as deadly as a common flu, they would use the media and pay artists and journalists to panic people and frighten people, because in this event, they reached an agreement with the Chinese to install tracking, control, domestication systems just like the Chinese in the Western world. All connected to the speed of 5G. So dr. Fauci ORDERED that his employees in Wuhan and, those left over at Fort Detrick and other American labore atories, release the strains of the coronavirus that were being researched. There was no more time because President Trump had cut funds for Coronavirus research
> So they knew that the mortality and infection rate of this COVID-19 (all strains) were as strong as the flu (yes, the studies at Bonn University are right, the rate of contamination and death are equal to a common flu). But it would be enough to cause people to panic. So dr. Fauci would receive more funds to continue his research (and get rich), the big pharmaceutical companies would earn many billions with useless medicines and vaccines (so useless and much more dangerous than Glaxo's vaccines against H1N1, because those against COVID-19 will be messenger RNA , never used before) and the Chinese government could install its surveillance and social credit systems in the western world (and even in India and Russia). And, of course, Bill Gates could gain a lot from vaccines, install his nanochips on people, and use his messenger RNA vaccines for who

Once again, we find a near-dizzying array of actors whose shared interests in an international clandestine conspiracy involve a byzantine plot involving incalculable logistical challenges. The above is less about explaining the world—even if it purports to do so—than reconciling the narrative holes and internal conflicts that emerge when various conspiracy theories meet online.

A "degenerating research program" in conspiracy study refers to new layers of conspiracy being added to rationalize each new piece of disconfirming evidence that becomes available over time (Clarke 2002:136). Whether a conspiracy theory must be internally consistent or can contain contradictory elements is in the eyes of the reader, because if disparate information conforms to a core belief, those already inclined toward that belief are unlikely to care. Several of the CTs we have just observed fall under the label "deception by officialdom" (which we are classifying as "enemy from above"), which is a huge category when sorting conspiracy themes, and relies on a common core belief that contains several rhetorical techniques that can cover a multitude of logical inconsistencies and new evidence.

We talked earlier of competing narratives being left side by side if they pointed to the same villains. That said, conspiracy theorists in an online community may demand that specific narratives be internally consistent, particularly if the group shares a set canon of stories or has a particular aesthetic of what is acceptable. Conspiracy-minded individuals will challenge others on inconsistency, as seen in the Wuhan threads earlier. The issue is further complicated by the unique approaches of participating individuals; some spend time researching and polishing various narratives, while others, equally conspiracy oriented, are content to let inconsistencies stand. Likewise, there is the problem of performance and competency; some people write or speak well enough to paper over problems with logic or data with passion or charm. It can be difficult to separate an incompetent performance of a conspiracy theory from a text containing internal inconsistencies. Among other things, competency in performance is linked to the rise in cut/paste or click and share content on Facebook groups, where even the most inept wordsmith can share a macro or a testimonial on their page if they believe it expresses their beliefs. In short, the success of the poster's narrative above is not measured in its explanation, but in its internal logic and reconciliation with traditional patterns of conspiracy theory construction. In this we must agree that the above is masterfully composed.

The conspiracy as history

The battle over Covid-19's origins is about meaning more than veracity. Where that meaning is tied into history is harder to see because the pandemic is so new and raw; writing about events in 2020 will not seem like history until time passes and circumstances also change; hindsight only comes with distance. But as we saw in the final example above, the author rooted the subsequent unspooling of events in 2004. A complete conspiracy theory reaches backwards in time to secure and explain the origin of contemporary events. In the words of Peter Knight, "If a conspiracy theory serves no other purpose, it is often the way that nonprofessional historians try out ideas about the nature of historical change" (2003:17).

In part such attempts to root modern CTs in history hinge on "conjunction error" and "misperception of chance." Misperception of chance is about timing; someone who has a car accident feels they are unlikely to be in another one soon, because they've just had one. Statistically, that's not true, yet it feels accurate to most people. Conjunction error is a little harder to explain. Try this: John is Latino, drives a Prius, believes in climate change, and attends a Unitarian church. Based on this information, is John likely to march in a Black Lives Matter protest? Conjunction error says yes. Conjunction error says that more things are at work than probability when people put ideas together; cultural signals may be read to influence what is no longer a 50–50 proposition. Unfortunately, those signals may be ambiguous, or not present a full picture. Suppose you learn that John is also a police officer who voted for President Trump. None of these things are mutually exclusive; based on just a few casual pieces of information about John, a conjunction error is easy to make.

In fact, CTs and history almost inevitably overlap; both are interested in the origin of things; CTs use history as bids for authentication. Indeed, conspiracy theories often pretend to be history, donning academic clothing and historic language in order to exist at all. The question of what history actually is proves surprisingly complex. History to most of us means what has occurred: the facts of events in places at certain dates, like a string of birthdays, the presents and type of cake at each, stretching back in time. This is a popular way of thinking historically; the problem is that there are several different ways to think historically. For example, we might imagine a series of knowable events whose causes and consequences are possibly also knowable. Interpretation seems based on solid facts, while explaining how and why helps explain cause and effect—i.e., if you bomb a country, that country will bomb you back. If you give aid to a country, it might support you when you bomb someplace else. In conspiracy theory thinking, with enough data and the right kind of theoretical models, all of history will make sense in just such a cause-and-effect relationship. In this way of seeing history, it can and should be a science, as precise as physics and as rigorous as chemistry. A CT claims more precision in its "facts" and more confidence in its accuracy than a historian would ever attempt.

The rest of us may think that the job of a historian is to explain how the American Revolution happened, but historians can see it as discerning the how, the why, and the consequences and significance of the Revolution; interpretation meets cold hard fact. Over time, one main reason for an event happening will emerge as the dominant narrative, and be somewhat accurate. But it won't tell the whole story, or even the inconvenient parts of that story. As an old Scottish proverb says, history books are written by the winners; songs and stories are written by the losers. The same holds true for conspiracy theories; facts can be interpreted to favor the losers as well as the winners. The differentiation lies in interpreting them accurately.

And since we are on the subject of historic interpretation, the next chapter delves directly into that topic, covering how anti–Semitic and related White Power theories dating back to the Black Death have been recycled in the time of Covid-19.

The virus is a hoax

Finally, at the same time as the Wuhan origin theory was circulating, some theorists expressed a mutually exclusive CT: the whole virus was one big hoax. Initially we dismissed this idea as something too silly to be discussed. Anyone who has organized a family wedding knows that getting 50 people with a common goal to work together is next to impossible; imagine trying to orchestrate an event with 50,000 or so actors, all in mistrustful countries with different aims, encompassing individuals ranging from country leaders to hospital janitors. Not even the greatest event director in the world (whoever she may be) has that level of skill.

Yet this strange belief persisted, fluidly moving between the kernel narratives "the whole virus is a hoax" and "the response to the virus is inflated." These were often attached to world leaders, particularly in the U.S., Italy, and Brazil. In fact, that first kernel circulated in the United States from a misinterpretation of a Trump quote. On February 28, 2020, at a rally in South Carolina, President Trump said: "Now the Democrats are politicizing the coronavirus. You know that, right? … It's all turning, they [Democrats] lost, it's all turning. Think of it. Think of it. And this is their new hoax." The quote was erroneously contextualized in several publications as a claim that Trump denied the existence of the virus. Trump actually proposed that Democrats were using the virus to attack him as part of an endless string of criticisms (election hacking, Russian collusion, Ukrainian meddling, etc.) which Trump categorizes collectively as "hoaxes." During the same speech he did downplay the virus, claiming it was less dangerous that the seasonal flu. For an archive of Trump's quotes about the virus up to April 21, see Keith 2020. From March 30, 2020, these two simple statements appeared in an extensive 4chan thread discussing the Covid19 hoax:

No.251023300: But the real question is why the world is in hiding? Are the Deep State trying to flex muscles with a fake media pandemic and economic shutdown? Where is all the money going?

No.251023465: They are also repeating "coronavirus-caused crisis" over and over again. Apparently it's very important to them that we get through our heads that this crisis was caused by a pandemic and absolutely nothing else. Even the normalfags at work are seeing through this bullshit as the scapegoat it is.

Soon after, others argued—and continue to do so—that while the virus may exist, its severity has been overplayed, from infection rates to mortality figures; anti–Trump forces (or other populist leaders worldwide) and/or shadowy authoritarian cabals are misrepresenting the statistics to cause panic, compliance, state capture, fraud, etc. Here is an example from the same March 30 thread combining several elements into a complete conspiracy while denigrating a vast swath of minority and marginalized communities through offensive language. A few explanations of common slang terms have been added in italicized brackets:

No.251028484: And for what? The average age of the (30) people who have died here are 89 years old with severe comorbidities like beetus [*diabetes*] and heart disease.... Instead of ruining our economies and turning our societies into soviet globohomo big brother faggot central ... why don't we just offer these old fucks some sort of quarantine instead?

But whatever. It's obvious this is not about humanitarianism or reason or even fucking pandemic control at all. This is about the same old globalist faggotry these globalist faggots have been yammering about and drooling over for decades on end. We all knew it was coming, they've been trying to push it with their climatolology doomsday bullshit, only no one is buying it anymore. Here's a new angle. Look at the shit they're talking about. Digital monies, tracking the population with apps and other bullshit, digital certificates to access societal infrastructure.... Boomers and housewives are sperging [*freaking*] out. Go look at plebbit [*reddit*], they're fucking hysterical. Screaming for forced vaccinations. Expect that one to be pushed severely as soon as the kike big-pharma vaccine comes out.

As part of the conspiracy thinking around the nonexistence of the virus, a curious question began popping up on social media platforms, asking: "Do you know anyone with the coronavirus?" In the early days of the virus, of course, very few people did. Responses created within threads or Facebook groups a context for skepticism and the enlarging of the hoax or overblown response conspiracy theories. The question slowly petered out as the virus became more common through May and largely disappeared during the July explosion of cases in the Southern United States.

A juxtaposition between academic and popular terms needs to be clarified here: academics who study conspiracy thinking find that there is no room for the concept of a "hoax" within such thought. Popular use of the term defines it as a lie of commission for the purpose of deceiving a person or group and several belief traditions like crop circles, Big Foot, or various haunted houses have all suffered from famous hoaxes. But conspiracy theorists think deception around a phenomenon furthers an associated conspiracy of trying to hide secret knowledge from the public. In CT-land, false flags are the closest thing to a hoax. A false flag is an event that is faked to blame or implicate a third party, advance a particular narrative, or enable a hidden agenda—such as using the fake pandemic to seize guns or microchip the population. For a historic example of a false flag operation (because they were really used in international relations and warfare) google "Operation Himmler 1939."

In Chapter Eight you will read about a rather charming little legend and associated conspiracy theories known as Ong's Hat. The creator of this faux legend (don't be confused; Ong's Hat is a town) actually confessed that he made the whole story up. He literally told all those involved that he was its sole creator. And those who believed the theory dismissed his confession as an attempt to throw them off searching for Ong's Hat.

Before the hoax beliefs faded real world actions demanded by Covid-19 skeptics resulted in the "#filmyourhospital" hashtag which began March 28 and was most active in April (Gruzd and Mai 2020). The theory was that hospitals were complicit in the Covid-19 mass deception.

For Covid-19 skeptics #filmyourhospital, like many of the anti-lockdown protests, was an act of ostension—a kind of legend trip to the hospital that has three related functions. First, filming the hospitals fulfills the pragmatic imperative in conspiracy theories to gather data and information. Second, conspiracy theorists are encouraged to share information that support the conspiracy, which they dutifully do, often on monetized YouTube channels. Third, as we explained throughout the book, ostension and legend tripping is an ambiguous activity where it is difficult to determine anyone's level of belief and so it is a very democratic practice that invites believers as well as skeptics to participate. Conforming to research on legend tripping, narration by those taking video recount the conspiracy, explain to viewers what to expect when we get to the hospital, display ambiguous features as proof of their disbelief (empty parking lots, empty reception areas, etc.), and provide the audience with a summation of the experience at the end (McNeil and Tucker 2018). All of these features are hallmarks of a legend trip which in this case amounted to an individual's performance of disbelief that signals larger personal, group, and political identity.

As we will briefly outline in the conclusion, the information, narrative, social and health crisis brought on by the pandemic is not merely a problem of "information." And this isn't a new point but it seems to bear constant repeating: information is embedded in narratives and real world acts that are part of an individual or group's wider identity and fundamental worldview. Until we honestly and doggedly reconcile our public health initiatives and wider response to the pandemic we will continue to struggle with the tenacity, vibrancy and real world effects of conspiracy theories and conspiratorial thinking.

THREE

Recycling White Power Rumors After the Black Death

I don't speak because I have the power to speak; I speak because I don't have the power to remain silent.—Rabbi A.Y. Kook

There comes a time when silence is betrayal.—Martin Luther King, Jr.

The pandemic spread rapidly from China across international trade routes. By late 1347 it had crossed the Mediterranean and reached European shores. Over the next three years it swept across Europe, killing at least one third of the population. At the time people simply called it the pestilence or the plague, but centuries later it would be known as the Black Death.

The death toll varied widely by location, but few places remained untouched. Sometimes whole villages were wiped out. Towns and cities hit hard tossed their dead into mass graves with a minimum of ceremony. After the pestilence passed through, the survivors had to take stock of their personal and community losses, and try to rebuild lives. Then the devastating plague returned. It came back in 1361, and in 1374, and again in 1390, and then again and again—fortunately at longer intervals and as more localized epidemics—into the 17th century. The initial waves during the 14th century reduced Europe's population by about half, and the following waves through the 15th century kept the population from increasing. But the recurring plague made everyone aware of their constantly impending mortality.

Nothing and nobody could stop the spread of the pestilence. Kings and knights couldn't fight it, the prayers of the churchmen were not answered, scholars and doctors had no practical solutions, and people had nowhere to run. Desperately, they asked: where did the plague come from? Why are we suffering so much? How do we stop it? Answers were demanded. From the inevitable seeking of causes and solutions came the stories that led to scapegoats.

Finding someone to blame

Blaming one's enemies for causing any problem is a typical response. Michele de Piazza was a Franciscan friar from Catania in Italy who maintained a chronicle of events in his times (1347–1361). He blamed the sinful Genoese: "Twelve Genoese galleys, fleeing our Lord's wrath which came down upon them for their misdeeds, put in at the port of the city of Messina. They brought with them a plague that they carried down to the very marrow of their bones" (quoted in Aberth 2005:29).

As Gabriele de Mussi wrote in 1348, others blamed the "heathen" Tartars (a medieval term for Mongols) who had been inflicted by the plague while besieging the Christian city of Caffa in the Crimea. The Tartars loaded their dead onto catapults and lobbed them into the city, where the "rotting corpses tainted the air and poisoned the water," which infected the citizens. Italian merchants fleeing the siege in ships then brought the plague back to Italy (quoted in Horrox 1994: 17–18). Most likely, the plague was transmitted via multiple sources along the busy Mediterranean trade routes.

Of course, the suffering people prayed for God's mercy, and they also asked the church to intercede with God. Bishops ordered special Masses, while local parishes held processions and services offering prayers to God and Mary and the saints. None of it seemed to work. The scholars in the universities, also churchmen, offered their answers. The Paris Medical Faculty had observed the omens: an eclipse, an earthquake, excessive rains, droughts, and recent unusual behaviors of animals (such as producing young in autumn) all signified God's warnings of a great disaster. Then in 1345 occurred a rare conjunction of Mars, Saturn, and Jupiter from which their combined astrological properties corrupted the air. The air was then further corrupted by comets, thunder and lightning, and earthquakes. Thus, they claimed, began the pestilence (quoted in Horrox 1994). However, this diagnosis did not offer a cure.

The doctors tried to find one. Aware of the problem of contagion, they attempted to quarantine infected houses, and also prevent people who were sick from going out. They also had a good grasp of the symptoms and course of the disease. In 1348, while the plague was at its height, Louis Sanctus, an educated monk in Avignon described in a letter the pneumonic, bubonic, and septicemic forms of the disease:

Men feel pain in their lungs, from which there comes a shortness of breath. He who has this malady, or is contaminated by it in any way whatsoever, can in no way escape, but will not live by more than two days.... [He then describes autopsies of the bodies.] And thus it follows that this plague is indeed most terrible and dangerous to all, namely that it is contagious, because whenever one infected person dies, all who see him in any way straightaway follow him to their deaths without any remedy. There is also another kind of plague, that at present exists alongside the aforesaid: namely that certain tumors suddenly appear on both armpits, from which men die without delay. And there is even a third plague ... namely that people of both sexes are stricken in the groin, from which they suddenly die [quoted in Horrox 1994:33–34].

In their attempts to deal with the plague, doctors prescribed herbal remedies, required moderation in food and drink, and suggested careful bleeding to balance the humors. In addition to treating the patient directly, medical advice also included keeping all south facing windows closed ("as the south wind is the cause of putrefaction") and regular cleaning and fumigation of houses so no foul odors could penetrate (quoted in Horrox 1994). Some of the advice helped, but no real protection from the pestilence existed.

The scholars and doctors were all careful to attribute the prime cause to God's Divine Will, from which all else followed. Thus, as the suffering continued without alleviation, the questions shifted to: Why did God will this? What have we done to incur the Divine Wrath? The answer seemed that surely mankind sinned too much. Writers and preachers throughout Europe wrote and spoke in detail of the multitude of sins into which Christians had fallen. The seven deadly sins seemed to run rampant: sloth, greed, gluttony, lust, wrath, envy, and pride. Some argued also that priests were unchaste (violating their vows of celibacy) and that "women were no longer bound by the restraints of their sex" (quoted in Horrox 1994: 125–126). From this focus on sin causing God's wrath, and the resulting demand to purge the world of sin to please God, rose the flagellants.

Whipping, or flagellation, had long been used to punish the flesh which had fallen into sin. Some monasteries particularly used self-flagellation as a means for monks to purge themselves of sin. When the plague hit, self-flagellation emerged from monasteries in central Europe and rapidly spread across Europe. Groups of people would wander from village to village, some carrying large crosses, and most carrying whips. They would enter the village in a procession—one thinks of Easter processions with the carrying of the Cross and the whipping of Christ—and then proceed to engage in emotional sermons followed by whipping themselves or one another bloody. Many villagers would join in, and some would accompany the flagellants on their march to the next village. The blood-flecked frenzy signaled the panic this unstoppable plague kept—no pun intended—whipping up in the population. Fortunately, the flagellant movement did not outlast the first plague outbreak, as both secular and religious authorities vigorously condemned the flagellants.

Jewish scapegoating

Then there were the Jews. The rumor that the Jews were responsible for the plague probably began in Switzerland in the autumn of 1348.[1] From there the rumor flowed quickly up and down the Rhine river corridor, and spread inland east and west. Accusations followed a similar pattern: containers of some liquid found near wells or other water sources were poisons. Jews placed them there in order to kill Christians and destroy the One True Faith. In response to these stories, armed lynch mobs in dozens of towns across Europe attacked the Jews within their communities and slaughtered thousands. In order to control the disorder, many town authorities took charge and formalized the persecution by arresting the Jews for trial. They would be tortured to extract confessions, and then burned to death in public squares in front of crowds of angry Christians. Thousands more Jews suffered from these judicial murders. In some towns the entire Jewish community was wiped out. Fortunately, as with the flagellants, the wave of pogroms largely stopped after the first plague outbreak ended in 1350.

Some leaders opposed the pogroms against the Jews. In 1348, the Pope himself forbade and condemned their torture and killing (quoted in Aberth 2005: 158–159). Both the Pope and other rational leaders, like Konrad of Megenberg, understood that the rumors were false, that torture only provided the answers you wanted, and that this was all mass hysteria (quoted in Aberth 2005: 155–157). Some rulers even gave Jews protection; the city of Cologne was one example of such level-headed leadership (quoted in Horrox 1994: 219–220). However, fear and prejudice too often outweighed reason and these pleas were generally ignored, the protections not copied by other regions. Part of the problem was that these intolerant leaders, and their predecessors, had been actively promoting anti–Semitic conspiracy theories for many years before the plague arrived. The Black Death just gave them additional fuel for their fires.

As secular and church leaders consolidated their lines of authority during the 12th and 13th centuries, they supported certain narratives to claim that outsiders, such as Jews, Muslims, and Heretics were a threat to a unified Christian community.[2] Much of the rhetoric involving Jews started with church propaganda that condemned them for rejecting and crucifying Christ. However, over time the rhetoric turned from opposition to the religion—anti–Judaism—to hatred of the Jews as a people—anti–Semitism.

Secular rulers created their own narrative. Many owed money to Jewish bankers, so they not only adopted the prevailing Christian attitude, but added the stereotype of the greedy, unscrupulous Jewish banker. These stereotypes reinforced secular and religious authority by defining religious outsiders as threats to their Christian kingdoms. Stories once told take on a life of their own. When a crisis develops, such as the plague, fearful people use the polemics as reasons to eliminate—that is, kill—the perceived enemy.

The main stories feeding plague era anti–Semitism had already emerged by the 12th century. The image of the greedy, grasping, Jewish merchant or banker was particularly ironic because, by the 11th century, various kingdoms had banned Jews from owning land, or from joining craft guilds. Virtually everywhere they were banned from public office, and even suffered restrictions on mingling with Christians. Hence, Jewish communities lived in their own segregated part of towns called ghettos. One of the few businesses Jews could practice which Christians benefited from was banking, as Judaism permitted lending with interest while Christianity, at the time, did not. Thus, most interactions between Christians and Jews centered on banking. More specifically the relationships centered around Christians in debt to Jews. This socially-forced relationship provoked resentment of the Jewish money lenders, birthing the stereotype of the wealthy unscrupulous Jewish banker.

The second conspiracy theory was even more pernicious than the first. Jews were tolerated within Christian doctrine since they followed the Old Testament, and according to the Revelation had a role at the End Times. However, they were also condemned for rejecting Christ, and for the crucifixion. Over time the polemics grew ever harsher as the alleged Jewish hostility to Christ and Christianity expanded into the Blood Libel charges. In this classic legend and conspiracy theory, Jews were increasingly described as sorcerers who had made a pact with the devil to destroy Christianity. (Several centuries later Protestants would ascribe the same Satanic pact to witches and witchcraft during the Witch Hunts of the Reformation period). The Blood Libel that the "Satanist" Jews were accused of involved charges of ritual murder (often by crucifixion) of Christian children or babies during Passover. Sometimes they were accused of eating the children as part of the Passover feast. Innocent babies, killed and eaten by Satanist Jews, was a powerful story that worked on several different potent fears and horrors.

The first recorded Blood Libel trial happened in Norwich, England, in 1144, but similar cases quickly emerged on the continent. The accusations followed a fairly standard trope. The discovery of a dead or missing child would be blamed on the Jews performing their Blood Libel. The local authority would put a portion of the local Jewish community on trial, they would be found guilty, and most of them subsequently hanged, thus appeasing the Christian population. As the Blood Libel trials spread, various Popes repeatedly denounced them, claiming the accusations were irrational. But they were generally ignored at the local level.

Jews were also accused of trying to hurt Christ by torturing his body through desecrating the Host—that is, Christ incarnate, transubstantiated into the wafer given out during Holy Communion. Transubstantiation is the belief that, when consecrated, the elements of communion—the wine and the bread—are literally transformed into the blood and the flesh of Christ. Desecrating the Host echoed the accusations of Jewish responsibility for the Crucifixion. Allegations of Jews stealing communion wafers, and then stabbing and burning them in some form of ritual murder of Christ, began in the mid-13th century, after the Feast of Corpus Christi developed into a major Christian festival. The feast involved processions of the Host around towns on Corpus Christi day, and included the entire populace either marching or watching. It is still celebrated today in countries practicing traditional Christianity. The desecration accusations were considered very serious, so when Jews were found guilty—again in a process whereby authorities appeased angry mobs more than sought accuracy—a number of victims from the local Jewish community would be burned at the stake. Popes also denounced these accusations and trials, but were again ignored.

One response by authorities was to make Jews servants of the crown. They became virtual serfs to the king. This provided some protection, but also risked exposure to abuse, either by the king, or by others if the monarch elected not to protect them. Eventually several rulers chose expulsion to rid their Christian kingdoms of Jews, and also to eliminate their debt to Jewish bankers. Wrapping the religious, authoritarian, and money motives for anti–Semitism all neatly together meant the Jews were expelled from England in 1291–1294, and from France in phases from 1306 to 1394. Many also fled Germany, which had become the epicenter of the desecration accusations. Most of these refugees went to eastern Europe, where the anti–Semitism was less systematic.

The scapegoating of Jews during the Black Death became a major turning point in violence and emigration. Well poisoning grew into the ultimate plot of the Jews to destroy Christianity. Once that fear took hold, the pre-existing persecutions and polemics were fertile ground for rationalizing the mass slaughter of Jews by an angry and frightened population. The re-emergence and power of conspiracy theories in a time of fear and uncertainty is a lesson worth remembering.

Anti-Semitic legacy recycled into Covid-19

Anti-Semitism persisted long after the Middle Ages. During the 19th century, however, it mutated into racism as race became an important defining identity. Race became defined by more than certain physical traits; it began to include ethnicity, and which ethnic grouping was or wasn't granted the attribute of "whiteness."[3] The latter was defined by place of origin, language, culture, and religion. Thus, for example, Anglo-Saxon was considered a race. In the United States, Catholic immigrants did not fit the ideal Anglo-Saxon/Germanic Protestant pedigree and were refused the status of "White." This was especially true of the Irish, Italians, and Poles who were immigrating to America in significant numbers at the time. Over time they would become more accepted as European Christians, especially since they actively positioned themselves as White in contrast to African Americans and the increasing number of Jews also migrating to the United States. Between 1881 and 1914 masses of Jewish refugees escaped from a wave of pogroms by the Russian government. (For movie buffs, these pogroms form the setting for the musical *Fiddler on the Roof*, and the viewer will note a number of the Jewish families leaving for America.) When these refugees arrived in America, they too were refused White status and the old anti–Semitic stories migrated to the New World to suit the new prejudices.

One prejudice of the modern period is to classify ignorance and brutality as located in the past, as Dana Milbank did in a *Washington Post* op-ed: "Could America's pandemic response be any more Medieval?" (2020). Classifying significant failures in United States pandemic policy as medieval is founded on a prejudicial belief that society has evolved, and we are somehow better than people in the past, and to feel that ignorance and brutality, when they occur, must be throwbacks. That assumption may make us feel better about ourselves, but it is not the slightest bit true: at least, history does not consistently bear that out. We have seen how the medieval doctors and others worked to understand the plague, and then use that knowledge in methods such as quarantine and cleanliness to fight it. In 2020, medical professionals applied their skills against Covid-19, and benefiting from centuries of accumulated knowledge had greater success. However, both in the Middle Ages and today, many people also rejected medical advice, and delved into conspiracy theories. Basically, there is little change in people between now and then.[4]

So it would be that in the "modern" era the old conspiracy theories about Jews would be recycled to fit the fears and uncertainties of the pandemic. The Covid-19 pandemic spread from China in late 2019, with the first cases in the United States reported in January 2020, and was global by March. Like the Black Death, it spread from wild animals to humans through zoonotic transfer. Centuries after its original devastation, Black Death bacteria (*Yersinia pestis*) would be identified as transmitted by fleas, hosted by rodents, to domestic animals and people. The virus responsible for SARS-CoV-2 (AKA Covid-19) seems to have been transferred either from bats (as was another coronavirus, SARS-CoV, in 2003) or from pangolins directly to domestic animals and humans. Zoonotic transfer has been a supplier of multiple diseases since humanity began agriculture and started living alongside herded or companion animals.[5]

Since Covid-19 has both a considerably higher mortality rate than the flu and a higher R0 (rate of contagion), medical authorities from WHO on down deemed it very dangerous.[6] Countries around the world ordered large-scale stay at home orders and quarantines. Covid-19 had nothing like the death rate of the Black Death, when half of Europe's population succumbed to the first wave and the following social upheaval. Still, the coronavirus and its effects in the economy proved deadly enough to cause considerable suffering and untold fear.

As with the Black Death, governments, churches, scientists, and doctors all responded within their various realms of knowledge and authority, but now with centuries of accumulated knowledge and technological development to help. Many of the interventions proved effective and saved lives. However, the fear persisted, and combined with the heavily restrictive "flattening the curve" measures, it led people to look for explanations and scapegoats. When discussing China and the current Chinese government, an established, visible enemy is easier to blame than a microscopic one. Jews were historically set up as the perfect scapegoat.

As winter melted into spring, populations spending weeks stuck at home, between 25 percent and 50 percent with reduced income, according to worldwide news reports, began to chafe at the restrictions. Frustration increased when reopening businesses enforced mask-wearing, as well as limits on numbers of customers inside buildings. The frustration and boredom left a lot of people open to the various conspiracy theories circling around the Internet—not to mention giving ample fuel to those already conspiracy-inclined. The contrast with reactions to the Black Death are stark. During the first outbreak of the plague there was a terrible fear of the world ending due to the horrendous number of fatalities. However, although further outbreaks entailed terrible local devastation, neither deaths nor CTs about the world ending were as widespread as in the first wave. Each outbreak may have been bad, "but no one any longer expected the world to end" (Horrox 1994:13).

With Covid-19 the fear was less visceral, especially for those living in areas with lower population density where it initially hardly hit. Instead, fear was stoked by the constant noise generated on the Internet and on cable TV—which bored, anxious, and frustrated people spent hours and days monitoring during lockdowns. The anti–Semitic conspiracy theories generated online were effectively the same, again involving plots of Jews to destroy or enslave Christians. Also, some of the theories accused Jewish bankers of profiting from the pandemic. A typical theory would look like this one from 4chan: "the jews are unstoppable and make money no matter what my being a useful idiot means nothing. Stay inside while pappy bezos ships everything and the united jewfro stock fund shorts the markets. Maybe one day you'll figure out that if they use the media to create a crash they can concentrate wealth in their hands. Soros is famous for this" (13 May 2020). This type of story clearly had its foundations in the Middle Ages, persisting across the centuries to be revived at the next crisis.

Recognizable tropes adapted to the new situation. The core accusation accused Jewish banks of funding manufactures of the disease as a bioweapon to kill Christians. "Zionist" controlled organizations, such as FEMA, would enslave the rest.[7] A linked story claimed the same Jewish banks profited from the coronavirus by selling vaccines, taking advantage of market volatility, and giving loans to desperate people. These two central themes are clear descendants of the well poisoning and greedy Jewish money-lender motifs of the Middle Ages. Fortunately, 2020 hasn't yet encouraged such hysteria that pogroms have broken out against Jews. However, these stories encourage increased violence, harassment, and discrimination.

These various anti–Semitic conspiracies became mixed together in the modern period under an alleged Zionist political agenda. According to the anti–Semitic definition, Zionism went beyond supporting a Jewish national state to plotting for world domination. In terms of Covid-19, the assumption was that Jews were exploiting the crisis, regardless of whether those spreading this rumor saw the virus as a hoax, or as real but produced by Jews.

The problem of anti–Semitic messaging grew much bigger than a few tweets or posts. Typically, well-known White supremacists with numerous followers would use social media platforms to push their hate messaging. These were retweeted and reposted by their followers, and then by their friends, and then by others suspicious or on the fence, in a rapidly expanding chain reaction not dissimilar to the expansion of a virus itself. In fact, conspiracy spread on social media can be accelerated by various algorithms which respond to views and likes. Most of the messages bypassed the algorithms and monitoring by any social media companies filtering for hate speech, through calculated design. Typically, the posters used careful wording to avoid the filters—for example the Echo triple parentheses around a word "(((…)))" to represent Jews. It was not uncommon for some partisan media outlets to pick up on some of the less wild rumors and then take them up themselves. Also, American politicians occasionally repeated these stories. Usually the worst offenders were local politicians who were under less severe scrutiny, but such activity also occurred at the national level—at which point the rumor could become legitimized and amplified simply through its presence, even if debunked (Heath, Wynn and Guynn 2018; ADL 2020a). The use of political and religious leaders in adopting and circling anti–Semitism has parallels with the medieval precedent of consolidating power through describing perceived outsiders as threats.

Puppet Master

Many of the stories combined the stereotype of the greedy Jewish banker along with the plot to harm and enslave Christians under a broader Puppet Master concept. Puppet Master conspiracy theorists believed in individual Zionist masterminds controlling governments and global institutions to help with their plot to control the world—often under the so-called New World Order, an End Times dog whistle mentioned in the introduction. The stories were enhanced by visual imagery of the "Happy Merchant"—a caricature of a Jew who is hook nosed, bearded, rubbing his hands together gleefully. With the stereotypes well established, they rarely need much explanation. The allegations fit images and stories which virtually everyone had heard and seen in some form or another. For example, this social media post stated:

> Corona virus is a hoax by the vax kikes teamed with the banker kikes.
> As usual the vax kikes want to pump you and your kids full of aluminum and mercury to turn u into a nigger tier retard who's content doing a menial job for 50 years.
> As usual the banker kikes want to crash the economy and tighten the money supply so that (a) small indie businesses go out of business, then large US-UK-Israel companies can move in and take the market (b) people default on their mortgages and lose their homes to the banks (c) large businesses plead for loans from western banks (d) governments plead for loans from western banks which they can repay by taxing the people.
> Same kikery that's been reoccurring for centuries [quoted in CST 2020:5].

This post, which appeared in various social media platforms after its appearance on 4chan, lumps everything together quite succinctly. "Vax kikes" and "banker kikes" use slurs to refer to the Jews who want to harm White Christians through vaccines, as well as the Jews who profit from White Christians' misfortune. Note that "banks" and "western banks" assume control by Jewish bankers. As long as the reader holds the classic stereotypes about the Jews, the logic of the piece falls quickly into place for them. Jews were similarly linked to other coronavirus conspiracy theories about harming White Christians, as in this Twitter post: "Good morning guys. Quick update there are no 5G Towers in Jewish areas I wonder why" (Twitter post quoted in CST 2020:3).

The average social media participant lacks the resources, time, and knowledge to check on claims like 5G tower locations, and so is susceptible to at least consider the comment plausible. Even those who are not overtly anti–Semitic still receive a barrage of such unfiltered misinformation. Thus, a short post like this Tweet can simultaneously feed off and reinforce a stereotype, such as the greedy Jewish banker: "My goyim friend you are wanting virus vaccine? Only 10 million shekel for limited time only" (quoted in ADL 2020d). Goyim is the Hebrew word for foreigners, and the shekel is the Israeli currency. The use of Hebrew and the affected broken grammar creates an "authentic" sounding voice. The reader can even visualize and "hear" the stereotypical Jewish Happy Merchant in their head as they read it. Other stories can contain a lot of insider information, which the knowing reader has already accepted; the unknowing reader does not know its veracity or lack thereof. "Martial Law has been decided by FEMA which is controlled by the Chabad Lubavitch movement centered around their Rabbi (their Messiah being Jared Kushner and his wife the future Queen Esther). Martial Law is WalMart" (quoted in ADL 2020d).

The kernel conspiracy narrative in the Twitter post above is a classic trope that government agencies—in this case FEMA, the Federal Emergency Management Agency—have been captured by the Zionists. The Chabad Lubavitch is a Hasidic Orthodox, Jewish sect. This sect has been growing rapidly in popularity across the globe, mostly due to its relative openness (Csillag 2018). Its specific mention in the above quote may be because its last Head Rabbi died in 1994, leaving the movement even more decentered than before. However, both the rapid growth of the Chabad along with the "mystery" of whether there is a secret Head Rabbi has led to conspiracy thinking about them.

Meanwhile, Donald Trump's elder daughter Ivanka converted to Orthodox Judaism in order to marry Jared Kushner in 2009. Two Jewish people so close to the presidency produced extreme alarm in anti-Semites. The problem is worsened by the fact that some pro–Israel commentators have compared her to Esther (Mandela 2020). The biblical Esther is celebrated for stopping her husband the Persian king from killing the Jews, and for pushing him into supporting them instead. However, that support included permission for Jews to kill their enemies. A "Queen Esther" so close to the president sets up fears of the government supporting the Jews in killing their enemies: White Christians. The final phrase, "Martial Law is Walmart," references another series of conspiracy theories that Walmart is logistically supporting FEMA in their construction of concentration camps, where they will imprison Americans after martial law is announced during an emergency. Thus, a couple of sentences reveal an evil Jewish sect, allied with the powerful Kushners, using the Federal government and a large corporation to take advantage of the manufactured or faked Covid-19 pandemic to imprison and then enslave and kill White Christians.

Another modern theme evolved from a combination of the historic claim of Jews spreading disease with the 19th century idea of Jews as an inferior race. The racist stereotype, a fairly typical one, described Jews as dirty and unclean, almost as animals (Dundes 1997).[8] They were, therefore, sources of disease, which they would either accidentally or deliberately spread.

In the early 20th century Jews, along with Catholic Irish immigrants, were blamed for outbreaks of cholera and typhus in American cities. Then in 2019 the United States suffered a major measles outbreak, the worst in 15 years. Most of the cases occurred in communities with low vaccination rates. However, outbreaks also developed in Orthodox Jewish communities in New York City. The outbreak immediately caused a spike in anti–Semitic harassment, "pedestrians crossing the street to get away from visibly Jewish people, bus drivers barring Jews from boarding, and people tossing out slurs such as 'dirty Jew'" (Green 2019). The cause was likely travelers from Orthodox communities in the Ukraine infecting the large number of small children in the NYC community. However, the rumor had quickly spread that Orthodox Jews not only refused vaccinations, but of course lived in unhygienic conditions. Rather than compassion and concern, the "dirty Jew" attack very quickly emerged in response.

Unfortunately, during the coronavirus crisis, members of Christian, Muslim, and Jewish religious groups insisted on holding crowded services and ceremonies; an Islamic conference held in India in March 2020 became another target for coronavirus anger and contamination conspiracy theory (discussed in the Apocalypse chapter). Included were some of the Orthodox community in New York.

In response, Mayor de Blasio Tweeted out an ill-worded message, "My message to the Jewish community, and all communities, is this simple: the time for warnings has passed. I have instructed the NYPD to proceed immediately to summons or even arrest those who gather in large groups. This is about stopping this disease and saving lives. Period" (de Blasio 2020). By singling out Jews he fed into the stereotype that they were particularly unclean spreaders of disease, and gave unintended reinforcement to anti–Semitic beliefs. Soon after his tweet the Internet filled with demands to isolate Orthodox Jews, and to violently punish them for gathering. They were frequently labeled as unclean, lazy, welfare dependent, with a disregard for civilized laws (ADL 2020e). Like the fear that "dirty Jews" were spreading measles, now the fear was they were spreading Covid-19.

During the pandemic, the role of Puppet Master (the ultimate symbol for the evil, greedy Jew) was filled by George Soros: wealthy investor, philanthropist, and Holocaust survivor. Soros became the modern face onto which anti–Semitic stories could be manifested—eclipsing the Rothschilds as the archetypal puppet master in recent years. Since the 19th century the wealthy banking family of the Rothschilds had been the center of many conspiracy theories. The accusations that they profited from wars almost precisely mirrors the accusations that Jewish banks profited from Covid-19. Because of their vast wealth and international links, the Rothschilds could easily be pointed out as the conspirators behind just about any global event (see Barkun 2013; Landes and Katz 2012). Conspiracy theories about Soros became mainstream after the election of Barack Obama. In October of 2010, Conservative radio host Rush Limbaugh dedicated a portion of his show to explaining how Soros had supposedly funded Obama's election win, and was now "pulling his strings" (Limbaugh 2010). A month later the popular Fox News pundit Glenn Beck spent an hour using elaborate props to explain how Soros was literally a "puppet master" (Beck 2010). After these broadcasts and others, Soros became nationally recognized as a "controversial" figure—although the Rothschilds still appear as the master puppeteers in European conspiracy theories. A depiction of Canadian Prime Minister Justin Trudeau as a ventriloquist's dummy set upon Soros' knee circulated widely on Canadian anti-lockdown groups (collected April 20).

More recently, President Trump repeated allegations that Soros was involved in funding the migrant caravans of Central American refugees walking to the U.S. southern border in 2017 and 2018 (Samuels 2018). The idea of Jews supporting immigration of brown-skinned people is another element of the anti–Semitic belief that Jews are trying to eliminate White Christians, and the President used the already "notorious" Soros as the puppet master in this too.

Therefore, it is no surprise that Soros would be dragged into the Covid-19 crisis. In this case, he had financial ties with a biotech lab in Wuhan, China (apparently one of his trusts owned a few shares in a small pharmaceutical lab). That was enough for the usual social media rumor mongering, which would be picked up by commentators such as Alex Jones of InfoWars, who claimed Soros funded the coronavirus as a bioweapon designed to bring in the New World Order and the Mark of the Beast (Jones 2020b).[9] As expected, a number of politicians picked up and repeated the rumors, including at least two GOP congressional candidates. In this story Soros in particular, rather than Jews in general, was held responsible for the whole thing.

Yet it was not only Jewish or Asian people who found themselves in enhanced difficulties relating to White privilege or power during the pandemic. Militias were on the rise as well, and the White power movement elements in them and among the Boogaloo bois[10] proved as difficult to untangle as they were easy to see coming.

FOUR

"But My Cousin Said"

Covid-19 and Black Communities

The conspiracy theories that unite all Black People are about the government. Now, I know you white people out there—you're all laughing. You think Black peoples is crazy and gullible.... But this is serious when you realize how many conspiracy theories against us turn out to be true.—Roy Wood, Jr.

Immunity: virus free for the culture

When the coronavirus first appeared, there was a belief that Black people might be immune. The first positive Covid-19 tests returned in the United States were mostly of White patients, and many of those tested had made trips overseas (V. Jones 2020). Further, early results showed a very low rate of infection in Africa. The news outlet *France 24* reported in March that only three cases of infection were recorded in Africa: one patient in Egypt, one in Algeria, and one in Nigeria, with no deaths. To add to the theory, the Nigerian case was reported as an Italian working in the country, who later tested positive for the virus in Lagos. The patient had arrived in Nigeria from Milan in February 2020 but was asymptomatic, and he was subsequently quarantined four days after his arrival in a local hospital.

Africa having so few positive tests when the rest of the world had 86,000 cases and nearly 3,000 recorded deaths (out of the 60 countries where Covid-19 patients had been found by then) paved a fairly straight road to making assumptions that perhaps something genetic about Africans, or at least naturally present in Africa, put the coronavirus out of play (*France 24* 2020; Agência Angola Press 2020).

Even professionals began to wonder about the coronavirus and

Hally Mass Jobe
@HallyMassJobe

Coronavirus cannot spread in hot countries plus black people can't get it. Crushed Garlic and hot water will cure you immediately, let's just all go and pray together in one big mosque and shutdown all the 5G towers that we don't have. #Coronavirus #Goodnight

8:59 PM · 2020-04-05 · Twitter for iPhone

6 Retweets and comments **48** Likes

○   ⇄   ♡   ⬆

Greeno-philic @ajikor · 2020-04-05
Replying to @HallyMassJobe
😂😂😂 someone is tired. I totally understand your frustration. It's discouraging.

♡ 1   ⇄   ♡ 2   ⬆

Hally Mass Jobe @HallyMassJobe · 2020-04-06
You don't even know lol. Let's just keep praying because people will believe what they want to believe.

○   ⇄   ♡ 1   ⬆

Figure 4.1. A tweet parodying African-American Covid-19 conspiracy theories.

Africa. Professor Yazdan Yazdanpanah, head of the infectious diseases department at Bichat-Claude Bernard Hospital in Paris stated "[p]erhaps the virus doesn't spread in the African ecosystem, we don't know" (*France 24* 2020).

Initial information on cases in Africa could be one of the reasons that the rumor mill began to churn out the belief that Black people were immune to Covid-19 (Watson 2020a). The rumors persisted even after Kem Senou Pavel Daryl, a Black man from Cameroon, contracted Covid-19 while studying abroad in Jingzhou, China (Vincent 2020). This could be in part due to three news articles that incorrectly reported Daryl's illness, the first from a now-deleted *African Daily Mail* article. The article stated that the student "escaped" coronavirus because "he has black skin, the antibodies of black are 3 times strong, powerful, and resistant as that of a white" (*African Daily Mail* 2020; Watson 2020b). A second article from website *City Scrollz* was also retracted. It had been titled: "Chinese Doctors Confirmed African Blood Genetic Composition Resist Coronavirus After

Student Cured" (Watson 2020b). The article also cited an "African" man (with no specific country given) named Zanomoya Mditshwa who shared his opinion: "Caucasians is always at war with our black skin because they know our melanin is our defense against all that they throw at us. This proves yet again that the black man is indestructible, our bodies are made of the same substances that make up this Earth because we are owners of this universe they will never wipe us off, history has already proved that" (quoted in Watson 2020b).

The Zambian Observer article copied *CityScrollz* verbatim (Watson 2020b). Similar articles shared by the *Zambian Eye* in February 2020 (again copying *City Scrollz*) and *Faces of Malawi* in March 2020 continued to spread misinformation about the ability for Black people to contract Covid-19 (Chitsamba 2020).[1] While all of the articles proved false (Palma 2020), Black people around the globe, including the United States, continued to circulate the idea of their own immunity through social media and the grapevine (Breslow 2020). A Twitter post cited below illustrates the circulation of this immunity theory; by July 1 it had been shared more than 56,000 times since publication on March 9, 2020, with upwards of 380,000 "likes."

During the height of the pandemic, an unidentified woman filmed her encounter with a Baltimore, Maryland, police sergeant who purposefully coughed on her as he walked past. The video was subsequently shared on the social media site Instagram where it gained in popularity and fomented disdain for the officer. The woman in the short clip loudly exclaimed in reference to coronavirus: "Oh, I ain't worried about that shit! Y'all get that shit, black people don't. So you can cough your white ass back where you live at! You ain't gonna infect nobody but your coworkers!" (Anderson 2020). While the action of the officer was clearly distasteful at best, dangerous at worst, the woman's perception of her invincibility to diseases as a positive side effect of her blackness has actual historical roots.

In the 1740s during a yellow fever outbreak in American coastal port cities, physician John Lining recorded observations from an inspection of a docked slave ship and its cargo of captive Africans. He found that the disease was not impacting the captives, only the White people in the area (Mock 2020). Then in 1793, Lining's work was used by Dr. Benjamin Rush during another epidemic of yellow fever in Philadelphia. Rush was, among other things, a signer of the Declaration of Independence and would later be named the "father of American psychiatry" by the American Psychiatric Association. While White people fled the city, many African Americans remained behind to nurse—and dig graves for—those dying of yellow fever. Rush asked Black people to stay behind due to Lining's work. As an abolitionist, Rush was a friend to several Black clergymen who helped to

Brian
@_ValTown_

Had no idea Black people haven't been affected by
Coronavirus. Always knew we were superior.

4:20 PM · 2020-03-10 · Twitter for iPhone

47 Retweets and comments **102** Likes

key.
@keywilliamss

So NONE of these Corona Virus cases have been black
people?! LEMME FOUND OUT WE IMMUNE. It's the least God
can do after slavery.

2:31 PM · 2020-03-09 · Twitter for iPhone

56.4K Retweets and comments **383K** Likes

Figure 4.2. A tweet parodying African-American immunity theories.

convince Black people to remain behind. However, Rush was incorrect
about African American immunity, and hundreds of Black people died
because they did not flee the city. In *Medicalizing Blackness,* Dr. Rana Hogarth wrote about the Philadelphia epidemic that "[t]he idea of innate black
immunity placed an undue burden on the city's black inhabitants. For those
black people who did stay behind to help, it meant buying into a belief that
at its core defined their bodies as being distinctive and unequal to whites"
(2017:30). The roots of the ideas and theories about Black immunity are
found in the racist history of the United States, at least, and have had a desperately negative impact on communities of color in the States long before
Covid-19 appeared on the horizon.

Conspiracy theories aside, while some Black people rested in the narrative that they were indeed immune to the virus, it was actually ravaging
Black America. As evidence emerged that Covid-19 could be more deadly
to those with chronic health conditions, the racial injustice of medical care
provided to Black communities reared its head (Aubrey 2020). In April

2020, data emerged showing that 89 percent of people hospitalized with Covid-19 also had at least one chronic condition; roughly half had high blood pressure and obesity and a third had diabetes or cardiovascular disease (Aubrey 2020).

In addition, at that time the Centers for Disease Control (CDC) found that 33 percent of people hospitalized with Covid-19 were Black Americans, despite the fact that they comprise only 13 percent of the U.S. population (Aubrey 2020). Taking a glimpse into three hard hit states we find that Black people comprise 43 percent of Covid-19 deaths in Illinois, 40 percent in Michigan, and 70 percent in Louisiana, all of which are disproportionate to their demographics (15 percent of Illinois, 14 percent of Michigan, and 32 percent of Louisiana's populations are Black) (Plater 2020). The higher prevalence of obesity, high blood pressure, and diabetes among Black American communities partially explained this disproportionate infection and death rate (Aubrey 2020).[2] Further, the high stress levels as a direct result of the discrimination experienced by Black Americans could also be a contributing factor, as chronic stress can impact the body's immune system, exacerbated further by how chronic stress is linked to poverty, which increases the risk factors in low-income communities to Covid-19 (Aubrey 2020). Research out of Johns Hopkins Bloomberg School of Public Health found that 25.6 percent of Black Americans live in so-called "healthcare deserts" which are zip codes with few or no primary care physicians. Only 13.2 percent of White Americans live in a healthcare desert (Harriot 2020). Dr. Anthony Fauci, director of the National Institute of Allergy and Infectious Disease, said:

> It's an exacerbation of a health disparity. We've known literally forever that diseases like diabetes, hypertension, obesity and asthma are disproportionately affecting minority communities, particularly African Americans. … We're very concerned about that. It's very sad. There's nothing we can do about it right now except to give them the best possible care to avoid those complications [quoted in Bicks 2020].

While the medical world continued to wrestle with the issues of systemic racism in healthcare, Black communities began to wake up to the real dangers of Covid-19. In March, several Black NBA players tested positive for the disease, including Donovan Mitchell, Rudy Gobert, and Kevin Durant (Magee 2020). Finally, actor Idris Elba who had also tested positive, took to Twitter intent on dispelling the theory that Black people could not contract Covid-19: "My people, Black people, Black people: Please, please understand that coronavirus … you can get it, all right? There are so many stupid, rediculous conspiracy theories about Black people not being able to get it. That's dumb, stupid" (Elba 2020; Espinoza 2020; Magee 2020).

Expendability of Black communities

Meanwhile, there was a shift from safer at home policies to a keen focus on reopening the United States for business in order to salvage the economy (Evelyn 2020a). Once that occurred, the narrative changed from thoughts of immunity to rumors that Black lives, once again, were expendable.

As reopening began with a fervor to bolster up the lagging economy of the United States, Black Americans began considering and realizing who exactly was going to be on the new frontlines. In May 2020, nearly all states were reopened to some degree and Black Americans were feeling as if their health, safety, and rights didn't matter compared to others (Reeves 2020). By that time, America had seen several protests calling for the return to "normal" and the reopening of restaurants, bars, entertainment establishments, and personal care businesses. Most, if not all, of the participants in these protests to reopen businesses were White men and women, and Black Americans became concerned because statistically people of color would be the ones risking their health and safety to return to the jobs that would open up those industries (Reeves 2020).

The impact of reopening would be a Catch-22 for communities of color. On one hand, the communities were being battered through financial insecurity and job loss. During the stay at home orders roughly 80 percent of Black workers did not have the ability to work from home, if they retained their jobs at all (Coleman 2020). Pew Research found in April 2020 that 44 percent of Black Americans reported that "they or someone in their household experienced job loss or wage loss" directly attributed to the coronavirus pandemic response measures (Evelyn 2020b). The United States Federal Reserve reported that out of households earning $40,000 or less, nearly 40 percent of those employed in February 2020 lost their jobs by the beginning of April 2020, and for Black Americans nearly half of their households were in that earning bracket (Evelyn 2020b). That same Pew Research data revealed that roughly three-quarters of Black Americans did not have emergency funds to cover expenses, and more than 45 percent of Black respondents could not pay all of their bills. For those Black Americans who owned their own businesses, data was equally as stark since Black businesses were less likely to be approved for the Small Business Administration's Paycheck Protection Program (Evelyn 2020b).

Yet on the other hand, with reopening looming Black Americans were deeply concerned about their health and wellbeing, as people of color were disproportionately represented in workplaces that have known occupational hazards. Black Americans were already more likely to be part of those occupations deemed "essential," who continued to work through the pandemic, than other racial and ethnic groups. *The Guardian* reported that "black workers were more likely to be employed in essential services than white workers, with 37% of black workers employed in these industries compared with 26.9% of white workers," and, specific to the healthcare industry, "[b]lack workers are about 50% more likely to work in the healthcare and social assistance industry and 40% more likely to work in hospitals, compared with white workers" (Hawkins 2020). In the United States' largest cities, more than 60 percent of warehouse and delivery workers are BIPOC and overwhelmingly considered essential during the pandemic (Evelyn 2020b). Another essential occupation, janitorial staff, is over 75 percent BIPOC in the United States, and more than one-quarter of them live below the Federal poverty line (Evelyn 2020b). In general, Black workers (along with their Latinx counterparts) were less likely to work in occupations that were "professional, management, or related occupations" which were better paid than other areas in the labor force (Coleman 2020). Adam Serwer of *The Atlantic* found "The lives of disproportionately black and brown works are being sacrificed to fuel the engine of a faltering economy, by a president who distains them" (2020). Denita Jones, a Black call center worker in Texas, echoed Serwer: "It's disheartening to know my country thinks that I'm expendable" (in Evelyn 2020b).

In the United States a historical precedent exists of Black people being devalued and sacrificed, beginning with slavery where Black bodies were sold for hard labor and made mere property, and moving through the founding of the country. In the Constitution, Black persons were only worth three-fifths of a person (Coleman 2020). In 1857, through *Dred Scott v. Sanford*, the United States Supreme Court determined that slaves were not citizens of the United States, and therefore were ultimately only valuable as property (Vishneski 1988). In the Jim Crow South, the idea of "separate but equal" continued to devalue Black bodies (Coleman 2020). During the pandemic, Black Americans were already gravely aware of the value of their bodies in comparison to the value of items such as loose cigarettes and possibly stolen goods from a vacant home (Coleman 2020).[3] Economist William Darity from Duke University found that Black lives are worth less than one-third of White lives, stating that "[t]he discount rate on black humanity has been enormous. A variety of metrics indicate that, even after the end of Jim Crow, black lives are routinely assigned a worth approximately 30% that of white lives" (Coleman 2020).

At the time of this writing, with majority Black counties accounting for more than half of all coronavirus cases in the United States, and roughly 60 percent of all deaths, Black Americans may have a good reason to think conspiratorially about being viewed as expendable. As re-openings occurred, cases of coronavirus continued to rise—disproportionately among Black populations. Dr. Chandra Ford, a UCLA professor and director of the Center for Racism, Social Justice and Health, states that "[t]he choice of governments to circumvent science to advance the cause of repairing falls on the backs of people of color, the poor and immigrants It is more than reckless.... You can't run a business when you aren't breathing" (Evelyn 2020b).

Conspiracy theory or real conspiracy

In *I Heard It Through the Grapevine: Rumor in African American Culture,* folklorist Patricia Turner refers to "unverified orally transmitted stories" in the Black Community as both rumors and legends or contemporary legends; the stories meld within communities over these commonly accepted terms (1993:3). The term "conspiracy theory" was barely in popular use in the early 1990s and folklorists tended to consider CTs as part of rumor studies. She defines "rumors" as "short, non-narrative expressions of belief"; "legends" as "more traditionally grounded narratives of belief"; and "contemporary legends" as "items containing particularly modern motifs" (5). Turner suggests that the spread of rumors and legends were more than mere gossip in the Black community, but a way to protect individuals and the full community from outside conflicts and threats (xvi). David Dennis, Jr., an adjunct professor of journalism at Morehouse College, points to the idea that Black conspiracy theories are different in form or function from others, noting that they are created to "make sense of illogical conclusions and inconsistencies in official accounts based on centuries of evidence regarding America's relationship to its black citizens, a relationship that certainly begs explanation" (2016). Conversely, Dennis juxtaposes the creation of Black conspiracy theories with conspiracy theories created by the political right during the 2016 election cycle; the latter were created to "offer escape from an inconvenient reality" such as the birther conspiracy theories that were a clear attempt to try not only to disqualify Barack Obama but also to "other" him as a foreigner (2016).

Generally speaking, rumors and legends specific to Black interests have been shared only within that community. Seldom are these rumors/legends shared with majority race communities.[4] In addition, even if the basis of the conspiracy theory is shared with primarily White communities, they will hold a slightly different narrative in part due to the need for Black American communities to use the theories as sensemaking tools. However, there are clearly some examples of conspiracy theories held in the Black American community which run closely along the traditional course of conspiracy theory ideology and may be exactly the same theory that majority race communities believe. For example, some Black Americans believe that '90s Rapper Tupac Shakur is still alive today, having sought refuge in Cuba (Parham 2015). Many people from multiple races and ethnicities believe that either Michael Jackson died in the 1980s and it was his impersonator who died in 2009 (Wells 2014), or that the pop icon lives on to this day (Thomas 2016).

There also are Black Americans who believe in the flat earth theory held by many majority race persons (Wolchover 2017; Pilgrim 2018). In 2017, rapper B.o.B. began a GoFundMe campaign titled "Show BoB the Curve," to find evidence that the planet is actually round, as he publicly espoused in a 2016 diss track against astrophysicist Neil deGrasse Tyson that the Earth was flat (Lui 2017).[5] The rapper, whose given name is Bobby Ray Simmons, Jr., was welcomed with open arms into The Flat Earth Society (Davis 2016). He is in good company with NFL player Sammy Watkins (Rapaport 2017), and NBA players Kyrie Irving (Gartland and Extra Mustard 2017), Draymon Green (*The Crossover* 2017), and Jaylen Brown (Joseph 2017) who all believe the earth is or could be flat.[6]

Oftentimes rumors/legends in the U.S. Black Community tend to be based or shaped by the residual trauma that actual historical prejudice and racism experienced since their arrival in 1619 as slaves. These beliefs in conspiracy theories seem to be tied to the social devaluation of African Americans (Davis, Wetherell, and Henry 2018). One example of a legend rooted in the historical terrorization of Black communities by White supremacy is the 1980s story that Church's Chicken, a popular fast food chain in the American South, was actually owned and operated by the Ku Klux Klan. Their goal was to sterilize Black men through additives in the food (Turner 1993:82–92; Manuel-Logan 2012a). Stemming from historic use of Black bodies in medical testing came the rumor/legend that the HIV/AIDS crisis was medical terrorizing of the community. Turner reported being told about the idea that "U.S. scientists created AIDS in a laboratory (possibly as a weapon to use against enemy in the event of war), and they needed to test the virus, so they go to Africa, as they [Africans] are expendable, introduce the disease, and then are unable to control its spread to Europeans and Americans" (1993:162).

In 2005, Rand Corp. and Oregon State University released findings from a study that showed these rumors and legends had a negative impact on efforts to prevent the spread of the disease among Black Americans (Fears 2005). Of those surveyed, nearly half believed that HIV was man-made; one-quarter believed that AIDS was produced in a government laboratory; and 12 percent believed it was created and spread by the CIA (Fears 2005). More than half of respondents (53 percent) believed that the cure for AIDS was being withheld from the poor, while 44 percent believed

DAP/ADOS TRIBE
@Black_Action

Never forget. It could just as easily happen again with this
current crisis, as it has happened so many times before. Black
People are considered the expendables by the rest of society.
#ADOS #coronavirus

5:22 PM · 2020-03-15 · Twitter Web App

66 Retweets and comments **110** Likes

Figure 4.3. A tweet featuring Hurricane Katrina photos, comparing ideas of Black expendability to the pandemic.

that people who took the then new HIV drugs were being government
guinea pigs (Fears 2005). Further, 15 percent believed that AIDS was a form
of bio-engineered genocide against Black people (Fears 2005). Psychologist Na'im Akbar stated in conjunction with fears about HIV/AIDS epidemic that Black Americans were not "...a bunch of crazy people running
around saying they're out to get us, [the belief] comes from the reality of
300 years of slavery and 100 years of post-slavery exploitation" (quoted in
Fears 2005).

For many Black Americans, just as with the 2005 HIV/AIDS study, the
government is a large villain in conspiracy theory, an "enemy above" type
of conspirator. Thinking about the tragedy of Hurricane Katrina, film producer and director Spike Lee discussed in 2005 that he believed the U.S.
government had possibly been involved with the flooding of the New Orleans Lower 9th Ward during Hurricane Katrina, stating that he "wouldn't
put anything past the U.S. government when it comes to people of color.

There is too much history" (Reuters 2005). Similarly, rapper Kanye West stated that "George Bush doesn't care about black people" in response to his perception concerning the lack of the U.S. government's efforts to warn, support, and rescue Black Americans who were directly impacted by Hurricane Katrina (Chappell 2010). Yet Spike Lee and Kanye are not alone; in 2018 researchers did find that Black Americans were more likely to believe that the government purposely flooded New Orleans' poor neighborhoods during Hurricane Katrina by breaching the levees to spare middle-class ones (Davis, Wetherell, and Henry 2018; Dolan 2018). Carl Lindahl noted that the legend took on even greater conspiratorial hues in several tellings where the flooding was a government plot to use Katrina to wipe out poor Black neighborhoods (2012). The fear of government conspiracy was rooted in historic precedent; the government did dynamite the levees during the Mississippi Flood of 1927, flooding St. Bernard Parish next to the Lower 9th Ward (Lindahl 2012).

Tuskegee

Suspicion of government and powerful outsiders has been earned in many ways, not least the infamous Tuskegee Experiments. The *Tuskegee Study of Untreated Syphilis in the Negro Male* began in 1932 under the U.S. Public Health Service (USPHS). A human experiment intended to last six months, it instead ran until 1972 (Nix 2017). The USPHS recruited 600 African American men, mostly sharecroppers, of whom 399 had syphilis. They told the participants they would be treated for "bad blood," a common term for several ailments including but not limited to syphilis. In return for consent to be studied, they would receive benefits: free medical exams, meals, and insurance to cover funeral expenses (Nix 2017). In reality, the USPHS experiment was tracking the full progression of untreated syphilis for documentation (Nix 2017).

Test subjects diagnosed with latent syphilis were not given medical care, only provided placebo medications such as aspirin and mineral supplements for the duration of the experiment (Nix 2017). The men in the study were never told they were not being properly treated, nor offered lifesaving penicillin, in spite of the fact that in 1947 it was not only readily available, but recognized as the correct medical intervention for the disease (Heller 2017).

Local physicians were part of the unethical study, having been persuaded by USPHS to not provide medical treatment for any of the Tuskegee patients. The investigation team watched the men die, go blind, and experience other severe health problems due to their untreated syphilis (Nix

2017). In 1968, USPHS investigator Peter Buxton found out about the Tuskegee Study, and promptly informed his superior that its failure to treat patients was unethical (Nix 2017). The USPHS opted to continue with the goal of tracking the participants until all test subjects had died, autopsies were performed, and the project data was analyzed. Buxton then told his story to a reporter friend who passed it to Jean Heller, a journalist with the Associated Press (Nix 2017). On July 25, 1972, Heller broke the news about the Tuskegee Syphilis Study, rocking the American medical establishment (Heller 2017).

The ensuing outrage from the 1972 AP story finally forced USPHS to cancel the study three months later (Heller 2017). Further, an October 1972 advisory panel found that although the men had freely consented to participate, they were never told the study's true purpose (CDC n.d.). By November 1972, 28 participants had already perished from untreated syphilis, 100 more from medical complications of untreated syphilis. In addition, at least 40 spouses of study participants had contracted the disease, and it had been passed to 19 children at birth (Nix 2017).

When the news story broke, Don Prince, an official with the CDC in 1972, said: "I don't know why the decision was made in 1946 not to stop the program…. I was unpleasantly surprised when I first came here and found out about it. It really puzzles me" (Heller 2017). Dr. J.D. Millar, then Chief of the Venereal Disease branch of the CDC, confirmed that the 74 Tuskegee Study survivors could not be treated in 1972, due to their age. Possible side effects for penicillin therapy would "constitute too great a risk to the individuals, particularly those whose syphilitic condition is dormant" (Heller 2017). Millar confirmed that the subjects could have been given penicillin after the end of World War II: "Looking at it now, one cannot see any reason they could not have been treated at that time" (Heller 2017).[7]

Tuskegee, as the debacle came to be known in mainstream America, resulted in two Federal regulations covering studies that use human subjects: each participant must fully understand and agree to the purpose of the study, and the standard of care provided all human subjects must at least equal the minimal available treatment currently known.[8] Complicity from Tuskegee Institute's leadership became a big part of the breaking story. Robert Moton, who succeeded Booker T. Washington as the second principal of the all–Black college, knew the study would investigate untreated syphilis when he was asked to help set it up; Moton agreed, with the proviso that Tuskegee Institute and Black researchers be significantly represented in the credit resulting from the study.

It is impossible to overestimate the crop that sprang from the seeds of mistrust sown by Tuskegee. Racially-based conspiracy theories focused on health mistrust almost inevitably stem back to this very real conspiracy as justification (Thomas and Quinn 1991). Sadly, tragedies like the Tuskegee Experiment were not the last conspiracy to be perpetrated upon the Black American Community, and all caused deep and lasting mistrust of public health officials—which can be seen in the Covid-19 conspiracy theories and ideas of 2020 (Nix 2017). Yet another example that caused long-lasting distrust of the medical establishment is how U.S. Southern Black fertility had historically been controlled by White people, inciting years of sterilization abuse via the medical establishment in the 1950s and 1960s. One such sterilization program was run by the State of North Carolina. While the program began in the 1920s as a way to reduce spending on poor White women and men, the state shifted its focus to target more women and particularly Black women as it moved forward. Between 1929 and 1974, when the program ended, 40 percent of the victims were people of color (Kessel and Hopper 2011).

One North Carolina victim, Elaine Riddick, was raped by a neighbor in 1967 and became pregnant. A five-person state eugenics board approved the recommendation that she be sterilized as she was "feebleminded" and "promiscuous," despite the fact that the pregnancy was the product of criminal rape. The procedure occurred after she gave birth, without her consent or knowledge; Riddick did not find out she was sterilized until she was 19 and married, seeking to find out why she was having trouble conceiving (Kessel and Hopper 2011).

Denied representation and marginalized in mainstream media, government communication, and public health initiatives, for many communities of color, sharing information on social media sites such as Facebook, Instagram, and Twitter provides opportunities for education and information dissemination between and among each other. Such was the case during the pandemic. This information integrates authentic news reports but involves historic and culturally appropriate reading and interpretive strategies that reframe this information in the context of community norms and values. Some of those norms include traditions of distrust and disbelief which provide interpretations of information that may be unintelligible to outsiders but perfectly logical and useful to insiders. These traditions of sharing, interpreting and transmitting information have become even more strained in a digital environment of misinformation, disinformation, and conspiracy.

They have also been strained by extraneous elements of pressure rising from Covid-19, but not as a direct result of them. White power militia predate Covid-19, but the acceleration of the Boogaloo movement and their expectation of a coming race war in America is a result of the pandemic.

Militia movements, the boogaloo, and accelerating Armageddon with a racial twist

To fully understand the militias and their involvement against communities of color, we have to return to Chapter Three and anti–Semitism. In the Middle Ages secular and religious leaders used attacks on perceived outsiders to consolidate authority; these days leaders in the modern U.S. try the same thing. However, in the Middle Ages a major crisis caused the fear and distrust to erupt into bloody massacres beyond the control of even kings and popes. Similarly, in the U.S. a growing movement of militia men are preparing for a bloody civil war against the government, and also against the Jews, who they think influence or control said government.

As of this writing the White power (also referred to as the militia or patriot movement, with each containing subtle variations) militias in the United States are difficult to quantify. Following surges in membership in 1992 and 1993 (because of Ruby Ridge and Waco, both famous confrontations between law enforcement and alternative living groups) membership surged again in 2008 with the election of America's first Black president. The groups are also difficult to quantify, says the Anti-Defamation League: "Most white supremacists do not belong to organized hate groups, but rather participate in the white supremacist movement as unaffiliated individuals. Thus the size of the white supremacist movement is considerably greater than just the members of hate groups. Among white supremacist groups, gangs are becoming increasingly important ... (adl.org)."

Also, according to the Anti-Defamation League, militias tend to encompass five main groups: (1) neo–Nazis; (2) racist skinheads; (3) "traditional" white supremacists; (4) Christian Identity adherents; and (5) white supremacist prison gangs. Most of these are familiar terms, easily explained with a simple Google search if not, so we will focus here only on explaining the Christian Identity history. The contemporary White power movement in the United States emerged after an accumulation of crises: defeat in Vietnam, the Watergate scandal, and the expansion of civil rights movements (racial, feminist, and gay). The result for some White Americans was a massive distrust of government because it was seen as no longer working to ensure their comfortable continuance as the most powerful American voices. Shortly after Vietnam, the "spitting on soldiers and calling them baby killers" legend was invented (Lembcke 1998). In response some disgruntled veterans developed an aggressive, masculine, paramilitary culture.

The paramilitary culture of resentful veterans showed a remarkable parallel to German veterans after World War I. These men felt their defeat was due to betrayal by politicians, communists, and Jews. Many German veterans joined paramilitary units called *Freikorps* and participated in political violence. The Nazi party also had their own paramilitary group called the *Sturmabteilung* (the SA), commonly known as Brownshirts. A key difference in the U.S. paramilitary movement was its resistance to the state, rather than trying to influence or run it as the Nazis succeeded in doing. Hence, White power is not synonymous with White nationalism. In fact, the American White power movement dovetailed neatly with the broader conservative anti-government rhetoric, which had evolved in response to the civil rights movements. These various movements had a lot of cover from one of the mainstream political parties.

During this period the White power movement also linked with, and for the most part merged with, the Christian Identity (CI) movement. In 1886, a man named E.P. Ingersoll published a book called *Lost Israel Found in the Anglo-Saxon Race*. In essence, he said German and Nordic people were the lost tribe of Israel. Soon after a lawyer named Howard Rand appeared on the scene, and coined the term "Christian Identity" while setting up the Anglo-Saxon Federation of America; with its anti–Semitism and extremism against all non-whites, the group found friends in the Ku Klux Klan and among the Brownshirts emerging in Germany. Only Aryans could be Christians, the group preached; Jews and non-whites were descended from Satan, and would in the Millennial reign of Christ be servants to the righteous (American, Canadian, and European Whites). Keep your eye on this belief as we discuss Covid-19 accelerating Armageddon, because at certain points it gets murky whether militia members mean a heaven-versus-hell war, or a second American Civil War between races.

"The Order," AKA the "Silent Brotherhood" or even the "Aryan Resistance Movement," were White power groups based out of the CI movement, and responsible for a crime and killing spree between September 1983 and December 1984 that brought militia groups to public awareness. "The Covenant, the Sword, and the Arm of the Lord" was active in the 1970s and 1980s. Most organizations fell apart over time as leaders died in prison or in police battles; the names of some are still seen on martyr flags carried by contemporary White supremacy groups. Just like the White power movement it spawned, the Christian Identity movement had always been fragmented, sharing a common belief rather than a strategic sense of united purpose. Since the 1980s White power militias have prepared for war on the state in whatever country they are in; Canada and various European nations also have White power groups, although the United States tends to take up global bandwidth on the subject.

The White power movement of today consists of a mass of small independent organizations, each with their own agenda, but more or less in agreement if not alliance with others. Occasionally, they had support from members of the American Republican party. A recent example was Matt

Shea, GOP Representative in Washington State, who actively supported several militia groups, and published his own manifesto calling for a Holy War against non-whites and non-believers (Gutman and Brunner 2019).

It is important to point out that not all militias are White power groups.[9] Some emphasize politics over race; some blend both. Those who identify with the boogaloo movement (AKA the Big Igloo and the Big Luau, among others) are not easily defined as specifically White supremacists. Ironically, where other militia groups emphasize race, the boogaloo movement emphasizes weapons, and its beginnings on 4chan equated its future with disrupting police and government activity through the free use of weapons and violence. This succinct explanation from reporters Jason Wilson and Robert Evans of Bellingcat.com might help differentiate the boogaloo movement from armed militias overall.

> The white supremacist upsurge in the last half-decade has been repeatedly linked (including in Bellingcat analyses) to the intensely racist, misogynist, and queerphobic culture that characterised /pol/ boards on 8chan and 4chan.
> The Boogaloo subculture's origins also can be traced in part to 4chan, but to a different board, /k/, which is devoted to weapons…. /k/ is hardly a bastion of sweetness and light (like all 4chan boards, it is littered with every imaginable slur), but unlike /pol/, militant white nationalism is not the default ideological position [bellingcat.com].

Militia participants tend to be alt-right individuals, as do boogaloo bois (as their members often call themselves) although some identify as libertarian or anarcho-capitalist. On their platforms, some groups deny being militia or anti-government (The Three Percent, for example) while others boast about their revolutionary aims. In an exchange that will not be reproduced here, a May 30 Facebook thread from one group showed the deep divides. The thread began with "Evan" quoting from Ephesians, lamenting that America had lost its moral direction. Several members suggested Evan had introduced fake news, with comments ranging from "you're deluded" to "you need to be taken out." One member said he identified as both gay and Muslim and thought Evan was preaching hatred. Two members said they had agreed with Evan until he mentioned "the sky fairy" and derided the Islamic poster as a left-wing plant or troll, as well as being another kind of "fairy."

Combining Rapture theology with CI militancy leads some White power militia members (such as "Evan," perhaps) to believe themselves tasked with ridding the world of the unfaithful (which often means non-whites, Muslims, and Jews) before the return of Christ. Among militia members who espouse a Christian as well as a Christian Identity worldview, they would understand the coming civil war to be part of Armageddon as described in Revelation. And they would see themselves on the theologically correct side of that war. Hence, White Christian racial theology reinforces the militia and survivalist mentalities.

A common trait among the White power movement is to protect Whites against what they see as state sponsored or supported genocide of European descendants. Government support of abortion, birth control, immigration, and inter-racial marriage are all deemed efforts to wipe out White Christians. White women, therefore, had a key role in breeding, and so had to be protected by men. The duty to protect one's family was another reinforcement of paramilitary gun culture. This roared into view during Covid-19 with protests over economic hardships caused by lockdowns; men surged into capital buildings with guns to protect their families from a threat that was part immediate peril because of poverty, part long-term harm because of the stock market. And, as always, against government overreach and creeping totalitarianism. The most striking of these was the April 30 protest inside and outside the Michigan state capital.

In the Canadian context, Western Canada, most notably Alberta, has been a hot-bed for anti-government and White supremacy movements since the 1980s. As in the United States, groups have been growing over the last few years in response to the election of Justin Trudeau in 2015, and encouraged by the election of Donald Trump south of the border the following year. The main difference between Canadian and United States groups is that Canada does not have a cultural history that glorifies militias and subsequently has few outside of the Three Percenters. Gun control regulations also prohibit parading around with semi-automatic rifles or any firearms as were on display during pandemic lockdown protests in the United States. The less radical political face of the anti-government movement is Wexit Canada, formed in January 2020. This party seeks secession of the western provinces of Alberta and Saskatchewan from the more populated, influential, and liberal central and eastern provinces, and the movement (if not the official political parties) has considerable support from anti-government and White power groups (Hutter 2018; Wakefield 2019). Canadian militia members are against both their own government and that of their neighbors to the south (except for President Trump), as one sees in this exchange from "The Canadian Revolution" Facebook page (21 May):

Oh Canada, going after one party is not gonna do nothing, the entire lot of em are all in it together. They will never step down, release power, unless it is taken ... and even then, the UN, USA or whomever will send in troops to take out all the dissidents, brand them as terrorists, fake c19 spreaders, looters etc etc ... removing Trudeau will literally change nothing, he is an actor, a puppet, just another minion. The NWO is the enemy, don't get mislead by the whole China BS, they are just the model they want to enslave us with. Zionist dogs are hiding in plain sight, trying to take your very souls, and you wanna punch the actor Trudeau? This is far bigger than playing the same old political game ... refocus!

FEMALE COMMENT: Keep up the good work.

COMMENT: Lets drain the Canadian swamp

COMMENT: Been saying this since the puppet was elected. hes nothing but a sheep ones hes lost his usefulness he will be disposed of like any other piece of trash...

FEMALE COMMENT: I sure hope so, daily, I hope so.

RESPONSE TO FEMALE COMMENT: they always do. once enough ppl wake up and the pressure is on they will toss him and find a new puppet to further push the agenda.

COMMENT: I agree. So what's the fix? I strongly believe that Trump is the solution to the removal of the old guard in the USA.

The "enemy outside" conspiracy of creeping totalitarianism via the Jewish New World Order conspiracy is inserted into the general anti–Trudeau political talk common in the group, and the comments highlight a general acceptance with this worldview with a hint of Deep State from the final comment. The growth of White power in the 1980s and 1990s, and its comingling with certain branches of Christianity, prompted White Christian militiamen to turn their attention to Jews. The terminology of the global plot they set themselves up to fight against started with references to the ZOG (Zionist Occupation Government), and then picked up on the pre-existing rise of the NWO (New World Order). The NWO had increasingly come to mean the onset of Armageddon for many Christians, precipitated through a One World Government. The general theme was that through control of the United Nations, banks across the world, and the U.S. Government, the Jews would enslave and slaughter Christians under the New World Order: as part of the process to bring this about, the Jews manipulated communists, liberals, non-whites, journalists, and academics, all to help eradicate the White race. Rhetoric formed around these beliefs, for example with frequent references to "Jewish abortion doctors who murder children" (Belew 2018a:146). Therefore, recruitment into the militia armies was deemed essential to defend against the Jewish menace.[10]

Note also the female voices in the "Canadian Revolution" group and how they position themselves in contrast to the male poster. Congratulatory, hopeful, but always reflective of what men said. The role of women in militia movements is rarely as fighter; women tend homes and raise strong children, as is their role in the struggle against White genocide. They keep order. It echoes the masculinity of the antebellum South, in which men protected White women from the dangers of the world around them—especially the dangers of Black men. Consider 1915's *Birth of a Nation* by D.W. Griffith, which worked to revive the Ku Klux Klan by depicting them as saviors in the postwar South, while depicting Black people as savage, unintelligent, and predatory. Most specifically, it showed the Klan rescuing pure

White women from Black men who were attempting to rape them, perpetuating a racist mythology of the savage and criminal Black man (Clark 2019). This remains a thriving value in several militia groups.

After 9/11 the focus in both Canada and the United States turned to Islam as the greater threat to White Christian civilization. However, during the presidency of Barack Obama, the movement merged anti–Islamic sentiment with both anti–Semitism and race as threats (Potok 2010). After the election of Donald Trump, a massive jump in anti–Semitic acts ranging from harassment to discrimination to violence occurred in 2017 and 2018, presaging more than 2000 such incidents in 2019 (ADL 2020b). The year 2019 was the worst for anti–Semitism since the Anti-Defamation League began measuring in 1979, with 2017 second and 2018 third. The increase in anti–Semitic acts was part of a significant overall jump in right-wing extremism after the election of Trump (Jones 2018). By 2019 the Department of Homeland Security (DHS) belatedly acknowledged the level of threat on their website. Meanwhile, the Network Contagion Research Institute (NCRI) reported the word "boogaloo" had increased in use by 50 percent on Facebook and Twitter in late 2019 and early 2020, and the DHS predicted an increase in violence over the summer (Tucker 2020)

For the general public, the marches and violence in Charlottesville, Virginia, in 2017 put the White power movement on the radar. It was the first time terms such as "boogaloo" began to penetrate mainstream media, even though subtle differences had not yet emerged between the intentions behind White militias and the aims of the boogaloo movement. News video showed neo–Confederate and neo–Nazi militia groups marching to "protect" a Confederate statue while shouting chants such as "Blood and Soil," and "Jews will not replace us," at counter-protestors. At the larger protest the next day, just before a counter-protester was killed, chants of "Sieg Heil" were heard, while "torch the Jewish monsters" appeared in an online forum (Stutman and Spitalnick 2020).

Although the militias grew less overt after this incident, they have reappeared in the Covid-19 anti-lockdown protests in several states. Sporting semi-automatic rifles, ammunition vests, and often flying confederate flags, they protested against what they saw as dangerous government restrictions on White Christians, including wearing masks and accepted a vaccine (when it arrives) as unquestioning obedience to an unworthy government. Despite the greater caution on public display, evinced once the supremacy groups recognized that mainstream media covered their participant at the protests negatively, some anti–Semitic symbols still appeared. During an April 18, 2020, protest in Ohio, a member of the National Socialist Movement held a sign of a plague rat, but with the Star of David superimposed, and the phrase "The Real Plague." (Integrity First for America identified that protestor via private email.) At a May 1 Chicago protest, a sign reading "Arbeit Macht Frei" (work sets you free) was prominent; those words appear on the main gate of the Auschwitz concentration camp.

The decentered and leaderless approach of the White power movement means bombers and shooters frequently get described in the media as lone wolves. This allowed the movement as a whole to remain invisible for years, until the problem was officially acknowledged by such entities as the Department of Homeland Security. The movement's massive social media presence and tacit encouragement by sympathetic media corporations allowed for the normalization of armed protests, abetted by news narratives of false equivalence with, for example, antifa.[11]

The irony of this false equivalence, and one reason White power groups have been included here as part of conspiracy theory study during the pandemic, is that these groups enjoy dealing in CTs. They benefit from perpetuating them. In a 2017 paper on extremism at George Mason University, Sam Jackson, a Syracuse University doctoral student studying militias, explained that the groups use conspiracy theories as cohesive elements to create community in their otherwise fractured organizations. His work showed how militias benefited from circulating prominent and pervasive anti-government conspiracy theories, including those focusing on "gun control, the Federal Emergency Management Agency (FEMA), and the United Nations as key components of the threat posed to the lives and liberty of Americans by the federal government" (Jackson 2017). Jackson acknowledged "racist conspiracy theories (for example, those positing that Jews control the federal government, referred to as ZOG [Zionist Occupied Governmentor Zionist Occupation Government])" as part of the group but did not encompass them in his work.

Black lives not mattering

Such groups are monitored by many researchers and domestic terrorism experts alike, and it is important to note that the use of White privilege or power against Jewish communities or communities of color during Covid-19 was not limited to militia groups. When America's pandemic-stressed population added four killings of unarmed Black citizens in rapid succession by police, plus a jogger named Ahmaud Arbery killed by alleged White militia members (unproven as of this writing), their culmination in Floyd's murder became the scream heard around the world. Unfortunately, the fact that Black American communities were hit harder by Covid-19, with more cases and higher death rates, was only retroactively acknowledged following the explosion of support for a growing awareness that systemic bias and institutional racism had to be accounted for.[12]

One example of this dissonance came from comments made by the U.S. Surgeon General Jerome Adams, a Black man, on April 10, 2020, when he simultaneously admonished the BIPOC communities to take personal responsibility for their welfare during the pandemic, and admitted that the Trump administration's plan to prevent future deaths of BIPOC's was still incomplete. Adams stated that BIPOC Americans should "avoid alcohol, tobacco and drugs" and that they needed to "step up" and do better for their "abuela, do it for grandaddy, do it for Big Mamma, do it for pop pop" to save themselves from Covid-19 (Branigin 2020). Earlier that week, while speaking on BET, a primarily Black-focused network, the Surgeon General acknowledged that Black Americans and other persons of color were much more vulnerable to Covid-19 due to existing health disparities and historic racism around key issues such as housing, education, and employment (Gray 2020). In that interview Adams stated:

> I want people to understand that African Americans [and] communities of color are at higher risk for COVID-19 than the average population out there for a couple of reasons. Number one, unfortunately in this country we know that being Black means that you are likely … to be of a lower socioeconomic status and the things we're telling people to do to protect themselves—social distancing, staying home from work—are not options for people who are part of the gig economy or who were relying on a job which may or may not have health insurance to keep them safe. And when they do go home, in many cases, they aren't as able to be as far apart from others as someone would if they're living in a nice big house in the suburbs. So that's one reason why communities of color are at higher risk. We also know the communities of color unfortunately have a higher incidence of diabetes, of heart disease, of lung disease. And so that puts them at higher risk also [2020].

The difference between Adams addressing a Black versus a White audience did not go unnoticed, nor did the Trump administration's failing to release a plan to address the impact of Covid-19 on BIPOC communities. In a syndicated opinion piece from May 2020, the Rev. Jesse Jackson, Sr., wrote: "The virus didn't discriminate. The society enforced the discrimination; the virus just preyed upon its victims. We have gone too long, struggled too hard to adjust to the reality that it is dangerous to be Black while jogging or to be Black in a pandemic" (Jackson 2020). Black communities have long understood the dangers that accompany darker-skinned bodies moving through predominantly White areas (Powell 2020).

In 2017, a study found that Black men living in predominantly White neighborhoods were less likely to engage in physical activities, including jogging or running, in the areas surrounding their own homes due to incidents; these ranged from neighbors quickly moving to the other

resources positions in pan–African drug trials became tantamount to using human test subjects with little regulation for participant safety, hidden behind a combination of at best naiveté, at worst complicity, from NGOs. A web of international laws made prosecution, let alone proof of exploitation, nearly impossible as well. Using humans as the equivalent of laboratory guinea pigs finds echoes in several Covid-19 conspiracy theories, as mentioned in the chapter on conspiracy theories in Black North America.

So does making money at the cost of public health and human lives. It is impossible to overestimate the damage caused to medical trust in rural working-class regions of America based on the 1990s explosion in the production and prescribing of OxyContin and related painkillers. This is particularly true of some rural hinterland regions considered unimportant by elitists on both coasts, and it plays into a well-known rural/urban divide in American public health policy; in essence rural dwellers can be perceived as a marginalized group, which complicates White privilege and White supremacy narratives in ways public health is still trying to examine within its own policies.

Maine's logging camps and Appalachian coalfields are two specific examples of communities decimated by prescription painkillers (Welch 2020). Small wonder, then, that in 2018 some 22 states were suing Purdue Pharma, arguably the most influential of the corporations that convinced the Food and Drug Administration to approve the new class of "wonder drug." Approval came, according to internal documentation presented at the lawsuits, despite both the government agency and the private entity knowing the drug's addictive properties.

The social justice issues behind protecting all people equally during drug trials is a huge topic explored in research, lawsuits, and investigative journalism. So is the influence of companies bent on making money no matter the human cost; suffice it to say that the explosion of litigation against the unethical behavior of large pharmaceutical corporations in the years just prior to the pandemic should not be forgotten when considering the issue of mistrust toward official medical advice. Distinctions between for-profit corporations, governmental, and extra-governmental agencies like the Center for Disease Control or World Health Organization, tend to fall away, as most subtleties do, within arguments related to conspiracies around healthcare.

Online platforms are not known as places for reasonable and nuanced discussion; even those that start well tend to get caught up in amplification and possible astroturfing. The international Facebook group "Vaccine Talk: a forum for both pro and anti vaxxers" (VT) strives in its rules for members to keep the group even-handed and deep-diving. Conducted in the English language, VT includes people from diverse Canadian, American, and

European classes and regions. Most of the participants say they reached their positions for or against after careful investigation, a description that encompasses the continuum from listening to friends on social media, doing original research on who has what economic ties to which corporations, consulting naturopathy practitioners, and stopping at many points in between. Participant's lived experience is privileged in posts as a valid and unchallenged form of knowledge. Many of the position examples used in this chapter are from this Facebook group.[3]

In late May 2020, a poll from the Associated Press–NORC Center for Public Affairs Research found that half of surveyed Americans said they would refuse a Covid-19 vaccine; refusers fell into two camps, with 40 percent saying they would refuse, period, and the remainder wanting questions answered before accepting vaccination (Neergaard and Fingerhut 2020). Separating vaccination attitudes and fears specifically within Covid-19 conspiracy theories is complicated, especially when theories tend to be bundles of thought wrapped by strong feeling, rather than straightforward narrative.

Incompetency and social justice

For instance, one refuser who wished to remain anonymous said by private message, "Trump is such an idiot, he would approve anything just to make people think he was doing something right. Especially in an election year" (12 May 2020). Conspiratorial thinking expressed in kernel narratives weave into something fuller only when warranted by the teller. One important element in each CT cluster is who the teller thinks the villain is.

Globally, anti-vaxxers tend to consider their own government as untrustworthy, perhaps also incompetent. Within this group, those who were pro-vaxx before the pandemic doubted whether the first vaccine presented for Covid-19 would work, but felt confident that one would roll out soon, all too soon. The central conspiracy theory here revolves around previously discussed governmental indifference to lives of people of color and other marginalizing factors (such as poverty), combined with a cover-up of the vaccine's rushed release. And this dubious attitude toward the first vaccines offered is not limited to Black people; White people were expressing solidarity that people of color, women, and the working poor would be offered the vaccine first. And that the probably shoddy product would be rolled out via economically manipulative programs. To these theorists, "expendable" and "essential" are the same: having already been put in danger by continuing to work in public facing services while others were told to shelter at home, essential workers and healthcare providers are most in need of the vaccine, but vaccine hesitant posters argue the "reward" should not be an untested one. If healthcare providers don't get offered the vaccine at the same time, it is highly unlikely other essential workers will deem it safe. Nor would general public opinion.

The idea that the government might push an untested solution to the pandemic on the most unprotected members of the public (women and people of color) gained support because of the mixed messages about hydroxychloroquine, an anti-malarial medication tested as a treatment for Covid-19. Despite no endorsement from his own health agencies, President Trump asserted on several occasions its efficacy and noted once that he took this drug; at the same time, multiple medical studies posted on social media linked it at best to no effectiveness and at worst to deaths caused by the drug itself. Vaccination Facebook discussion groups, concerned that the White House did not take its responsibilities for safety seriously, cited these events repeatedly in online discussion as proof the administration would encourage or even force the public to take unsafe medication and vaccinations. The drug was pulled from trials not long afterward. Meanwhile, anti-lockdown Facebook groups shared discredited studies and misinformation on the drug in an effort to support the President.

In fact, quite a few medical missteps have occurred globally in relation to vaccination creation and trials that uphold social justice concerns for communities of color worldwide, particularly when intersecting with financial disenfranchisement. First, in April 2020 French doctor Jean-Paul Mira faced a deluge of criticism from people around the world after he suggested that Africa should be the testing ground for a Covid-19 vaccine on the French television channel LCI (Wong 2020). Mira said: "If I could be provocative, shouldn't we do this study in Africa where there are no masks, treatment, or intensive care, a little bit like we did in certain AIDS studies or with prostitutes? We tried things on prostitutes because they are highly exposed and do not protect themselves" (Wong 2020). During the interview Dr. Camille Locht, the research director at the French National Institute of Health and Medical Research, Inserm, agreed with Mira.[4] The negative response to the interview came from celebrities, medical personnel, and common citizens. Senegal striker Demba Ba said on his Twitter: "Welcome to the West, where white people believe themselves to be so superior that racism and debility become commonplace" (Wong 2020). Oliver Faure, a member of France's Socialist Party, stated in response to Mira's questioning about if he "could be provocative" that the idea was "not provocation, it's just racism. African is not the laboratory of Europe. Africans are not rats!" (Rosman 2020). The World Health Organization (WHO) condemned the comments as racist, with Director General Dr. Tedros Adhanom Ghebreyesus stating, "African can't and won't be a testing ground for any vaccine" (*BBC News* 2020). Ghebreyesus went on to state that "[i]t was a disgrace, appalling, to hear during the 21st Century, to hear from scientists, that kind of remark. We condemn this in the strongest terms possible, and we assure you that this will not happen" (*BBC News* 2020).

Then in June 2020, while speaking at the Forbes 400 Summit on Philanthropy, Melinda Gates of the Bill and Melinda Gates foundation stated that when considering vaccinations, they should not go to the "highest-bidding countries." Rather they should be distributed to healthcare workers around the globe first as they are on the "front-lines." Then "you have to start to tier from there, based on the countries and the populations. Here in the United States, it's going to be Black people who really should get it first and many indigenous people, as well as people with underlying symptoms, and then elderly people" (Wong 2020). While the statement may have been innocent, Black people did not tend to interpret it in that way. On a Facebook posting of the *Time* magazine article focused on Gates's speech (Ducharme 2020), one person stated: "Shouldn't people with underlying conditions be right after healthcare workers. Why Black people and minorities? Oh helllllllll no. They definitely operate an agenda. Kill them quick and silently" followed by another poster stating: "always of course ... we've been tested on countless times."

Additionally, in June 2020 it was announced that a Covid-19 vaccine trial program began in South Africa through the partnership of the University of Witwatersrand, the University of Oxford, and the Oxford Jenner Institute, which developed the vaccine (Savage 2020). The program is supported by the Department of Health and the South Africa Medical Research Council, and funded through the Bill and Melinda Gates Foundation. The vaccine candidate, ChAdOx1 nCOV-19, was set to be used in a trial study involving 2,000 people including 50 HIV patients. South Africa at the time had more coronavirus cases than any other country in Africa with more than 7,200 cases recorded in a single 24-hour period on June 27 alone (Savage 2020). Each subject will be tracked for a year to see how well the candidate is protected against the virus.

While vaccination pilot programs have begun around the world to battle the coronavirus pandemic, the testing in South Africa raised the concern and ire of Africans, not to mention Black people internationally. By July 2020, protestors in Johannesburg were burning their face masks to display anti-vaccine sentiment. Seth Berkley, CEO of the GAVI vaccine alliance, stated that the anti-vaccine beliefs in Africa were "the worst [he'd] ever seen" (Anna 2020). Protests held up signs saying "we not guinea pigs" and "No safe vaccine." An organizer of the protest, Phapano Phasha, referenced the comments of Mira from earlier in the year and his desire that Africa not be considered a "dumping ground." Phasha then stated that he believed the vulnerable were being manipulated in the Oxford study since "people chosen as volunteers for the vaccination, they look as if they're from poor backgrounds, not qualified enough to understand." Phasha said, "I believe in science. And I believe that science has managed to solve most of the problems society is faced with. I'm not against vaccinations, I'm against profiteering" (Anna 2020).

There was also concern that a vaccine developed in any African nation might be ignored by Europe and North America. In the 21st century, African nations have dealt with pandemic governance, harm reduction, and vaccination projects far more often than European and North American countries. In addition to the persistent concern supported by historic conspiracy theories that poor people will be given the drug first, a second looms: African research is being overlooked either because of neo-colonial prejudices or because it does not benefit pharmaceutical companies in more powerful countries. In *The Guardian*, Afru Hirsch asked why Africa's coronavirus successes were being overlooked. She pointed out that Senegal, with a population of 16 million, and Ghana (30 million) had only 30 Covid-19 deaths each. In other words, projecting Eurocentric ideas about the state of healthcare in African nations meant ignoring their admirable success rate in fighting Covid-19, particularly in per capita comparison with the United States, the United Kingdom, Italy and other European nations (Hirsch 2020).

Among the successes ignored were links between malaria resistance and Covid-19's less severe cases, as well as the possible uses of *Artemisia annua*, or sweet wormwood, a member of the daisy family.[5] This herbal connection treatment rarely appears in the American or European-based social media discussions, even in groups where the core of their anti-vaxx stance is that a natural cure is always available and better than vaccines. (Hirsch 2020).

Meanwhile, in India, the "poor people will be offered the vaccine first, not out of altruism" theory showed up on Twitter under the hashtag #castesystem #castepolitics and sometimes #COVIDcaste. The City Editor at *The New Indian Express*, founder of the #RiceBucketChallenge, posted on her Facebook page about starving people accessing services during the pandemic (both food and healthcare) at some length. The *Express* also reported on the starvation of migrant workers stranded in Delhi, unable to get home or to feed themselves after being laid off (Mitra 2020). Had these workers been offered a vaccine, or even money to test it, what would have been their response?

As vaccine trials began in summer 2020, a call went out for more Black Americans to volunteer in Covid-19 clinical vaccine trials. Jacksonville, Florida, was one site asking for more volunteers who identified as Black to participate in trials. The concerns were that without Black participation, the vaccinations would have barriers to efficacy. However, even the trial staff understood the concerns that Black communities would have because of present and past medical tensions.

To add to the mistrust, on July 4, 2020, Minister Louis Farrakhan of the Nation of Islam made a three-hour long address that discussed the development of a vaccine for Covid-19. In his speech entitled "The Criterion," Farrakhan referenced the racist roots of the United States medical establishment, and requested that Black Americans be skeptical of any medications created to treat a virus that has disproportionately impacted them. While Farrakhan did not outright state that he was anti-vaccination regarding Covid-19, he urged Black Americans to be cautious and to consult Black doctors and physicians before proceeding with any drug created to combat or protect against the coronavirus. Farrakhan also suggested specifically that his African brothers and sisters should be cautious if a vaccine was established, which could be a nod to the vaccination trials in South Africa: "Do not take their medications. We need to call a meeting of our skilled virologist, epidemiologist, and students of biology and chemistry. We need to give ourselves something better. There are 14 therapies we can treat it with. The virus is a pestilence from Heaven. The only way to stop it is going to heaven" (*NewsOne* 2020).

In his "The Criterion" speech, Farrakhan also referenced the individuals who are, in his perspective, supporting vaccination: "They're plotting to give 7 billion 500 million people a vaccination." Referencing the now ubiquitous conspiracy theory that a cabal of enemies from above were plotting to use the pandemic and vaccinations for a global eugenics experiment, Farrakhan commented, "Dr. Fauci, Bill Gates and Melinda, you want to depopulate the earth. What the hell gives you that right?" (*NewsOne* 2020).

Big pharma, deep state

The next conspiracy theory group moves from social justice to suspicion that big pharma is corrupt and quite possibly in bed with the Deep State government. This conspiracy theory bundle is espoused in a YouTube video that appeared briefly in May, called *Plandemic*.

The video features Judy Mikovits, Ph.D., whose research results linking vaccination to a mouse coronavirus that led to Chronic Fatigue Syndrome were discredited because her lab results could not be replicated by other researchers. *Plandemic* became an almost immediate hit with the anti-all-vaccination-including-Covid-19 thinkers from the day it dropped—aided, unfortunately, by slow responses by YouTube and

Facebook trying to take the short film down as it popped up. Attempts to suppress its scientific misinformation were categorized by these two companies as social responsibility to avoid proliferating dangerous misinformation (among other things she encouraged going to the beach and not washing one's hands). The CT crowd and anti-vaxxers with little interest in other conspiracies swiftly interpreted these

Figure 5.1. A meme circulated in April 2020.

removals as censorship and an unwillingness to let people make up their own minds. More than 1.5 million views of *Plandemic* occurred in its first week on the Internet. The suppression of the video proved counterproductive to those wishing to point out its flaws, in part because anti-vaxxers are statistically the most educated and diverse of the conspiracy theory groups, except for climate change deniers. In June 2019 the Harris Poll surveyed more than 2,000 U.S. adults; 45 percent had doubts about vaccine safety. The top three reasons were based on "online articles (16%), past secrets/wrongdoing by the pharmaceutical industry (16%) and information from medical experts (12%)" (Infection Control Today 2019)

Kitta suggested in her 2011 work *Vaccinations and Public Concern in History: Legend, Rumor, and Risk Perception* that anti-vaxx conspiracy theories posit several reasons why vaccines are harmful. These mirror concerns listed here by Deborah T, an anti-vaxx mother who is not necessarily against giving her children a Covid-19 vaccination when one becomes available. But she did keep them from basic childhood immunity vaccinations. In her own words:

> Thank you for giving me this opportunity to share my thoughts on vaccines, and why I chose not to adhere to the recommended vaccination schedule for my school-age children. Ultimately, I believe individuals should have the right to make an informed choice on the safety and efficacy of vaccines, and that no one should be coerced either through legislation or from the mouth of a doctor to submit to vaccinations.

I did not arrive at my current understanding of vaccines (their efficacy and safety) overnight, but rather it came about as a result of my own health journey. After experiencing a myriad of health problems to which the traditional, allopathic model of medicine failed me, I began pursuing a more holistic form of healing and seeing doctors who were indeed MD's, but who were holistic in their practice. The way I am defining allopathic is the model that tells you for every symptom or evidence of disease, there is a drug or therapy that will counteract that symptom or kill the disease. When I say "holistic" model, I am referring specifically to the idea that the body was created with the ability to heal itself when the underlying stressor is removed and it is given the things it needs (nutrients, sunlight, fresh, air, water, etc.) to achieve healing. This is not an opposition to acute care or emergency care (treating infections, accidents, etc.), which our current medical system does well; but it is in opposition to the way we do preventative care or treat minor or even chronic degenerative diseases.

…Without going into number details of vaccine injuries and deaths, here are the things that motivated me not to immunize my newborns and later my school-age children: • LACK OF EFFICACY: Diseases were already on the decline when the disease was introduced and there were continued outbreaks of diseases in highly vaccinated areas, for instance the outbreaks in 1985 in fully immunized school populations (source: *New England Journal of Medicine*). • NUMEROUS SIDE EFFECTS and vaccine injuries that had been reported ($4 billion paid by the Federal government to date for vaccine injury claims) Incidentally, I met a woman during the time of my research whose son was severely injured from either the MMR or DPT vaccine (I can't remember which), and at the age of 3 or 4 had to learn how to walk and talk again. • FRAGILE IMMUNITY of newborns and children and the sheer number of antigens they are exposed to through the current vaccination schedule. "A child who receives all the recommended vaccines in the 2018 childhood immunization schedule may be exposed to up to 320 antigens through vaccination by the age of 2" (source: CDC). • NUMEROUS ADDITIVES in vaccines (things I avoid in daily life and in foods), which are added to vaccines (thimerosal/mercury was taken out of pediatric vaccines by 2003 when my 2nd born was two, but is still in the influenza vaccine). • ETHICAL CONCERNS: "Human cells from the tissue of aborted fetuses have been used in vaccines since the 1960s, and currently they are used in 11 vaccines. Aborted human fetal cell cultures are used for growing viruses, which are then used in the preparation of inactivated and live virus vaccines" (source: National Vaccine Information Center). • UNNECESSARY: newborns receive their first dose of HepB before they leave the hospital, and this is a disease they are at risk for only if their parents have more than one sexual partner or use intravenous drugs. [The CDC began giving this to all newborns when they had trouble convincing adults in high-risk groups to give consent for their newborns to receive the vaccine.]

Am I opposed to every vaccine? Not necessarily. If I or one of my children were going to a country where there was a prevalence of a particular disease that had been eradicated here, the risk of contracting the disease would then outweigh the possible side effects of the vaccine. This would be determined on a case by case basis considering the age and health of the person receiving the vaccination. Several of the diseases on the vaccination schedule (measles, chicken pox, etc.) are not life threatening to someone with a healthy immune system.

… I do want to mention something to show you that we try to be consistent where our health is concerned. We practice a holistic lifestyle that is in general different than the majority of people we know. For instance, we eat primarily organic fruits and vegetables, grass fed meats, farm-raised eggs, and minimal dairy products. We do not use sunscreens as a rule, drink reverse osmosis or spring water, make our own yogurt and kombucha. We turn off wifi at night and don't sleep with our cell phones in our rooms. We get regular chiropractic care, have bloodtests for vitamin and mineral deficiencies. We all take at least 3 grams of fish oil a day, take extra vitamin D in addition to getting adequate sun exposure, take a multivitamin, magnesium, etc. It is rare that we ever take an aspirin or ibuprofen, never take cold or cough medicine, and use homeopathic remedies for sore throats or headaches. My two oldest children have each had the flu once in their lives, have never had strep throat or any other illness besides a cold, and they are 21 and 18 years of age. They have each had antibiotics one time for acute infections.

Your last question, "Why do you think vaccinations are mandated if they are unhealthy," is a great one. I know that this might sound like I'm given to conspiracy theories, but I think the answer is both simple and complicated. There was a point in the early 1900's when all of the teaching in medical schools in the US was standardized. Not only is medical education standardized, but treatment is as well, and allopathic treatment of disease whether through vaccination or drug therapy is the standard. Different states have different rules in how doctors of natural health practice, but to be a part of the AMA there are standard practices you must follow. Deviation from that is not acceptable. It is considered quackery. For instance, doctors that practice alternative treatments for cancer could not be part of the AMA and are in danger of losing their licenses. My doctor just took a job at an alternative cancer treatment center in Arizona, so I know that some states allow that type of thing, but I think they have to be classified differently.

I also don't think it is a conspiracy to say that money is behind it. With all the good that we do in research and development, there is still a lot of money in "big pharma." Consider also that a lot of doctor education is in pharmaceuticals both within medical school and after they leave. Consider these organizations whose sole purpose is to "educate" and push this vaccination agenda on the public. American Academy of Pediatrics, Every Child By Two, Immunization Action Coalition, the Institute for Vaccine Safety and more recently the Bill and Melinda Gates Foundation.

I have already described how I have been treated and coerced by doctors, and I can point you to many parents to whom this has happened. You have seen how people respond even to your query on FB, as if everyone who chooses not to vaccinate is some ignorant backwoods no-nothing, intent on bringing harm down on their communities. There should be ongoing debate within the medical community regarding vaccines.

In a follow-up question, Deborah T dismissed the idea of a coronavirus vaccination having any sort of additive related to fertility control as "silly." Yet that is the next bundle of conspiracy theory narrative.

Covid-19 vaccination as a Trojan horse

The Gates Foundation, Black health, and conspiracy theories have long been known to one another. A common conspiracy theory that affects Black and White communities of faith equally circles large corporate entities, governments and individuals (almost always including Bill Gates, sometimes involving George Soros, the World Health Organization, and a shadowy, non-defined group of governments) working together to bring about a New World Order. These narratives usually include the motif that Gates and his pals engineered the virus in order to further their agenda. Sometimes that agenda is depopulating the world, sometimes it is tracking everyone for unspecified reasons or retail gain, sometimes it is causing specifically engineered deaths based on gene traits or even voting history. (This is not possible; in case one wonders.)

Some CTs suggest the virus was engineered by Gates in order to make him rich through the cure. The belief is particularly prevalent among people who believe the tabletop pandemic response exercise called Event 201 was an exercise in creating a pandemic. Others believe that Covid-19 was a naturally occurring virus that Gates and his evil actors took advantage of to bring about their agenda. This conspiracy theory bundle is espoused in a YouTube video that appeared in May.

Opinions on what the Gates vaccine additive will contain and what its end goal is depends on whether the conspiracy theorist was anti-vaxx or vaccine hesitant prior to the pandemic, or whether they hold a worldview that encompasses an End Times theory of Armageddon. The first group shares two basic concerns and both are built off the basic scaffolding of contemporary anti-vaxx beliefs. First, they worry that the pandemic will be used to install mandatory vaccination regimes not only for Covid-19 but for all vaccines. Second, and anticipated with vaccine side effects mentioned above, they fear unintended health outcomes caused by the Covid-19 vaccine, similar to the ubiquitous autism hypothesis or general concerns about weakening one's immune system. Concerns raised by these anti-vaxxers rose with the introduction of the relatively novel RNA vaccine system. Without going into medical details, vaccines based on RNA are dissimilar from traditional vaccines because they enter human cells and instruct them to produce proteins against specific disease antigens. The ability of RNA vaccines to act as a kind of "trojan horse" to deliver packets of data within cells has led to various conspiracy theories about the true purpose of the vaccine, which include[6]: harming all takers, making them permanent consumers of further medicines and healthcare services; killing specific ethnicities or races; occasioning birth control or sterility. As we have seen these concerns are part of the general discourse surrounding medical intervention and vaccines in contemporary conspiracy thinking. Take this example, shared on Facebook and on many other platforms:

> This is coming from my husband who is a microbiologist. He has worked at many institutions helping to create vaccines, and better science. But during his time at many

many world renoun institutes he saw very deadly unethical practices—he no longer works in that field because of how corrupt it had become.

HEED HIS WORDS OUR LIVES DEPEND ON IT

We are moving to step 5. Mandated MRNA vaccines are coming. The fear campaign of Covid has failed. People are not scared any longer of Covid, but that's not the problem anymore and truthfully Covid never was.

The problem is now that Covid failed and you are seeing this chess game of totalitarian control unfold, let me tell you what is really coming. If this is a mandatory vaccine campaign and it gets rolled out rapidly, you better be aware, educated and terrified.

Globalist in the next 2–3 months will magically find the cure for Covid and roll it out in a mass vaccination campaign. This vaccine is MRNA vaccine. This roll out will come out very fast for two reasons.

(1) so that you have no choice but to comply, your stuck in your house and you'll beg for it to get out.

(2) so the side effects are not revealed until the vaccine has been widely distributed.

Why is this relevant. Well, MRNA virus carry the instruction to replicate and build its viral protein right away. It doesn't require anything other than the host cell machinery to operate. In other words, it cuts down the manufacturing process significantly.

Why is that a problem? Well, MRNA has direct coding. It will do what they are programmed it to do.

In this case the RNA cause direct DNA mutation which leads to cancer, they can change your emotion, give you autoimmune diseases, autism, anything that it is programmed to do. Possibly even worse.

There is no coronavirus vaccine and there never will be one. You think that you are getting a vaccine for immunity, when in reality it's a trojan horse for something different. I tried to make this as reader friendly as possible.

This is real. I never thought in my life this would ever be real. Just because we can manipulate biology in ways doesn't mean we should.

I left research biology for ethical reasons. Bioethics is a major problem. Data is falsified for the sake of rapid profits. I have personally witnessed it (VT forum, May 2020).

[The thread was shared by Megan, who added the following:] I'm sitting here thinking about how folks share their concern that they're gonna get microchipped and tracked by the government from a vaccination using a device that they can be tracked by the government on as they type.

I also want to know why I find myself so boring yet other people think they are so interesting that the government wants to know all about them. Like, can I borrow some of that confidence? [shrug emoji] [Megan, May 18, 2020, Facebook]

The relatively novel addition to this list is that one of the additives will be a microchip that acts as or could become a personal identifier or tracker.[7] Some CTs around this idea suggest the chip might activate via 5G waves.

The second additive theory is part of a separate bundle of concerns about Covid-19 that breaks across secular and religious lines. For secularists, tracking individuals is part of a super-conspiracy in which the New World Order pushes systems of total surveillance and control as preparation for installing itself. This is part of the creeping totalitarianism that animates several conspiracy theory groups, particularly militias that display strong anti-government tendencies. Not limited to anti-vaxxers, the idea of biomedical control is a powerful metaphor uniting several disparate concerns. A popular protest sign and poster seen at lockdowns and online declares "COVID-19 IS A FALSE FLAG OPERATION TO USHER IN THE NEW WORLD ORDER. They are forging death certificates to inflate figures Do your research! Say no to masks mandatory vaccines one world currencies...."

Another meme that appeared in several variations on anti-vaxx threads integrated the idea of a vaccine or antibody immunity passport that would allow people to work. The idea was in fact rejected by the WHO on April 20, 2020. Still, the meme's connection about being asked for your identity papers in historic totalitarian regimes added fuel to the conspiracy theories. The meme stated:

> YOUR PAPERS PLEASE How forced vaccinations actually work. They don't come to your door with armed guards and a doctor to force a needle on you. They will tell you, "No vaccine papers? Then you get no state id." No id means no job. Boss man cant get insurance unless all his employees have been vaccinated.... Kids cant go to school without their papers. Can't get a bank account without your vaccine papers etc. If you can't make it completely off grif than you will be forced to submit as the gras of the governments tighten. They don't have to force you, they just have to lock you out of the system that we have become so dependent on.

Such memes were accompanied by a multitude of affirmative conspiracy statements like the following, which appeared on a Facebook lockdown protest site: "Jim: Just wait until they start the (C)ertificate (O)f (V)accination (ID) agenda and people can't enter into any public buildings without a verified vaccine on their microchip. Gabriele: Just like animals, you chip your pet to find them if they go missing. They want to control us but we need to fight them when this hits."

For religious anti-vaxxers the New World Order becomes an acceleration agent for what Christians call the Great Tribulation or Armageddon, and Muslims call the Great Massacre or Last Day. This is discussed in a later chapter.

The idea of a harmful agent in the vaccine, intended to cause us to spend all our money on healthcare, walks hand-in-hand with a larger conspiracy that American hospitals are making money off of the pandemic by either getting government subsidies or charging unreasonable amounts. Or possibly by falsely claiming to treat Covid-19 patients; each have appeared in various social media formats. On April 18, 2020, in a Facebook post that circulated often during this time "Les" reposted on his timeline a classic FOAFtale (Friend-of-a-Friend Tale) or contemporary legend as a true report:

This is pitiful. I have a friend who is a friend of Joe.... They labeled his death as a covid-19 death and it wasn't! So the family asked why it was listed as the COD and the nurse told them they've been labeling as many as they can with the virus because that's how they're getting funding. So there ya go! Now we know that the numbers are false because many who have passed didn't die from the virus, but another cause. That's how they're getting the $$$$ and that is the truth.

The logic of economic exploitation of the vulnerable by for-profit healthcare corporations breaks down in countries like Canada and the United Kingdom (among others) with universal coverage; however, narratives about big pharma remain partially relevant and in circulation because most citizens in these countries fear being exploited by predatory drug companies.

The bio-engineering of a vaccine to kill specific groups finds its echoes in the smallpox blankets history of North America, among other legends and rumors like Kool cigarettes, a menthol brand popular among, and advertised to, Black Americans. They were rumored to contain particular additives that accelerated lung cancer (Turner 1993:171). Even the Church's Chicken legend echoes specificity. The virus and vaccines as a form of targeted biological weapon was briefly covered in the origins chapter. The concerns of any group who supports this conspiracy thinking will invariably be tied up in asymmetrical power relations with untrustworthy outsiders. For example, Al Jazeera reported that Iranians believed the virus targeted people of Persian descent partially because they were hit hardest and first in the Middle East and that America is antagonistic towards them. Black and Latin communities have their own versions of being targeted, as do a subset of White supremacists in the United States who subscribe to the White replacement and White genocide conspiracies discussed earlier. The strangest one appeared when an individual member of the Blazing Patriots Facebook group posted on his personal Facebook page that the vaccine would be bioengineered to kill Republicans. Most of his fellow patriots left that alone, although a few posters did point out that this was not realistic.

The theme that vaccines will cause sterility is pernicious because it imperils a population now and into the future. As we saw in the chapter on Black communities and conspiracy theories, sterilization narratives are promulgated by politically marginalized groups, documented most among Africans and Black North Americans. Both are grounded in the convoluted relationship explored earlier between big pharma and small developing countries: including aid, trust, NGOs and governments, human clinical trials and international law. Sociologist Amy Kaler noted how sterility rumors had an impact on Western health intervention in Africa, including but not limited to vaccination programs, and compiled a list of sterility rumors dating back to the 1920s (2009). She also stressed that although "rumors of sterility surrounding public health interventions cannot be reduced to

Extensive documentation of rumors in Africa that vaccines cause sterility, 1950s-2006*

Date	Country	Health intervention	Details of rumor	Source
1950s	Rhodesia	Childhood vaccination	Causes sterility	Kaler 2004
1959	Congo	Polio vaccine	Makes children sterile	Hooper 2004
1960	Nyasaland	Smallpox vaccine	Causes sterility	Vaughan 1994
1980	Uganda	Polio vaccination	Makes children sterile	
1983	Burundi	Childhood vaccination	Makes children s	
1986	Kenya	Childhood vaccination	Contains co	plus Philippines (1990s),
1990	Cameroon	Tetanus toxoid	Makes c	Madagascar (2007),
1992	Nigeria	Childhood vaccination	Makes	Pakistan (2013 onward),
1994	Tanzania	Tetanus toxoid	Is "ant	Kenya (2015)
1996	Kenya	Childhood vaccination	Make	
1996	Malawi	Childhood vaccination	Makes	
1996	Uganda	Polio vaccine	Contain	Often associated with
1997	Kenya	Polio vaccine	Contains	mass vaccination
1998	Angola	Childhood vaccination	Contains co	campaigns
1999	Mozambique	Childhood vaccination	Causes sterility	
2003	Niger	Childhood vaccination	Makes children sterile	
2003	Nigeria	Polio vaccine	Causes sterility	Yahya 2006
2003	Zambia	Measles vaccine	Makes children sterile	Kokic 2003
2004	Somalia	Polio vaccine	Makes children sterile	Chitnavis 2004
2005	Guinea	Childhood vaccination	Contains "family planning"	Millimouno 2006
2006	"West Africa"	Childhood vaccination	Causes sterility	Jegede 2007
2006	Djibouti	Polio vaccine	Makes children sterile	IRIN 2007

*from Kaler, *Soc. Sci. Med* **68** (2009): 1171-1719

Figure 5.2. A chart of vaccination rumors, attribution included.

monocausal explanations, many African societies have undergone very broadly similar experiences during colonial and postcolonial history, similar enough to allow ... for the possibility of developing a general framework to account for these rumors" (2009:1713–1714).

Under the apartheid regime the government actually wrote up a plan to sterilize Black South Africans without their knowledge. It really was a conspiracy; it was just never implemented. In 2013, the Health Professions Council of South Africa found Dr. Wouter Basson, former head of the country's chemical and biological weapons program, guilty of anti-fertility research among other crimes against humanity (Jackson 2015). The United States and Canada each engaged in sterilization of Black and Indigenous women, either without consent or through coercion, well into the 1970s (Schoen 2011; Carpio 2004); like Tuskegee, these practices eventually entered mainstream knowledge for most Canadians and Americans. A 2018 lawsuit by Indigenous women in Saskatchewan catapulted sterilizations into the news and reignited discussions of the practice across North America (Longman 2018; Zingel 2019).

So we return to the problem suggested at the beginning of this book: sometimes conspiracy theories form because there was a historic conspiracy to which a group can point and say, if it happened before, it can happen again. Little wonder that BIPOC women continue to make up the largest group of those who fear the Covid-19 vaccination will contain a Trojan Horse of sterilization.

Beware of Gates bearing gifts

Hardly any conspiracy dealing with Covid-19 health beliefs would be complete without Bill Gates. As early as April 17, 2020, *The New York Times* identified Gates at the center of a host of circulating coronavirus conspiracies: "In posts on YouTube, Facebook and Twitter, he is being falsely portrayed as the creator of COVID-19, as a profiteer from a virus vaccine, and as part of a dastardly plot to use the illness to cull or surveil the global population" (Wakabayashi, Alba and Tracy 2020). Such popularity may have stemmed from an April 14 tweet in which Gates wrote that President Trump withholding funding from the World Health Organization was a bad idea; following this, evidence points to increasing anti–Gates hysteria due to amplification via right-wing media, if not outright astroturfing. Most of the voices chivvying up fear and anger directed toward Gates came openly from far-right pundits with established conspiracy track records, such as Alex Jones or Laura Ingraham. Using their media platforms, they promulgated links between Gates and shadowy actors, conspiracists, and companies that stood to gain in money or power because of the pandemic.

The following is a representative sample from Facebook on July 3, 2020. A 2018 story from *Business Insider* with the title "Bill Gates thinks a coming disease could kill 30 million people within 6 months—and says we should prepare for it as we do for war" (Loria 2018) was shared by a user who added this commentary:

> From 2018. How did he know? [thinking emoji]
> The next deadly disease that will cause a global pandemic is coming, Bill Gates said. An illness like the pandemic 1918 influenza, but it might not even be a flu, but something we've never seen. And he added, "The world needs to prepare for pandemics in the same serious way it prepares for war."

Among the first comments:

> **CODY:** Hmm almost like it was planned... [eye roll emoji]
> **ALLEN:** This guy is scaring the shit out of me.
> **ALLEN:** Antichrist?
> **GEORGE:** But he's already designing a cure, what a POS
> **CHRIS:** They invent the disease and sell the remedy.

Gates has since its inception remained the star in the center ring of the Covid-19 conspiracy theory circus. The most enduring attack involved covert sterilization, casting him as a genocidal eugenicist, which relied on proven falsehoods. In a May 12, 2020, article from *Type Investigation*, journalist Kathryn Joyce explained the origins of this concept that will not die—as well as its astroturfing and amplification.[8] In 2010, a news story circulated that a Gates Foundation funded initiative had used a contraceptive called Depo-Provera on unknowing villagers in Navrongo, a rural region of Ghana. Promptly denounced by Ghanaian health professionals and traditional leaders who pointed out that the Navrongo project had not tested any medications at all, the story still gained traction, pushed by Mame-Yaa Bosumtwi, a disgruntled employee in a lawsuit with an agency whose director once worked at the accused clinic. By 2011, wide circulation of the Depo-Provera falsehood in Ghanan newspapers offered the U.S. pro-life movement a new strategic partnership by reframing abortion and contraception as violating women's safety and racial justice. Pro-life groups

> hired Black activists and highlighted uglier aspects of the history of reproductive health care—in particular, the courting of the eugenics movement by Planned Parenthood founder Margaret Sanger in the early part of the 20th century. A right-wing documentary, *Maafa 21: Black Genocide in 21st Century America*, used a Swahili word that refers to the holocaust of African enslavement to denounce Planned Parenthood as racist. Billboards in Atlanta and Manhattan carried messages like, "The most dangerous place for an African American is in the womb" [Joyce 2020].

Black feminists weren't buying it; they called the strategy out as an attempt to stop abortions, rather than showing concern for BIPOC pregnant women. But the rhetoric employed drew on the earned mistrust people of color in America directed toward American healthcare. Enter the Rebecca Project (RP), a non-profit focused on social justice issues for women of color. RP released a report in 2011 called *Non-Consensual Research in Africa: The Outsourcing of Tuskegee* that mixed verifiable problematic practices with more nebulous allegations, including the Navrongo project that was backed by the Gates Foundation. This report was followed in 2013 by *Depo-Provera: Deadly Reproductive Violence Against Women*. Both reports were written by Kwame Fosu; unbeknownst to the Rebecca Project, Fosu was the father of the disgruntled employee Mame-Yaa Bosumtwi's child. Kathryn Joyce, the journalist who investigated the story, described Fosu's first report as poorly sourced, the second as a fulsome conspiracy theory (2017). The reports eventually caused a fatal schism within the NGO, and its dissolution.

When the Gates Foundation started a new effort to increase African women's access to contraceptives in 2014, the framework established by the RP reports and American pro-life organizations framed the conflict that followed. No longer a fight over faith-based morals and the sanctity of life, this was about biomedical neo-colonialism perpetuated under the guise of altruism; Gates was waging chemical warfare on poor women. Recognizing that this strategy worked best when told by indigenous African voices, the conservative backers of the colonialist argument made themselves less visible than in previous iterations of anti-abortion initiatives. The strategy would succeed because it was embedded in a long tradition of health legends, rumors, and conspiracy theories present in both African and Black North American communities espousing skepticism and antipathy to foreign health initiatives, particularly when they mimic worldwide neo-colonial development initiatives.

That same year, Zimbabwe's Registrar General suggested modern contraceptives were a Western ploy aimed at limiting African population growth, while Kenya's Conference of Catholic Bishops announced without evidence that the WHO/UNICEF tetanus vaccine was laced with a sterilization hormone. The Kenyan Parliament spent significant sums of money on testing to prove that it wasn't.

If both the CTs and the methods of transmission sound familiar, it is because current attacks on Gates follow the same template, now to a global audience rather than African or anti-abortion centered audience. In April 2020, Candace Owens, a Black woman who speaks on conservative issues, called Gates a "vaccine-criminal" and claimed he had used "African & Indian tribal children to experiment w/ non–FDA approved drug vaccines." She suggested that she would refuse any vaccine created by so ethically tainted a source, and people of conscience should follow her example. In both her original Facebook post and a follow-up Twitter post, Owens linked Gates' purported involvement to the WHO and broader global conspiracy theories.

Despite Reuters and Snopes declaring them false, photographs purporting to prove that the Gates Foundation runs a "Center for Human Population Reduction" spread throughout 2020. *One American News*, a far-right network, also amplified the idea of Gates seeking population control in numerous broadcasts. Other villains of the pandemic were pictured (whether real or photoshopped) in the company of Gates to either sully their mutual reputations or advance a Deep State narrative. A short list of such suspects includes Soros, Fauci, Justin Trudeau, members of the WHO and CDC, and more. In fact, Gates has been woven into super-conspiracy theories linking him to a global system of biomedical power and control akin to the anti–Semitic puppet master stereotype.

The above chart is reminiscent of Rothschild's NWO maps that have appeared in conspiracy theory publications for nearly a hundred years. The iconography of anti–Semitic scapegoating is embedded in anti–Gates conspiracies.

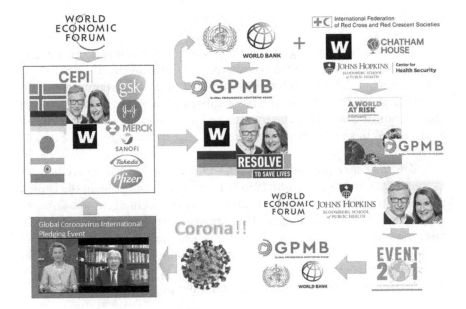

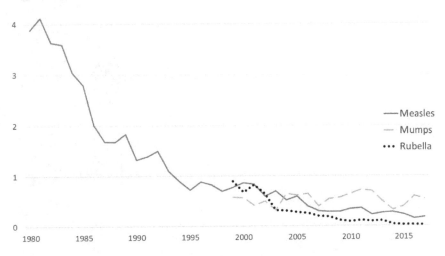

Figure 5.3. Anonymously circulated Gates conspiracy chart.

Vaccination has helped reduce global cases of mumps, measles, and rubella
Reported cases 1980 to 2017

— Measles
— Mumps
••• Rubella

Figure 5.4. WHO chart of vaccination success, from BBC website.

Conclusions

This chapter's catalog of Covid-19 vaccination conspiracy theories might give some insight into why 50 percent of Americans (for a start) would reject a vaccine if offered it immediately. Such a significant number is disastrous to public health messaging, and in fact contributes to that accelerationist conspiracy theory attached to an auto-identification object being added to a Gates-backed vaccine. These are the subject of the next chapter.

Before we leave this one, however, let us revisit the idea of vaccinations as a force for good. It took from 1953 to 1979 to eradicate polio in the United States through vaccination. Eradicate. Because vaccinations are as much about public as individual good, they are not always perceived as being in one's personal best interests. The good of the many and the good of the recipient can be weighed in the balance and found uneven. But whatever one may say as an individual, statistically it is impossible to deny the global effectiveness of vaccines on creating a healthier population worldwide.

Six

Apocalypse Now, or Later?

End Times and the New World Order

The truth is that every interpreter thinks her/his position
is the average Christian position.—Ken J. Purscell, retired
pastor, teacher, researcher

For Christians, knowledge of the past does not just put the
present into proper perspective, it orients us to God's meta-
narrative. All of our holy days are remembrances of the past
that emphasize our hope for the future.—Elizabeth Stice

Some of the conspiracy theories circling Covid-19 pertain to a
New World Order and extra-biblical approaches to End Times, making a connection between vaccination, contact tracing and "The Mark
of the Beast" (which is part of the "Great Tribulation"). When you mention that you are writing about such beliefs and the pandemic, the
response is pretty standard: "but that's just a small group of—." The
next words will be particularly telling. "Nut jobs" with its undertone of
conspiracy-theorist-turned-prepper? "Evangelicals" tends to be the most
common finale: tidy, quantifiable, inaccurate. Sometimes "fundamental-
ists" or even "Americans" replaces evangelicals.

The conspiracy of Covid-19 accelerating plans to bring in a One World
Government—and why that is a bad thing—requires a bit of baseline information to understand, which may raise a question to readers. Aren't we meant
to be debunking rather than sympathizing here? Perhaps, but when a conspiracy theory affects public health policy to such a significant degree that roughly
half the world's population is prepared to refuse a vaccine not yet invented,
understanding why becomes vital to public health (AP-NORC 2020). Man-
dating compliance to public health best practices does not increase its likelihood; the very act of seeking compliance exacerbates resistance. Humans are
stubborn creatures; for example, we continue to experience the fallout from
the American 1902 court case *Jacobson v. Massachusetts*.

Dismantling a concern within a faith community can turn all too easily into why that religion is "mere superstition" in the first place. This would be disrespectful to internal community views, and indeed to at least two of the current authors who share End Times concerns yet don't believe their interpretations support conspiracy theories about Covid-19. Voluntary compliance to sound health practices is most easily achieved when messages are carefully constructed toward those least compliant, addressing rather than dismissing their concerns. Public health theory calls this skill cultural competency, sometimes cultural humility. It hinges on listening to the community, and then using the words and values of the suspicious group to persuade.

Christians and evangelicals

But even if one accepts trying to understand and express empathy to a community's terms as a best practice, one might be tempted to ask, why bother? Isn't this group a fringe element, a negligible community in terms of size and influence? The short answer is no; End Times believers are a huge swath of the population, and not limited to Christians. About a third of the world's current eight billion inhabitants are expecting Jesus to return, some of them as early as 2050 (Pew Research Center 2010); this encompasses Christians, Muslims, Bahai, and even non-religious people. Christian communities are not always aware that Islam also preaches a final showdown involving Jesus returning to Earth as an authoritative leader, in what Muslims call "The Great Massacre"; we will return to this concept shortly.

There are 2.3 billion Christians around the world. Of America's 330 million or so population, 240 million self-identify as Christian. In Europe, only 28 percent of those who self-identify as Christians (roughly 570 million people) are active in churches or hold the Bible as a final authority; no survey was found seeking Second Coming belief among this group, but it is statistically likely to be about half of that 28 percent (Pew Research Center 2018). In Canada 55 percent identify as Christian. According to the 2011 census, Muslim Canadians make up 3.2 percent of the population. Of that general population 29 percent say that religion is very important, making Canada ever so slightly more secular than her southern neighbor (Lipka 2019).

Evangelicals are a subgroup within Protestant Christianity. This group is important in conspiracy theory because of its perceived support for President Trump. Among Americans identifying as Christian, about one in four chooses the additional description of evangelical. The National Association of Evangelicals (NAE) lists four beliefs and follows with a summation:

- The Bible is the highest authority for what I believe.
- It is very important for me personally to encourage non–Christians to trust Jesus Christ as their Savior.
- Jesus Christ's death on the cross is the only sacrifice that could remove the penalty of my sin.
- Only those who trust in Jesus Christ alone as their Savior receive God's free gift of eternal salvation.

These distinctives and theological convictions define us—not political, social or cultural trends. In fact, many evangelicals rarely use the term "evangelical" to describe themselves, focusing simply on the core convictions of the triune God, the Bible, faith, Jesus, salvation, evangelism and discipleship [NAE 2015].

"Evangelical" has become a term that some Christians will correct if it is applied to them, even if they identify with the four statements above, because it has become synonymous in media discussion (liberal and conservative) as a group that is primarily White, Republican, and admiring of the current president tasked with addressing the pandemic during his White House tenure. The sometimes-overlooked presence of a left-wing Christian evangelicalism in the United States (Corp 2020) also complicates the pervasive narrative that conspiracy theories based in evangelical Christianity are synonymous with Republican politics.

Statistically, American evangelicals are 76 percent White and 24 percent disagree with President Trump on all or nearly all issues; 14 percent have a bachelor's degree and 7 percent an advanced degree. Name rejection is not a global issue. Christians globally identify at a 25 percent rate as evangelicals (de Senneville and Besmond 2016) and evangelicalism is rising worldwide while falling in the United States.

Christians in America could not under normal designation be described as a minority, let alone a marginalized one. Pew results in 2020 list America as 70.6 percent Christian (Pew Research Forum 2014). The same is not true worldwide; in fact, religious freedom in North America skews stats from other countries. Statistically, 1 in 8 Christians lives in a country where their beliefs are persecuted (Watt 2020). A 2019 Pew study found that 143 countries persecute Christians and 140 persecute Muslims, with 87 for Jews. In each case, persecution had risen from 2007, when Christians faced persecution in 107 countries, Muslims 97, and Jews 51. Eastern religions were at 50 in 2019, up from 33 (Chandler 2019).

Part of a conspiracy theory's appeal to an individual rests on how much that person feels part of a group likely to be victimized by what the CT suggests. When the overarching narrative is about resilience in the face of threat (and temptation), the self-identification of "being persecuted" is an inherent part of one's worldview, irrespective of how free one actually is.

Muslim belief in the Last Day

A 2012 Pew study in Islamic countries found that 50 percent of Muslims expected Jesus to return "soon" (Casper 2016). In Africa, where 40 percent of people self-identify as Christian, and 45 percent as Muslim, one could figure half of the continent's 1.3 billion population has some level of belief in a Last Day (LeMarquand 2000).

Islam anticipates The Great Massacre; it follows a prolonged period of moral decay, which some scholars say lasts as long as 500 years. By that reckoning, the world is somewhere around year 475 of this decay, give or take. During this time the Deceiving Messiah (Al-Mashih ad-Dajjal) and a Beast (Dabbat al-ard, literally Beast of the Earth) presage the Second Coming of Jesus (The Last Day or the Last Judgment). Jesus doesn't come as a prophet, but to lead a millennial reign of peace under his authority. While paralleling some End Times beliefs with Christianity, Muslim holy texts are silent on a piece of Armageddon very much to the fore in Christian belief: The Mark of the Beast, sometimes abbreviated as The Mark. Islam has a Beast but neither the Qur'an (Islam's Holy Book) or the Hadith (stories of the life of the Prophet that form an auxiliary "scripture") mention a Mark.[1]

The Qur'an and the Hadith between them mention a handful of greater signs, and dozens of lesser signs, that herald the beginning of the End. The Greater Signs include: sexual immorality leading to new diseases; famine and oppression resulting from crooked business operations and wealth hoarding, and drought resulting from judgment of bad behavior; those who are not true believers fight with each other and with the true believers. About the Beast/False Messiah, the Hadith says little specifically:

> Verily, among the first signs to appear are the rising of the sun from the west and the emergence of the beast before people at noon. Whichever of them occurs first, the other will soon follow.—Ṣaḥīḥ Muslim 2941
>
> Nothing between the creation of Adam until the establishment of the Hour is a greater tribulation than the affair of the False Messiah.—Ṣaḥīḥ Muslim 2946
>
> I surely know what the False Messiah will have with him. He will have two flowing rivers, one that appears to be clear water and another that appears to be blazing fire. If one of you sees that, let him go to the river of fire, lower his gaze, put his head down, and drink from it, for it will be cool water. The False Messiah has one covered eye with thick skin over it. Written between his eyes is the word of unbelief. Every believer will be able to read it, whether he is literate or not.—Ṣaḥīḥ Muslim 2934
>
> I saw a vision last night by the Ka'bah in my sleep. There was a brown-skinned man, as beautiful as I had ever seen. His hair fell between his shoulders, a man whose head was dripping with water. He placed his hands on the shoulders of two men as he circled the House. I said: Who is this? They said: It is the Messiah, son of Mary. Then I saw a man behind him, with very curly hair and blindness in his right eye, resembling the look of Ibn Qatan. He placed his hands on the shoulders of a man as he circled the

House. I said: Who is this? They said: It is the False Messiah.—Ṣaḥīḥ al-Bukhārī 3256, Ṣaḥīḥ Muslim 169

Interpretations range widely, and prophecy is sprinkled throughout the Qur'an in ways different from the Christian scriptures, which confines it primarily (although not only) to Revelation and Ezekiel. Comparing Hadith verses to Revelation points out that Islam does not mention a specific Mark of the Beast, yet concerns about Covid conspiracies accelerating the Great Massacre are similar to those of Christians believing the pandemic has accelerated Armageddon.

It is unclear how many Christians and Muslims understand each other's religions enough to compare their End Times beliefs. A religion professor asked to discuss Muslim concerns expressed the fringe element theory with which this chapter opened, with the pejorative addition that only those bent on political gain would adhere to such a belief: "...it is difficult to think of any majority Muslim country that has a political faction as massive as American evangelicals, who are so intensely focused on apocalyptic thinking that they pay no attention to contemporary political realities. The ISIS group has manipulative apocalyptic imagery, but it remains a minority view" (email May 30).

At the political end of religion in both Protestant Christianity and Sunni and Shia Islam, adherents of each faith have at some point called the other out for being the spirit of Antichrist. Remember the idea that a regime based on evil, corruption, and falling away from God might not be led by a specific man; the Antichrist could be an ethos, an epoch—or a different religion, leading people astray. That possibility plays well into political maneuvering of Muslims against Christians and vice versa; indeed, it has precedents dating back past the Crusades. It is perhaps ironic that moral entrepreneurs seeking to lead a modern crusade have turned similar concerns about cruelty and corruption shared by these two groups, successfully against each other.

Conventionally, Muslims and Christians at extreme ends of their respective faiths have viewed one another as the enemy, to the point that the coming showdown between good and evil pits them against one another; the West has been called the Antichrist by some Muslims; the Middle East is the minefield from which evil arises to some Christians.

What are "those people" afraid of?

If one asks politely, North American church-goers will tell you, somewhat sheepishly, how they grew up expecting to be that all-important Last

Generation. Hubris meets prophecy; each successive teen youth group thought it would play the starring role in Armageddon. This is a surprisingly common belief, bolstering the idea that CTs appeal most to those who feel, as *The Conversation* podcast put it, narcissistic, either wishing or assuming their role in the world to be greater than it is (Bligh 2020). This is not uncommon in conspiracy thinking overall.

The authoritative piece of literature on End Times for Christians is the Book of Revelation, attributed to John. To some, Revelation is a description of things already past, namely Nero's reign. Christians got caught in the crossfire and faced mortal persecution as Nero scapegoated them to deflect public anger at him following the Great Fire of Rome.[2] Yet for many Christians, Revelation is what is yet to come.

John doesn't provide a key for interpreting his text; he just describes things in bald terms that don't seem to those outside the interpretive community of believers to make sense. Stars fall into oceans and kill everything. Numerous lamps appear that talk to him, and not at all in a Disney-esque way. Plagues take out quite specific percentages of the population by roasting, drowning, or starving them; one plague can be interpreted as saying it scares people to death. A dragon is trying to eat a newborn. The guide throughout this hallucinatory journey has a sword for a tongue.

John of Patmos (the island to which the writer of Revelation had been exiled for being a Christian) is traditionally identified as the "beloved disciple," namely Jesus's best friend during his time on Earth, and the author of the Gospel of John and three Epistles. Those three letters are among the sweetest books in the whole Bible: admonishing people to love each other; pastoral, gentle, and kind. The book of John is different in tone and structure from the other Gospels, incorporating Greek philosophical premises like God as the word (logos) and Jesus as the word made flesh. It holds the world's most famous Bible verse, John 3:16. The Gospel and Epistles are consistent among themselves, while Revelation is very different. Historians and theologians have long debated this identification of John of Patmos with the beloved disciple: arguments against common authorship are based on differences in grammar, tone, terminology, and theological approaches. (The beloved disciple would also have been pushing 90 by the time Revelation was written, around 95 CE—neither impossible, nor a strong argument for.) It's hard to reconcile Revelation's chained dragons and harlots drunk on martyr blood while astride horrific monsters with this sweet old man.

Running through it all, however, are poetic images about the all-powerful central figure of the book: The Lamb who was slain (a Biblical reference to Jesus). Revelation is a difficult book, evidenced by how often people get the name wrong (there is no terminal s). Ultimately, it is the revelation of Jesus as both lamb and lion. A sinless sacrifice ended the need for animal sacrifice forever; individual relationship with God became possible without an intermediary priest; and in Revelation, Jesus returns to claim all that was bought with that sacrifice. Gentle Jesus, meek and mild, is replaced by all-powerful Jesus, redeeming everyone who asked to be since Lucifer won humanity with a fuzzy logic claim made from within a snake suit. In essence, Jesus returns to kick butt.

But if you say it like that, Christians don't much appreciate the wording. And if you don't believe in Jesus being on Earth the first time, crucified and risen from the dead, the book looks like a mishmash of poetry, prophecy, and weirdness too open to interpretation to evince belief from a reasonable person. If you do believe in Jesus as a sinless sacrifice, then the central figure of a victorious Jesus stands out within the prophecies; believers see repeated displays of victory and stunning reversals as the meek inherit the Earth—open to wide interpretation as to how that will logistically happen. It still reads like an acid trip, but a good one.

To understand the layout of conspiracy theories spreading in Christian communities, we also need to understand the biblical context and characters involved—the kind of deep story that structures the seemingly chaotic expressions of pandemic panic. A few concepts will be crucial for this explanation, many familiar but often misused. Armageddon is the last battle on earth between good and evil. In Revelation, John identifies the events that will lead to Armageddon and the final reign of Jesus on earth. While there is some debate (addressed later) about the order of events, in general terms there will be signs that the End Times have begun, one of which is the rise of the Beast and a plague during which "ugly, festering sores broke out on the people who had the mark of the beast and worshiped its image" (Rev. 16:2).[3] When all of this has been completed, there is a final war between the forces of good and evil, ending with 1000 years of Jesus reigning on earth. This abbreviated summary hides a number of debates about the order of events, their particulars, and how Christians will be involved at any given point.

For our purposes, the most crucial debate linked to CTs about Covid-19 asks the question, "Who is this Beast?" In popular literature and media, the Beast and the Antichrist are often treated as synonymous, but this is not biblically specified. The Antichrist might be a world leader, or perhaps a spirit of an age, or an incarnation of the denial of Jesus as God (1 John 2:18–22). Either the Beast or the Antichrist becomes the leader of the New World Order (discussed below). The Beast demands to be worshipped to the point that those who do not are executed (Rev. 13:12). The Mark of the Beast is required to buy and sell:

> It [the Beast] also forced all people, great and small, rich and poor, free and slave, to receive a mark on their right hands or on their foreheads, so that they could not buy

or sell unless they had the mark, which is the name of the beast or the number of its name. This calls for wisdom. Let the person who has insight calculate the number of the beast, for it is humanity's number. That number is 666 [Rev. 13:16–18].[4]

Receiving this Mark demonstrates loyalty to the Antichrist regime. An angel warns in a loud voice:

"If anyone worships the beast and its image and receives its mark on their forehead or on their hand, they, too, will drink the wine of God's fury, which has been poured full strength into the cup of his wrath. They will be tormented with burning sulfur in the presence of the holy angels and of the Lamb. And the smoke of their torment will rise for ever and ever. There will be no rest day or night for those who worship the beast and its image, or for anyone who receives the mark of its name" [Rev. 14:9–11].

Those who took the Mark would face eternal damnation:

But the beast was captured, and with it the false prophet who had performed the signs on its behalf. With these signs he had deluded those who had received the mark of the beast and worshiped its image. The two of them were thrown alive into the fiery lake of burning sulfur [Rev. 19:20].

In contrast, those who refused would rule with Jesus for at least a thousand years:

I saw thrones on which were seated those who had been given authority to judge. And I saw the souls of those who had been beheaded because of their testimony about Jesus and because of the word of God. They had not worshiped the beast or its image and had not received its mark on their foreheads or their hands. They came to life and reigned with Christ a thousand years.

To Christians who believe Revelation is about the end of our world as we know it, the question is not whether there will be a Beast, but how to interpret what it will look like so one avoids falling prey to the Great Deceiver. Many dire warnings run through John's words about not being deceived which are echoed in chapter two of the Apostle Paul's letter II Thessalonians.

Armageddon comes at the end of the Great Tribulation, a seven-year period of intense persecution for Christians (and not that nice for anyone else, either; darkness, heat, and stinging insects are just a few of the plagues). Authorities differ on whether the Great Tribulation is preceded, interrupted, or followed by Jesus returning to collect the Christians, the event known as The Rapture. John Nelson Darby coined this term in the 1830s (Akenson, 2018) as a name for the Second Coming of Jesus, setting it firmly at the beginning of the Great Tribulation; many are surprised to find that the word Rapture never appears in the Bible, and that the Bible is silent on the issue of actual timing as to when the Christians reunite with Jesus.

The Great Tribulation involving the Mark of the Beast (expressed in both popular culture and the Bible as 666) as a way to exclude believers from society lies at the center of a group of Covid-19 conspiracies. In communities where the Great Tribulation, the Rapture, the Antichrist, and the Beast are not only real but immanent events, believers actively seek out figures in the pandemic crisis (as with just about every crisis in history) that could match Revelation's predictions. They are then taken as fulfillment of the prophecies—which perhaps helps explain the growing alarm that a New World Order has been accelerated in some way by Covid-19. One matchup is that Trump is the Antichrist, held more by leftwing Christians than right, for obvious reasons. Another is that Bill Gates is the Antichrist, planning to microchip us all in fulfillment of the 666 prophecy as he ushers in a global government.

The New World Order and a One World Government

American President Woodrow Wilson used the expression "New World Order" (NWO) to describe the post–World War I world; this appears to be its first recorded instance in the English-speaking world (although a conspiracy theory does exist linking the NWO to the 1913 establishment of the U.S. Federal Reserve: see Crozier 1912).[5] Since Wilson, and later Winston Churchill, used the phrase in establishing and describing the League of Nations (the inter-war effort at what would become the basis for the United Nations), the NWO soon became linked to a more global way of governing. Hence its sister phrase, One World Government, suggesting that the New World Order will be a One World Government. They are practically synonymous in End Times thinking.

Most of the NWO theories borrow heavily from anti–Semitic legends dating back to early days of money lender slander, when Jewish power was largely limited to financial circles, as we discussed in the Black Death chapter. The theory that Jews secured political power through back channels and influenced world affairs never really left NWO conspiracies, just updated and ramped up from individual "Uncle Shylock" characters to those all-powerful "puppet masters" (e.g., George Soros) taking control of governments through international banking.

Technology at the end of World War II changed rapidly enough to disquiet European and North American societies, while the formation of the Soviet Union brought a new (and mostly unwelcome) heavyweight player to a changing political field. Outside of the active conspiracy theories involving real world politics and economics, futurist writers such as H.G. Wells began to envision a dystopian technological society based on a New World Order (1940). Whether fiction or political writing, the idea of a NWO found itself in the hands of those bent on simultaneously sounding the alarm, and gaining significant social power, remuneration, and recognition as the one who had been smart enough to first ring the alarm bells. People who take on such tasks are often referred to as moral entrepreneurs, a term coined by sociologist Howard Becker (1966) for people who become rule creators or enforcers to solve a perceived social evil.[6]

Starting in the 1970s, many of those sounding the alarm about a New World Order referenced an ancient and now-defunct group called the Illuminati. Derived from the Latin for "enlightened," the Illuminati grew out of a society founded May 1, 1776, in Bavarian Germany. The group, comprising fewer than a dozen members at the start, wanted to privilege scientific reason over religion and politics for purposes of social justice and enlightenment. This put them at immediate odds with the Catholic church and, given the turbulent revolutions in the nascent United States and in France, the group soon found itself accused of fomenting civil unrest. Internal argument among members (below a thousand even at its heyday) added to their decline. By the early 1800s the actual group was a hollow shell, but their legend lives on.

Because the Illuminati attempted to recruit from the Freemasons after internal division and bad publicity reduced their membership, they are sometimes assumed to have merged with the Freemasons. The persistence of these two groups in conspiratorial thinking cannot be overestimated.[7] While the early Bavarian Illuminati are no more, the romanticized notion of a powerful renegade remnant continues in multiple and competing CTs, preserving the name and upgrading the group's intent from enlightenment and reform to malevolent world dominance. A reference to the Illuminati in a conspiracy theory does not always mean the speaker/poster believes in, or even makes a connection back to the Bavarian group and Freemasonry; the contemporary idea of the Illuminati acts largely as a boogeyman adaptable and flexible enough to be woven into various competing interpretative communities. For example, as you will shortly read, Freemasons and secret societies have been woven into the Satanic international child trafficking and exploitation rings associated with one aspect of the QAnon super-conspiracy. Liberal and leftist interpretations have seen machinations behind the International Monetary Fund, World Bank, and World Trade Organization as plots by Conservative economic and political leaders moving the world toward illiberal One World Government (OWG). Likewise, various Conservative and rightwing movements, of which the John Birch Society is a tentpole example, identified international "socialism" as the creeping OWG menace. While traditional super-conspiracy theories by professional CT practitioners eventually feature a historic and specific mapping of the Illuminati and their role in various contemporary phenomenon, most everyday conspiracists lump the Illuminati in with a One

World Government in a vague way, acknowledging it as part of a CT canon of beliefs but not necessarily central to their own interpretations. As we have noted, the specifics of any given CT are sometimes less important than their shared nefarious intentions. (A word to the wise: someone who knows enough about the Illuminati to distinguish between the defunct group and a modern cabal in a conversation holds more than a passing interest in conspiracy theories.)

In 1970, Hal Lindsey's influential *Late Great Planet Earth* cast the Soviet Union and the then-nascent European Union (known then as the European Economic Community) as the bad actors to watch in forming the OWG. Throughout the 1980s, several moral entrepreneurs and professional conspiracists capitalized on the growing interest in End Times eschatology, combining it with far-right politics. Whether those groups overlapped much at the time is subject to interpretive debate, and of less consequence than what happened next. As the date moved closer to 2000, NWO conspiracy theory seemed to jump the tracks from these two smaller groups into a growing mainstream awareness. An arguable boost in that came as George H.W. Bush gave a 1990 speech to Congress using the term; the resulting fear across various communities was swift (Berlet and Lyons 2000). The fact that Bush Senior's speech was delivered on September 11 would fuel a later CT that dogged his son. By September 11, 2001, NWO fear was sufficient to make George W. Bush engineering the terrorist attacks from within his White House on orders from his NWO cabal cronies a popular conspiracy theory to this day.

This was perhaps another turning point, the first seismic event in the new millennium, because after 9/11 the lid seemed to come off Pandora's box. From this point forward, almost any major international incident saw recycled NWO conspiracy theories, not only from Christian alarmists or right-wing circles, but also within mainstream speculation. Various NWO theories moved into the daylight, propelled perhaps by access to social media as a transmission tool, and by an as-yet-unremarked growth in White supremacy movements across Europe and North America.

The great falling away

If the age of the Antichrist were nigh, manifested in a New World Order, then the Second Coming—the return of Jesus to select the righteous who have remained true—must be immanent. Apocalyptic thinking pervades American culture, and not only among faith communities.[8] The use of Armageddon, the Second Coming, or the Great Tribulation in mainstream entertainment began an accelerating shift in the early 2000s, from "this is scary and real and important" to "this is silly," something on par with believing in the monster under your bed. Christians and Muslims soon saw amoralistic portrayals of events they held sacred, which fueled belief that making fun of these events was a precursor to their arrival; a great falling away from faith is also predicted before the Second Coming in both faiths.

From *Raptured* by Ernest Angley in 1950 to the *Left Behind* series (LaHaye and Jenkins 1995–2007), Christian literature considering the implications of the Apocalypse has focused on biblical interpretation and addressing world events as signs of the times. This genre provided moral lessons based on the assumption that readers were already familiar with Christian Apocalyptic themes. Secular science fiction focused on the end of the world had existed long before 2000, but began to merge with themes such as OWG/NWO in the beginning of the 21st century.

Shortly after the start of the new millennium, a proliferation of literature from outside the evangelical worldview began taking amoralistic approaches to those sacred themes. The protagonist in the *BBC* five-part series *The Last Enemy* (Berry 2008) was a slowly waking pawn in a government using "total information awareness" technology. What is perhaps most interesting about the series is that its discussion of ethics surrounding microchipping humans was grounded not in religion but privacy. No moral or eschatology implications existed to being a participant in a cashless society based on a unique body-embedded identifier (AKA a Mark). The same proved true of Suzanne Weyn's teen fiction series, starting in 2004 with *The Bar Code Tattoo*, followed by *The Bar Code Rebellion* (2006) and *The Bar Code Prophecy* (2012). The moral center of objection is that the tattoo moves from choice to mandate, ushering in unethical and secretive eugenics that furthers a divide between rich and poor society members.

Enter Tom Perrotta's 2011 novel, *The Leftovers*, in which the disappearance of about 3 percent of the world's population has no moralistic overtones whatsoever. In Perotta's world, people of all faiths and ages, including pagans and atheists, simply vanish. Everyone else is left behind to figure it out and keep going. The tone of the series (a cult forms of people who smoke constantly, believing their lives have no meaning since they have been disdained by God) amplified a growing sense of disdain for earnestly held beliefs, which evangelicals could begin to point to, alongside proliferation of other fiction and nonfiction treatments of The Second Coming outside Christian-specific markets. By the time *The Leftovers* premiered as an HBO series on June 29, 2014 (created by Damon Lindelof and Perrotta), and ran three seasons, the Apocalypse might be reasonably moved from the realm of horror to comedy—albeit dark—in the minds of mainstream entertainment consumers. In cultural awareness, Armageddon became not the stuff of nightmares so much as bemused condescension.[9]

Such theme recombination around technology, threatening governmental control, and either secular or religious apocalypses, combined with a global pandemic, have moved apocalyptic thinking and themes into mainstream discourse. While secular versions give less religious weight to a single threatening or evil leader, the progression of social control and OWG/NWO in many novels is now nearly indistinguishable from earlier Christian literature. As the fictional narratives have converged, so too have CTs cross-fertilized between religious and secular worldviews.

Recombining conspiracy for Covid-19

The rapid emergence of Covid-19 has given new life to theories around both the Mark of the Beast and the OWG/NWO in the minds of conspiracy minded individuals and groups. One theory purports that contact tracing, wearing masks, and complying with stay at home edicts are practice runs for the "New Normal," which is, in essence the New World Order. Across all social media formats comes the interpretation that compliant populations, or "sheeple," learn unquestioning government obedience through these health practices, and this is leading to a subtle slide into One World Government headed by a cabal of viral opportunists. Yet arguments over stay at home orders and wearing masks can also be interpreted directly oppositely through this eschatological frame, but here the debate advocates for optimal public health outcomes. A counter-conspiracy among leftwing Christian interpretation says resistance to masks, stay at home orders, and contact tracing show immoral values since these are all ways of showing care and concern for fellow humans. Those speaking most boldly against this type of shared care in the name of Christ are, it is said, in fact part of the false prophet culture, the spirit of Antichrist.

Donald Trump rapidly rose as a favorite for the role of Antichrist in June 2020 after clearing Black Lives Matter protesters from a D.C. church to pose with a Bible in front of its sign (Rogers 2020). Prior to that event, calling him the eschatological Antichrist was arguably more sarcasm and irony than actual belief. Still, keep in mind that the scariest person with power over you is the most likely boogieman for one's biggest CT villain; those who fear Trump may be the Antichrist are less likely to base this on his actions or placement inside other conspiracy theories. Conspiracy theories run on emotion. Also, most American presidents are cast in this starring turn during their tenure. When they leave office, the legend abandons them and hops onto the shoulders of the next occupant. Time will tell with Trump and leftwing conspiracy theorists.

Extra-biblical authorities

Prevalent almost worldwide among the myriad and sometimes conflicting conspiracies attributed to Bill Gates is the undying idea that any Covid-19 vaccine would involve some form of unique identifier—a digital tattoo or auto-ID chip implant—and these would later become the Mark of the Beast. This theory walks hand-in-hand with the "sheeple get ready" idea of compliance to false or freedom-reducing community health behaviors like wearing a mask and limiting outings as preparation for forcing compliance with a New World Order. Sometime in the 1970s or '80s, a cashless society managed through bodily implanted identification evolved as the leading theory among evangelists (not evangelicals) for what the Mark might be. Moral entrepreneurs cashed in on the explosion of prophetic interest in 1970s America to create a canon of accepted yet extra-biblical info around the Mark of the Beast.

Lindsey's *The Late Great Planet Earth* (1970) emerged in the context of what were then considered extremely high gas prices in a manufactured oil crisis; where one finds Middle Eastern Muslims inconveniencing Western Christians, or vice versa, End Times conspiracy theories will shortly follow for both groups. Although Lindsey's work predated personal computer culture, the advent of significantly more powerful and even home-based technology in the 1980s reinforced the cashless society idea. Computer fear became Beast fear. Lindsey and many evangelists spoke on such fears in later crusades and lectures, naming successive threats. As Australian futurist Katina Michael points out in her body of work on auto-ID and social resistance to the same, naming new technology as the Mark of the Beast pre-dated Lindsey, moving from ration cards, to magnetic strips on credit cards, through barcodes, to radio-frequency identification (RFID) chipping, to the current frenzy of fear surrounding Covid-19 vaccines. Each generation pointed to some revolutionary technology and said it was the Mark. None were (Michael and Michael 2009).

Considering how revolutionary the home computer became in that brief span of 50 years between Lindsey's seminal book and the current crisis of Covid-19 vaccine, it is not surprising that conspiracy theories could hardly keep up. As these changes took place, the idea of a Mark being the only way to participate in commerce synced with both computer technology and futurist predictions that we will eventually use e-data rather than money for our currency. The Mark became almost synonymous with an embedded computer chip, the RFID now being the suspect of choice. The build-up of trusted evangelizing voices has pushed this auto-ID and cashless society theory enough to make it difficult for many to delineate them from actual scripture. The American coin shortage that occurred because of the disruption of the pandemic added fuel to the conspiracy fire beginning around June 2020, when some businesses refused cash transactions.

Public opinion might characterize these ever-changing warnings that a cashless society system had arrived as too many near misses to continue crying "Beast" with every technological advancement. End Times believers might instead suggest each is a step toward the inevitable—supported by futurists and computer tech geeks producing headlines such as "Why You're Probably Getting a Microchip Implant Someday" (Weiss 2018). Or a YouTube video titled "I Put a Payment Chip in My Hand to Replace My Wallet" in which *Buzzfeed* writer Charlie Warzel had a computer chip implanted between the thumb and forefinger of his right hand. This was subsequently connected to his Venmo account, fulfilling his wish to become the first person to purchase a cup of coffee with his hand rather than his phone (*BuzzFeedVideo* 2016). Warzel's video and articles were part of a series on the future of money, but where people in general saw the pros and cons of a cashless society, evangelicals saw tech catching up to fears about End Times prophecy. A 2015 Pakistani governmental plan to track those on a terrorist watch list by implanting RFID chips (behind their knees) also met with immediate comparisons to historic Nazis identity tracking and democratic erosion (*Express Tribune* 2015). One need only read the comments on the Warzel video or the *Express Tribune* article to see the breadth of divided opinion.

After they were not legally allowed to mandate it, companies in Sweden asked employees to implant a device that would open security doors in a high-tech firm. By 2018 some 4,000 Swedes had voluntarily microchipped (Savage 2018). U.S. legislators took the matter seriously enough to prevent the problem faced by Swedish workers. More than a dozen states, including California, Colorado, Florida, North Dakota, Missouri, Ohio, Oklahoma, and Wisconsin currently have laws against forced implantation of RFID or other digital auto-ID forms in humans. Georgia's is called the *Microchip Consent Act of 2010* and "not only stated that no person shall be required to be implanted with a microchip (regardless of a state of emergency), but also that voluntary implantation of any microchip may only be performed by a physician under the authority of the Georgia Composite Medical Board" (Perakslis 2013:146; see also Michael and Michael 2013).

Yet conspiracy theories surrounding Gates and the Covid-19 vaccine persist, including that it will secrete within its serum an unwanted, undetectable fellow traveler. Not that every theory said undetected; a subset suggested we would be required to sign that we accepted the chip. That could not happen without repealing several state laws first—not to mention dealing with extensive civil unrest. Gates himself never mentioned a chip; he did speak of a digital tattoo. The chip concern may have come from a few misunderstandings, not least recent patents, house resolutions, and public health best practice.

WO2020060606—human body implant panic

On March 26, 2020, Gates applied for a patent. The abstract states:

Human body activity associated with a task provided to a user may be used in a mining process of a cryptocurrency system. A server may provide a task to a device of a user which is communicatively coupled to the server. A sensor communicatively coupled to or comprised in the device of the user may sense body activity of the user. Body activity data may be generated based on the sensed body activity of the user. The cryptocurrency system communicatively coupled to the device of the user may verify if the body activity data satisfies one or more conditions set by the cryptocurrency system, and award cryptocurrency to the user whose body activity data is verified [Abramson, Fu and Johnson 2020a].

The patent, in the words of University of North Alabama Business and Technology Studies Professor Daniel Ray, is "marking territory, not people. Patents are used in businesses all the time as property rights, things that have been set aside as the exclusive right of a particular company to develop. Then if someone else develops it first, they can't use it without buying the patent from the holder. It's a way of winning the race, even if you don't develop the tech" (2020b). In this case, the tech sounds like a frightening juxtaposition of human body activity with currency. However, the embedded device is more along the lines of a sensor, and data mining is not about retail; it involves solving a specific math problem by using as many data points as possible to find the one correct answer. "That, and the fact that this tech doesn't exist yet, Gates is just putting a marker down that this is his territory, is about as simple as I can put it," Ray said.

"Maybe it would help to say, I'm a Christian and I would never let anyone mark me, but I'd let someone do this to me if it didn't involve painful surgery. Which it might. Another reason this kind of thing isn't happening anytime soon" (D. Ray 2020a). Gates is doing what business geniuses do, Ray concluded; seeing space for a useful invention that hasn't been invented yet, and patenting it before someone else even made the tech. At some point in the future when someone does create this system, they have to come work for him, or buy out his patent. Either way, he wins.

That's not an easy thing to explain to a concerned public, where "patent number" WO2020060606 (really the publication number for the international patent application: Abramson, Fu and Johnson 2020b) features heavily in narratives casting Gates as the Antichrist, who will institute the Mark of the Beast through the Covid-19 crisis. It is an unfortunate patent number choice for a group primed not to believe in coincidence—particularly when conspiracy theory sites can do the following:

> Look up this MICROSOFT Patent, W02020060606. Notice the 60606 in it, like 666. This patent has to do with the human body, and currency, which connects with Revelation and the mark of the beast, which relates to a person's ability to buy or sell.

The publication date was March 26, 2020, a date with 49 numerology. 3/26/20 = 3+26+20 = 49 [Hubbard 2020]

"Computer" = **666** (English Sumerian)

C	o	m	p	u	t	e	r	**666**
18	90	78	96	126	120	30	108	

"Dollar Sign" = **666** (English Sumerian)

D	o	l	l	a	r	372	S	i	g	n	294	**666**
24	90	72	72	6	108		114	54	42	84		

"Internet" = **666** (Reverse English Sumerian)

I	n	t	e	r	n	e	t	**666**
108	78	42	132	54	78	132	42	

"Vaccination" = **666** (English Sumerian)

V	a	c	c	i	n	a	t	i	o	n	**666**
132	6	18	18	54	84	6	120	54	90	84	

Above and next page: Figures 6.1–6.6. Using numerology to explain coronavirus concerns.

"Mandatory" = **666** (English Sumerian)

M	a	n	d	a	t	o	r	y	
78	6	84	24	6	120	90	108	150	**666**

"Revelation" = **49** (Full Reduction)

R	e	v	e	l	a	t	i	o	n	
9	5	4	5	3	1	2	9	6	5	**49**

Still, as unfortunate as the March 26 patent number is, it pales before the next piece of fuel in this conspiracy fire.

HR 6666: contact tracing and social control

The state and federal legislative sessions banning involuntary chipping started as far back as 2006 in Wisconsin, 14 years before Covid-19 brought us the Testing, Reaching, And Contacting Everyone (TRACE) Act, also known as House Resolution 6666. Remembering that coincidences don't exist in conspiracy theory, one can see a problem with the resolution's name.[10] Introduced in House May 1 (and not passed as of July 2020), the bill says in its official summary:

> This bill authorizes the Centers for Disease Control and Prevention (CDC) to award grants for testing, contact tracing, monitoring, and other activities to address COVID-19 (i.e., coronavirus disease 2019). Entities such as federally qualified health centers, nonprofit organizations, and certain hospitals and schools are eligible to receive such grants. In awarding the grants, the CDC shall prioritize applicants that (1) operate in hot spots and medically underserved communities, and (2) agree to hire individuals from the communities where grant activities occur. (H.R. 6666, 116 2020)

Contact tracing may be one of the most misunderstood public health terms ever. Contact tracing generally includes phone calls to people who have been exposed, and visits to homes to provide testing or locate people who have not responded. Fear about contact tracing as a form of surveillance has gained traction worldwide, complicating efforts to identify COVID-19 clusters and slow the spread of the virus. Resistance is often linked to OWG/NWO theories. Here's one example, posted May 12 by Krista:

For those of us in Ohio thinking about going out to enjoy a little retail therapy since things are opening back up today...

** BE AWARE **

Masks are the least of your problems now. The Columbus Dispatch summed it up very nicely. Ohio has hired 2,000 "disease detectives" otherwise known as bounty hunters to trace, track, and ISOLATE people who have been in contact with infected people. They are specifically looking at households with children and elderly people. ISOLATE as in remove them from the home. This is very scary and we need to contact the Ohio legislature, and all our federal representatives. This may begin as early as this week. Just like Nazi Germany. May God help us.

All I can say, is let them try at our house!

Comment: Exactly the Army trained me well and I will protect my house

Comment: You can count on my AAA bail card to be available to ya! [police man, lock, and eye-roll emojis]

Pictorial comment [a photograph taken through a rifle site]: Glad I'm retired I'll be waiting

Comment: Do you have a link for this?

Comment: Oh wow that is scary as heck, I have an extra gun if you need one

The next day, Krista posted:

Now Dewine is sending out mailers to peoples house asking them to join in Contract [*sic*] tracing. This is being done by The Partners in Health.

The Partners in Health is funded by Bill Gates and George Soros. Oh yea. Chelsea Clinton is also on the board of Partners in Health!!

Same people same ties together. #staywoke[11]

This exchange encapsulates sentiments and public figures recurring in such posts, including a rather braggadocio tone that might signal hype rather than actual intent.

In other cases, resistance to contact tracing can be part of a broader anti-government and anti-lockdown movement that is not overtly Mark of the Beast or creeping totalitarianism but merely encourages conspiratorial thinking. These appeals are persuasive because they can tap into various communities. More importantly, we cannot rule out that they may be created by disingenuous actors as part of astroturfing projects which attempt to manipulate the public into serving the interests of unknown individuals or groups.

Such may be the case of the YouTube video entitled "Contact Tracing Scarier than you Imagined" (FreedomLover1977 2020). Uploaded on May 22, it opens with an unidentified woman who claims she received contact tracing class certificates. She says in a calm and reassuring voice that she wants to help us understand the process. In this way the woman takes on a traditional role in conspiracy theory, "the whistleblower." As we've said elsewhere, the whistleblower is one type of appeal to authority and is the only purveyor of reliable data from within corrupt institutions.[12] The video uses charts, graphics and screenshots in a fairly slick production to lead the viewer through the conspiracy. As the video goes along, our unknown narrator presents a seemingly even-handed explanation, pausing only here and there to point out the possible nefarious implications of language used in some documents, claiming, among other things, that Social Services could take children or pets from people with Covid-19. Neither is true. As a viewer we are almost watching the conspiracy theory unfold within this first-person account.

Here the technique is reminiscent of how paranormal television creates a feeling of truth and trust by imitating the real-life legend trip (see the chapter on QAnon, and Koven 2007). Two options exist; the first is that the entire production is a hoax parodying the conspiracy. Folklorists call this pseudo-ostension, where hoaxers use all the traditional features of a belief or story dishonestly; think fake hauntings or crop circles. What's curious about this process—and likely what the creators of this video are counting on—is that more often than not hoaxes actually reinforce belief. Even if they are discovered, this rarely proves fatal to the overall belief tradition. The second, if perhaps less likely, option is that the video is honestly delivered and genuine.

The way this contact tracing video first made its way onto the Internet—in daily uploads to different sites using slightly different titles each time—suggests purposeful seeding until it gained some traction. This is a media savvy task for the purportedly unemployed former contact tracer. This technique seemed to work since it was picked up by *The Gateway Pundit*, a rightwing webpage that routinely spreads conspiracy theory and misinformation. The video was attached to a piece attacking the qualifications of a particular contract tracing subcontractor hired by two states, and is cited as a good outline of the phenomenon (Hoft 2020). In a personal communication with Hoft he says that "someone referred it to me." In this way it entered, unvetted, the alt-news conservative ecosystem because it already confirmed the belief of the author that "Contact tracing is an attack on privacy. Having individuals, companies or governments involved means this practice will be corrupted, absolutely" (Hoft 2020).

Next the video is scraped by the site JoshWho.net, which pulls unaltered stories from the rightwing echo-chamber. JoshWho, AKA Josh Duffer, is involved in creating a censorship free social media platform Buddylist and expresses affinity for QAnon conspiracy theorists. He controls a network of related sites on various platforms that are used to game algorithms and advertisers through artificially increasing engagement and clicks (for gaming the system see Legum and Zekeria 2020). The content across most of the platforms is pro–Trump and conspiratorial—a perfect match for the video.[13] It was a professional job; successive iterations ranged from a few thousand hits to nearing 200,000.

In this brief example we can see how easy it is to agitate various groups with a simple YouTube upload, unvetted and unverified. But if contact tracing is not an excuse to swoop in and steal pets and children, whisk the elderly into nursing homes, and destroy privacy, what is it? From the National Academy for State Health Policy's website comes this succinct and very typical explanation:

- Individuals with Covid-19 are asked to identify whom they have been in contact with (closer than six feet for at least 15 minutes) in the last two weeks.
- Trained staff and volunteers then phone the contacts and tell them they may have been exposed without revealing the name of the infected person.
- Contacts are encouraged to quarantine themselves to stop the spread of the disease, get tested if they can, and offered health care, food, and housing assistance if needed [Kukka 2020].

Despite this evidence, misunderstanding remains rampant among the public. Another sample Facebook post targets contact tracing phone apps:

To all my contacts who intend to install the COVID-19 app AB TraceTogether, or any other tracking app, please delete me from your phone contact list and Facebook before installing the app on your smartphone, YOU DO NOT have my consent to use MY phone number in connection with your app to identify, track or locate me because you have this app. All your contacts will be known and theirs will as well, and it will be against their will or knowledge! and against the law!!!

I implore you to please stop and think before you give away your privacy to anyone especially the Government. They already know enough about you and quite honestly I'm concerned.

I don't want anything to do with this at all!

Thank you for your understanding and cooperation.

And I really hope I don't find out anyone has me being traced by this app, which I honestly think my friends are a lot smarter than to fall for a app that traces your every move, but again please delete any contact info you have of me before downloading a tracing app.

(Feel free to copy) [Janet, Facebook, May 22, 2020]

Launched May 1, the app cannot be used in the way Janet describes here. First, the AB in ABTraceTogether stands for Alberta, Canada; Janet is American and does not live near the Canadian border. When people react to titles and themes quickly, conspiracy theories flourish. The app doesn't share names, locations, bank details, or other personal data, but instead lets a person who has Covid-19 upload encrypted data that notifies other phones in the area that someone near them has tested positive. The devices "exchange Bluetooth-enabled secure encrypted tokens" (Government of Alberta 2020). As the tracing app home page reads, "The more Albertans who voluntarily download and use the app, the safer we'll be, and the faster we can reopen the economy" (Government of Alberta 2020).

This is only one of multiple phone tracing apps, which we single out only because of Janet's reaction. The first app was COVIDSafe, launched in April in Australia, which was downloaded by two million people in its first 24 hours. Multiple apps are available, with more to come, but with them some non-conspiratorial concerns:

> There are different proposals (and plenty of debate) about what information an app should gather and how much it should share with health officials. The Chinese government has taken phone tracking to an extreme, monitoring citizens' locations and purchases to gauge their risk and restrict their movement. GPS data from phones can identify potential hot spots and indicate who has been exposed. Government programs in South Korea, India, Iceland, and U.S. states including North Dakota and Utah are using phone location data to monitor COVID-19's spread. But GPS technology isn't precise enough to gauge short distances between two phones to determine which encounters are most risky. And widespread, automated GPS tracking raises privacy concerns that could lead to legal challenges in some countries.
>
> Many governments are instead developing apps that identify recent contacts by the exchange of low-energy Bluetooth radio signals. Each phone generates a random numerical ID that it broadcasts to nearby phones, which record such Bluetooth "handshakes." If a user experiences symptoms or tests positive, they can trigger notifications to phones they've recently been near [Servick 2020].

Loss of privacy is a prevalent human concern worldwide, and based on real governmental surveillance in many countries. Conspiratorial thinking has a fear of a police state that will lead to OWG as a central tenant in most contemporary enemy from above—elite based CTs.[14] In the religious concept of OWG, the "police state" is the "Satanic state," prophesied as the moral decay presaging the Last Day for Muslims, and by Christianity's Mark of the Beast.

Perhaps India is the best example of the juxtaposition of secular, religious, pragmatic and political concerns mixing into pandemic policy. Indian Christians and Muslims alike feared the April rollout of the Aarogya Setu Covid-19 tracking app. Downloading started as voluntary, but by May was mandatory for travel. Police wield varying levels of fines and jail time for those found outside their homes without the app, depending on the district (Christopher 2020).

In an interview by phone, "Dr. P," a medical colleague of one of the authors, related talking with relatives in her home state back in India. Asked whether Christians there feared the vaccine would be part of a New World Order conspiracy, the doctor came back with a surprising response. Muslims and Christians are hoping the vaccine will save them from surveillance, and from tracking technology leading to the Last Day:

Muslims are afraid the government will use it [the tracing app] to harm them as a minority. Christians talk about the restrictions as precursors to other restrictions. They don't fear the vaccine will have an added tracker; they are hoping desperately for a vaccine because they hate the phone app and want to get rid of it. To the Christians, the Mark of the Beast is the phone app. They cannot buy or sell without it, because they cannot leave their houses. And now the government knows where the Muslims are going [Dr. P 2020].

On March 25, 2020, India locked down its 1.3 billion-strong population, long before other nations reluctantly followed suit. As conferences were cancelled, including medical events Dr. P's family had planned to attend, an important multi-day Islamic conference in Delhi had already begun March 3. While many participants left the *Tablighi Jamaat* before the lockdown, some were apparently already sick. Others got stranded by the March 25 travel restrictions. Dr. P said that media reports attributed up to 15,000 cases of Covid-19 in India through contact tracing back to "that Muslim conference," as it became known in popular terms.

Churches in India had been cooperating with contact tracing up until the point it became mandatory. India's tracing app rollout reflects concerns worldwide about voluntary compliance becoming mandatory: when public good mutates into surveillance, conspiratorial thinking among marginalized communities is inevitable.

That said, American religious communities' concerns regarding contact tracing and other curtailing of freedom of movement don't reference India's experiences nor its Muslims' concerns, at least not on most online forums. Instead they focus on Mark of the Beast ideas arguing that after the phone app will come an implanted body device. Also, if discussions online are anything to go by, many Americans have not yet understood that contact tracers are humans who do follow-up work when a person tests positive for Covid-19, not a device to be implanted.

CBS News legal contributor Keir Dougall addressed this concern, citing *Jacobsen v. Massachusetts*, when he said that current pandemic efforts were trying to accomplish three things when usually only any two could be done at the same time: protect health, protect the ability to gather, and protect privacy. Sensitive as many are to privacy concerns, he pointed out that protections enacted under any pandemic regulations must be reasonable, not pretextual, and not beyond the scope of the health issue. If an app is overseen by a government rather than a private firm, Dougall pointed out, this changes the regulations on what information can be gathered. To some this makes the use of their information safer, to others, more likely to be breached (CBS News 2020). Despite possible astroturfing such as the aforementioned unattributed YouTube contact tracing video and the genuine concerns of lost privacy, during a May 15–18 Axios/Ipsos poll, three out of four Americans said they would give information on past contacts to a tracer if they found themselves Covid-19 positive (Talev 2020).

Dougall also covered employers who ask coronavirus health-related questions, and the right of employees to decline to answer versus public health needs. For instance, a person with no benefits working at a grocery store might hide symptoms in order to continue working (CBS News 2020). This returns to Dr. P, who works for a large health system covering multiple states. Dr. P described the reaction of fellow doctors in their cohort when offered free testing by their health system. At first Dr. P and colleagues were relieved that testing could be privately made available quickly (in April) but soon they realized that their employer would own their results:

> We began to realize how easy it would be for [the system] to say, "you have antibodies, you are immune, you can now work in a COVID unit." And there is currently no guarantee that having COVID once protects you from reinfection. Or, next time layoffs come because so many elective procedures are being cancelled because the patients fear coming to the hospital during the pandemic, then they would let go the infected doctors first. So, this suspicion you are researching, COVID is a game-changer for everyone.
>
> We are doctors, and we are concerned about our own privacy because our employer testing us means they own our test results. And what if they make the test compulsory? Right now, it is voluntary. Then will they remember which doctors said no at first? ["Dr. P" 2020]

Immunity passports, vaccine compliance, and the New World Order

We have discussed that unaware chipping is unlikely, and contact tracing is less scary than one thinks. What if the Covid-19 vaccine does not include a chip, but still requires a form of marked compliance? Disturbing (untrue) rumors of a required digital tattoo stem from a March 18 Reddit forum. Gates posted there: "Eventually we will have some digital certificates to show who has recovered or been tested recently or when we have a vaccine who has received it" (Gates 2020b). Gates is not the only person to mention marking people who have had a vaccine during a crisis, and in fact this has been done before in history. The International Certificate of Vaccination against Smallpox was proposed in 1944; prior to this time, travel to and within the United States hinged on the ability to display a smallpox vaccination scar. At those times, too, those who feared The Mark resorted to anti–public health rhetoric and deception; a brief and ignoble trade in faking smallpox scars using acid was available until the world wars broke out (Strasser 1989; Willrich 2011).

Discussion of "immunity passports" early in the pandemic played into fears of OWG/NWO–style restrictions from both secular and religious perspectives but they are also not a new idea. They were used during Yellow Fever outbreaks in several countries and proof of immunity or immunization has been a standard part of visa applications for at least 50 years (Kofler & Bayliss 2020). For natural immunity passports, a person is tested to prove they are immune and issued a document that allows them freedom of movement or access to particular areas. Public health authorities rejected the idea due to a high potential for harm, and by April the WHO had issued a statement explaining why they would not back or call for such documents, but the damage was done (WHO 2020). By May 2020, concerns over the idea of immunity passports had reached the point where a commentary in *Nature* appeared. After noting the danger of a "dystopian future," the authors stated that "In our view, any documentation that limits individual freedoms on the basis of biology risks becoming a platform for restricting human rights, increasing discrimination and threatening—rather than protecting—public health" (Kofler & Bayliss 2020).

In answer to the question of whether Covid-19 would bring about the Mark of the Beast, and paralleling immunity passports and digital tattoos, Richard Palmer of the Christian news site *The Trumpet* writes:

> The idea is that, soon, lockdowns around the world will be lifted—but only for those immune to the coronavirus. You will have to be tested to see if you've had the disease or be given a vaccine. Once that's happened, you'll be issued a certificate, identity card or tattoo. To travel and work freely, you'll have to show this proof that you're not infectious. In this way, millions will be tricked into receiving some kind of mark [2020].

This language may seem familiar, though slightly rephrased from what you have read above. Concern for the dangers posed by systems allowing freedom of movement to some and not others, with the pandemic as a background excuse, cross-pollinate between religious and secular communities with ease. Each reach the same conclusion: immunity passports or vaccine tattoos end in unequal societies and powerful world governments controlling the movement of all people. While implementation of immunity passports is unlikely after the initial explosive furor from all sides, it seems likely these concerns will continue to circulate and recombine with Covid-19, future diseases, and evolutions of OWG/NWO theories for the foreseeable future.

On the forehead

One final little sister legend exists to these concerns circling the Mark of the Beast. Set vaccine additives aside for a moment, and think again about the specifics of the warning in Revelation. The forehead or the right hand. Microchips to date have been embedded between one's thumb and forefinger (excepting Pakistan's brief proposal for behind-the-knee placement). That's the right hand, as foretold specifically, but not usable on a large scale yet.

But have you, since the lockdowns began to ease, been scanned by a digital thermometer? Where does that thermometer point? When people were told they could not enter hotels, restaurants, or most importantly houses of worship without being scanned by the digital thermometer, a whole new wave of "could this be it" swept through those already concerned. Mark conspiracies surfaced that temperature taking was the correct interpretation. This fear faded quickly in competition with tracing, masks, and vaccine compliance, but it is conceivable that increased use of digital thermometers as facilities reopen will cause a resurgence in concerns over The Mark. Expect to see this little sub-legend again in the future; like its big brother, it will emerge wherever fear meets misunderstanding.

SEVEN

QAnon, Pizzagate and the Pandemic

> American populists universally contend that those in positions of authority do not represent "the people," while conspiracies serve to identify the hidden controlling interests preventing a full representation of the interests of "the people."—Nathan Jessen 2019

This chapter is, in many ways, a dark mirror to the chapter on origins. Where most of the origin and biomedical legends, rumors and conspiracy theories were about dangerous outsiders, scapegoating and xenophobic reflexive labeling, this chapter looks at the other major theme in conspiracy theory, the clandestine threat from above via, in the case of QAnon, "elites" and the dangerous insider. As Campion-Vincent (1997) has noted, one of the key changes about conspiracy theory in the 20th century is the increased presence of narratives of "dangerous elites" within our own country or community.

Here we trace the shape of Pizzagate and QAnon, exploring how the latter has exploited the pandemic to widen its "vast conspiratorial system" (the Deep State hypothesis) as certain independent but integrated narratives within QAnon have grown in popularity. For example, the branch of QAnon that proposes that Hollywood and other elites are trafficking and exploiting children in a vast Satanic operation of sexual assault, torture and organ theft (the last in order to produce the semi-fictional drug adrenochrome) has become widespread during the pandemic, and an investigation of it will lead us from the present day, through the Satanic Panics of the 1980s and 90s (upon which the narrative is modeled) and eventually back to legends from the 12th century covered earlier. We will pay special attention to the way people act out legends and conspiracy theories and how these narratives demand our participation at all stages of their development: defining problems, identifying the guilty, and enacting a remedy.

QAnon and its version of the Deep State hypothesis is a significant force during the pandemic because of its reach into the very heart of the Donald Trump Administration and the GOP. It also became useful as a counter-narrative by those opposed to the pandemic lockdown and public health initiatives such as those discussed in Chapters Five and Six.

Part of what makes conspiracy theories dangerous are monstrous charges leveled against an amorphous "they": *they* carried out 9/11; *they* are building a totalitarian dystopia; *they* are raping and murdering children. *They* remain amorphous—the OWG, the United Nations, the Deep State, the Illuminati—but the need to identify specific individuals and uncover the actual plotters is a vital part of conspiracy ideation. For example, during the Illuminati rumor panic that overtook 1700s America, the Rev. Jedediah Morse proudly crowed that he had the names of the plotters, "I have, my brethren, an official, authenticated list of the names, ages, places of nativity, professions, &c. of the officers and members of a Society of Illuminati" (Johnson 1983). Morse's speech would be echoed on the lips of one of the great political conspiracy theories of American Politics, the Joseph McCarthy-led Communist witch hunt and his infamous claim: "I have here in my hand a list of 205 [State Department employees] that were known to the Secretary of State as being members of the Communist Party and who nevertheless are still working and shaping the policy of the State Department" (February 9, 1950). It was a charge that reappears most recently in claims that there is a Deep State acting against President Donald Trump and a rush to identify specific people involved. In fact, media scholars Whitney Phillips and Ryan M. Milner (2020) argue that many contemporary legends like Pizzagate and QAnon are expressions of a broader Deep State conspiratorial framing story that has a long history in America.

Deep state

Let's begin with the concept of a Deep State. In its simplest form the idea proposes that elements within the government, acting outside expected regulations under which the government should operate, control the actual mechanisms of administering the state. They work in concert with each other to advance a shared political project. For Republicans and those who support the President these Deep State actors are Democrats, especially those left over from the Obama administration. QAnon insists that it is "not just Democrats," which is a useful move to avoid the impression that QAnon is merely echoing a nakedly partisan political conspiracy theory.

The term is not native to American conspiracy theory tradition, although it has antecedents in influential 20th century political conspiracy thinking found in places like the John Birch Society. Ryan Gingeras, a professor in the Department of National Security Affairs at the Naval Postgraduate School, minutely details the term's history. He finds it first emerging in Turkey to explain the disparity between the apparent government and the relationship and influence of organizations within the government, the armed forces, and organized crime, each of which act as forms of parallel government (2019). Turkey's long history of coups, civil wars, and extrajudicial assassinations of political enemies makes the Deep State a common way for Turks to understand their government and history, according to Gingeras. After 2000 the term is widely used in academic literature to discuss not only Turkey but other Middle Eastern countries.

Gingeras traces its application to America through the work of Ola Tunander, who introduced the term "Deep State" to the man who would use it to analyze America and introduce it to the conspiracy communities, Peter Dale Scott. Scott was a literature professor at Berkeley and his early work was informed by his anti-war and leftist politics. Scott's writing on the Vietnam War and the murder of John F. Kennedy (1996) did not use the term Deep State; they did, however, contain the basic shape of the theory, and he reaches the conclusion "that a grand coalition of forces found within 'public government, organized crime and private wealth' engineered and profited from the president's death. Deep Politics muses that JFK's killing was just one episode within a string of cases that resulted in the continuation of the Cold War and the defense of illiberal practices at home" (Gingeras 2019).

It was in a similar vein that Scott used the term in his book *The Road to 9/11: Wealth, Empire, and the Future of America* (2007). This work brought him and Alex Jones, already a committed 9/11 truther, together on the InfoWars website in 2008. For the next eight years, as Jones' empire of conspiracy grew, so too did the concept of the Deep State, becoming associated with the Obama administration and its various machinations. Jones famously endorsed Donald Trump as the only man who could defeat the Deep State. The connection between Jones and Trump, and the term's use by the Trump administration, has given the theory credibility outside the conspiracy community.[1] The concept has also been partially shaped and nurtured into a more precise form of official political conspiracy theory by Steve Bannon, former chief strategist to President Trump. Published under a pen name (but most likely authored by Bannon) the term was introduced on his website Breitbart News a month after Trump's election (Virgil 2016) and heavily promoted ever since.

A Monmouth University poll in March 2018 showed that 37 percent of respondents had heard of the Deep State. According to the poll, "Americans of black, Latino and Asian backgrounds (35%) are more likely than non–Hispanic whites (23%) to say that the Deep State definitely exists. Non-whites (60%) are also somewhat more likely than whites (50%) to worry about the government monitoring them and similarly more likely to believe there is already widespread government monitoring of U.S. citizens (60% and 49%, respectively)." Asked more specifically if they believed "a group of unelected government and military officials who secretly manipulate or direct national policy" existed, just under 75 percent of respondents said yes.

The utility of the Deep State hypothesis to Trump is clear since it is an absent and voiceless enemy that excuses any and all of his failures. But the actual populist conspiratorial frame it is based on (whether based on countries with unstable democracies or from traditional conspiracism in America) places the power to manipulate the state into institutions and people who have been closely associated with the Republican Party itself: the military, religious institutions, the secret service, the Justice Department, and wealthy business people. Alex Jones for the last 12 years, and QAnon since 2017, have spent their time recycling and recontextualizing several traditional right-wing conspiracy traditions to repopulate the Deep State with the correct kind of enemies. Democrats are an obvious choice. For wealthy business people they have substituted George Soros (see Chapter Three), amorphous "elites," and Hollywood celebrities.

QAnon has amplified the rare appearance of a conspiracy category called "the benevolent conspiracy," arguing that Trump and a surprising gang of allies are conspiring from within the government to bring down the Deep State (Bergmann 2018:52). A final enemy tied to the Deep State is the co-opting and updating of the Satanic panic narrative of the 1980s and 90s. QAnon says a large secret society of Satanists were kidnapping children for nefarious purposes, but now they are part of the elite and will fall when Trump topples the Deep State. Originally part of Pizzagate, this kernel narrative is now one of the key ways QAnon has responded to the pandemic.

A brief sketch of QAnon

The basic outline of QAnon is fairly clear but constantly emergent and amorphous. Paris Martineau was one of the first reporters to write on QAnon:

> On October 28, someone calling themselves Q began posting a series of cryptic messages in a /pol/ thread titled "Calm Before the Storm" (assumedly in reference to that creepy Trump quote from early October). Q claimed to be a high-level government insider with Q clearance (hence the name) tasked with posting intel drops—which he, for some reason, called "crumbs"—straight to 4chan in order to covertly inform

the public about POTUS's master plan to stage a countercoup against members of the deep state [Martineau 2017].

At the time of this writing there are 4,483 posts attributed to Q in an online archive. Q's posts are purposefully cryptic in order to protect his cover (as Q and the QAnons claim) or, alternatively, to employ the common stereotype of the commercial fortune teller's trick: to make a statement as broadly applicable across any number of possibilities. For example:

2017-11-01 04:00:47 (UTC+1)
There are more good people than bad. The wizards and warlocks (inside term) will not allow another Satanic Evil POS control our country. Realize Soros, Clintons, Obama, Putin, etc. are all controlled by 3 families (the 4th was removed post Trump's victory).

11.3–Podesta indicted
11.6–Huma indicted

Manafort was placed into Trump's camp (as well as others). The corruption that will come out is so serious that deals must be cut for people to walk away otherwise 70% of elected politicians would be in jail (you are seeing it already begin). A deep cleaning is occurring and the prevention and defense of pure evil is occurring on a daily basis. They never thought they were going to lose control of the Presidency (not just D's) and thought they had control since making past mistakes [JFK, Reagan].

Good speed, Patriots.
PS, Soros is targeted.

The next 4,000-plus posts cryptically refer to a dizzying array of current events and various conspiracy theories. Mundane events, like the November 4, 2017, rounding up of Saudi royals by Crown Prince Mohammed bin Salman, are mentioned seven days later and tied to child trafficking. Then there are references to undying conspiracies like the death of Princess Diana and the New World Order. Overall, the conspiracies tend towards specific micro-conspiracies (that will obviously connect to others). Where they are prophetic, they tend to be in the near term. Take as an example the claim that November 2017 would see mass arrests of many members of the Deep State (nothing happened):

2017-11-02 03:56:16 (UTC+1)
Q Clearance Patriot

My fellow Americans, over the course of the next several days you will undoubtedly realize that we are taking back our great country (the land of the free) from the evil tyrants that wish to do us harm and destroy the last remaining refuge of shining light. On POTUS' order, we have initiated certain fail-safes that shall safeguard the public from the primary fallout which is slated to occur 11.3 upon the arrest announcement of Mr. Podesta [actionable 11.4].

The job of Q's followers (the anons) is to discover the meanings of these clues, put the pieces together, archive the information and act on that information, a process that Sarah Hartman-Caverly describes in her digital ethnography of the group's activities on 8kun (previously 8chan):

> anons collaboratively maintain a deep time line of political intrigue, compile lists of newsworthy resignations in the public and private sectors, follow law enforcement actions to thwart human trafficking, track the purchase and sale of stock by executives at major corporations, and count sealed federal indictments. Diggers take deep dives into the public record to report back biographical and historical findings of note, some draw network maps and time lines of associations between entities and events of interest, anons with coding skills develop post aggregators and searchable dashboards, and those with talent in digital artistry design images and iconography for memes.... Anons maintain a record of Q's trips and alert each other of spoof attempts. The bakers steward this content, beginning each thread with a running list of Q posts and notable submissions, links to dedicated research threads, tactics for social media campaigns, and a library of freely accessible online research tools [2019:189].

Several researchers have called this immersive and participatory construction of a super-conspiracy theory "gamification" because, as Rosenberg noted, "The best way to think of QAnon may be not as a conspiracy theory, but as an unusually absorbing alternate-reality game with extremely low barriers to entry. The 'Q' poster's cryptic missives give believers a task to complete on a semi regular basis" (2019). Researcher tendencies to highlight this novelty in the QAnon phenomenon is partially misplaced, because (as explored in Chapter One) *all* conspiracy theories are actually part of an interactive communal construction (snowball storytelling); the Internet has made that communal construction more visible and also more dynamically interactive as people move across various platforms, media, and use multiple digital tools to add pieces to a growing and changing narrative(s). A similar process of communal construction of a legend, and what may be the inspiration for QAnon itself, was Ong's Hat.

Ong's Hat began as an analogue pamphlet that recounted how a long lost transdimensional research group, "The Institute for Chaos Studies" and a neighboring Ashram in the Pine Barrens of New Jersey (the town of Ong's Hat) was formed. It proved successful but eventually was forced to escape into another dimension to avoid either an army raid or radiation from a nearby nuclear accident, leaving only one remaining building to act as a gateway into their world. On its face this does not look or feel anything like QAnon. Yet, documented by Jed Oelbaum (2019) in his Gizmodo column and Michael Kinsella's (2011) academic book *Legend-tripping Online: Supernatural Folklore and the Search for Ong's Hat*, when the legend moved online it became a participatory mystery with breadcrumbs scattered across newsgroups and later web pages where people attempted to put together the truth: "And anyone looking into the brochure for the Institute, long passed around in online conspiracy circles, would find it listed in a rare-book catalog called *Incunabula*, which first showed up around

1990" (Oelbaum 2019). The catalog claimed that the books it listed revealed a secret history of parallel dimensional research.

It turns out that the pamphlet, the book, and the legend itself were the work of one Joseph Matheny and his friends. For many years Matheny posed online as a fellow searcher for the truth of Ong's Hat, seeding the community with new bits and pieces of what his investigations uncovered.[2] As Oelbaum documents, "the exercise in collective storytelling ... online, amass[ed] a following of internet detectives who filled page after page on web forums and personal blog sites with research and theories about what really happened at Ong's Hat." Unlike Q (so far), Matheny eventually confessed to the hoax; many participants refused to believe his confession, and the search for Ong's Hat continues today.

While Q remains a mystery, reporters Brandy Zadrozny and Ben Collins (*ABCNews* 2018) uncovered three individuals who are responsible for spreading QAnon from its relative obscurity on 4chan to its rise as a near-mainstream theory of Trump's presidency. The researchers describe a process where two 4chan moderators, Pamphlet Anon (Coleman Rogers) and BaruchtheScribe (Paul Furber) teamed up with YouTuber Tracy Diaz. The three built and shepherded the Q-community by expanding it to more accessible platforms like YouTube and Reddit and finding homes for the community when various sites shut them down, like Reddit and 8chan eventually did. Along the way they gained followers and, in Diaz's case, monetized those followers to make YouTube her sole source of income. Rogers and Furber leveraged their labor to also achieve celebrity, appearing on InfoWars thanks to professional conspiracy theorist, Dr. Jerome Corsi, a fellow (if occasionally lapsed) believer. The partisanship of QAnon is mirrored, and perhaps nurtured, by Rogers, a "supporter of Donald Trump during the 2016 campaign, self-identifying as part of the 'meme war'—the creation and dissemination of images and internet-style commentary that internet agitators on the chans and Reddit credit with Trump's win" (Zadrozny and Collins 2018). This meme war is ongoing (and constant) in some parts of the QAnon community, as outlined by Hartman-Caverly:

> Veterans of the Great Meme War rally to the charge dubbed Operation Crystal Clear, establishing dedicated threads for tactical planning and a counter information armory to stockpile memes. Discussion shifts into war room mode. Anons create throwaway social media accounts as fallbacks and coalesce on a messaging strategy "to include crumbs that can be verified independently" and "assemble all of the publicly available research to connect the dots." They recycle successful posts from a prior #medialiesagain campaign and hold tactical briefings with lessons learned from past victories: select a common hashtag, curate text and image content, coordinate timing and volume of posts, plan the strategic deployment of original content. Anticipating censorship by automated social media filters and hands-on content engineers, anons prepare

a multiphased attack with secondary hashtags and backup strategies to co-opt the organically trending topic of the day [2019:188].

Hartman-Caverly argues that these meme warriors were more effective at electing Trump than the Russian disinformation and bot campaign, but her evidence is scant and this hypothesis remains hotly debated among academics. What is clear is that QAnon is the recruitment ground for a cohort of pro–Trump digital activists who try to influence news cycles and online discussion. They also attack Trump-negative messaging.

Since QAnon expanded into YouTube and Facebook, the movement has seen its ranks swollen by an unlikely demographic, Baby Boomers (those born between 1946 and 1964). White Boomers overwhelming supported Trump in 2016 and it is unsurprising that they would be receptive to a sympathetic message about him, but they have also become enthusiastic transmitters of the conspiracy theory via social media, earning the scorn of some of the younger and original adherents. The reply "Q-Boomer" denotes especially poorly done QAnon posts (Binder 2018). The convergence of the pandemic and the Q-Boomers may account for rise of the "Satanic child trafficking by elites" element in the QAnon saga; these would be ripe for recycling, since the Satanic panic and its various metanarratives and deep stories would be familiar, perhaps even still believed by people, who lived as adults through the 1980s and '90s. Certainly older Facebook posters have been active and effective users of anti-lockdown groups, which became vital conduits in the spread of various Covid-19 conspiracy theories.

The Satanism scare's epicenter was America, especially in smaller cities and rural areas. Its second key location was in Britain, with smaller outbreaks (usually regional) in Australia, Canada, New Zealand, France, and the Netherlands. The event that supercharged a simmering undercurrent was the publication of *Michelle Remembers* by Michelle Smith and Lawrence Pazder in 1980. The book introduced the concept of Satanic ritual abuse. Through workshops and conferences in the years that followed this publication's success, therapists trained in the techniques of accessing repressed memories spread the belief that a massive group of Satanists were kidnapping and ritualistically abusing and murdering children; meanwhile occult experts sold their services to train police and produce booklets like *Satanic Cult Awareness*, still available to police via the National Criminal Justice Reference Service website (Hurst and Marsh 1983). Finally, infotainment television, then in its infancy, used sensationalist programs to attract viewers and (accidentally?) fan the flames in such shows as *20/20*, *Geraldo*, and *Oprah* (Jarriel 1985; Rivera 1988; Winfrey 1989), to list just a handful from the dozens of news and daytime programming. (This is classic amplification.)

The resulting rumor panics swept up a number of innocent people falsely accused of ritually abusing children: nine people in the bedroom community of Martensville, Saskatchewan in 1992; and the McMartin preschool trial in Manhattan Beach, L.A., resulting in five people charged with 208 counts in two trials that lasted from 1984 to 1990. The sensational accusations in this case included secret tunnels, which forever attached them to Satanism legends. In 1991–2 nine children were removed from their homes in South Ronaldsay, Oakley, Scotland, because of ritual abuse allegations. Everyone in Oakley was cleared and subsequent inquiries were scathing in their assessment of social and criminal justice systems. However not everyone escaped jail; Daniel and Francis Keller, of Travis County, Texas, spent 21 years in prison due to false allegations.

For those who thought the Satanic panics were behind us, Pizzagate and its associated branch in QAnon have been a rude awakening. The persistence is partially explained by looking at the inner mechanism, history and social role of the story. First, Satanists are "enemies from within," they look like us, live among us and care for our children. Jeffrey Victor explains that "Satanic cult stories are part of a recurring cultural pattern in Western history involving the spread of subversion myths and a search for scapegoats to blame for social problems" (1993:75). The theme of "subversion myths" is picked up by Phillips and Milner who expand on the idea to point out that Christians' belief in the devil acting against God's people is a kind of deep story embedded in our psyche, proposing that we as individuals and communities as a whole could be perfect if not for subversion by the devil (2020). Under this system our failures are transferred onto a scapegoat and we don't have to examine either ourselves or the larger institutions we've built. This is partially why sociologists have suggested that these panics occur at times of social tension and upheaval (like the deindustrialization that was eviscerating many of the small towns that succumbed to the 1980s and 90s panics, or now during a global pandemic).

QAnon and Covid-19

QAnon slowly transformed parts of its sprawling narrative to respond to Covid-19 by politicizing the pandemic in favor of President Trump. From the archived Q posts it is clear they were late in addressing Covid-19. Only four posts mention the crisis in April, with 24 in May. Several posts reproduced quotes like "'Quarantine' is when you restrict the movement of sick people. 'Tyranny' is when you restrict the movement of healthy people" (15 May 2020) that had been circulating in memes for some time by then. In fact, during the pandemic most of Q's posts proved derivative, reinforcing standard conspiracy thinking about the virus. Anti-Fauci and anti-doctor sentiment was already baked into anti-lockdown communities in early April. Q likes to remind and reiterate; it is part of the breadcrumb and connect-the-dots gamification of the conspiracy theory. But it is clear that, unlike the supposed insider information that early Q drops pretended to offer, pandemic-era Q presents no secret or privileged information. Like most conspiracy theories and the communities that believe them, the virus presents a crisis to the worldview that QAnon narratives articulate. QAnon either had to integrate and explain the crisis, or risk irrelevance or internal dissonance within their interlocking narratives.

As Hartman-Caverly's meme warriors hypothesis noted, one purpose of QAnon is to support Trump through curating meme banks (a one-stop repository for when you need to find just the right weaponized meme for social media), planning information campaigns, aiding anti-lockdown supporters, and deterring criticism of Trump in online communities. From a post directing readers to the latest meme bank listing ("Meme Ammo" 16 May 2020) established categories such as Comey, Obama, and Schiff are joined by "Big Pharma," an acknowledgment of the influence vaccination skeptics have on the anti-lockdown dialogue. The category "Kung Flu" needs no explanation, reflecting the xenophobic scapegoating we covered in Chapter Two.

Within the context of the pandemic, QAnon is clearly working within a long tradition of weaponizing conspiracy to advance a political position. Integrating the virus into the Deep State narrative continues this project. Whether QAnon is driving the narrative or merely opportunistically co-opting and amplifying conspiracies and conspiracy thinking will have to be determined by big data research in the future. At this point all that we can say is that the ethics and aesthetics of QAnon align with the anti-lockdown movement, and that Q's followers use their digital activism skills to support and recruit those that they see as their natural allies.

Pizzagate

During the pandemic, QAnon pushed a far more exotic and noticeable cause than the mere ongoing politicization of conspiracy theories: Satanic trafficking of children. Q did this so well, it became amplified in mainstream media coverage. Anna Merlan, a journalist who spent years doing research among contemporary conspiracy theorists, describes Pizzagate as "a crystalline example of an internet creation that leaked into the real world in ways that were, by turns startling, comic, alarming, and violent" (2019:72). To briefly summarize the extensive and thorough coverage by Robb (2017), Merlan (2019), and Whitney and Miller (2020),

Pizzagate arose in the murky days leading up to the 2016 presidential election between Hillary Clinton and Donald Trump. The narrative emerged within and exploited three recent phenomena. First, since his original conviction in 2008 for sex with an under-aged girl, financier Jeffrey Epstein and his ties to the Clintons have been fodder for various narratives. Almost annual civil court cases against him, including being co-accused along with Donald Trump in a 2016 case, meant he was a well-known character. Second, former Congressman Anthony Weiner, then husband of Hillary Clinton aide Huma Bedin, was investigated in September 2016 and later convicted of sexting an underage girl: his laptop was searched and, thanks to private Clinton campaign emails found in the cache, it momentarily became evidence in the media scandal derailing Clinton's Presidential bid. Finally, Russian hackers accessed the email accounts of John Podesta, the chair of Hillary Clinton's presidential campaign, and the DNC office, and ran a disinformation campaign against Clinton for the purpose of getting Trump elected. As Robb reports, it was (and continues to be) common practice to seed disinformation on various boards like 4chan or Reddit in the hope of generating various rumors, legends and conspiracies to weave their way into the mainstream: Robb documents several beginning as early as July 2016. Folklorist Tim Tangherlini (2018) and his UCLA team of big data researchers (Tangherlini et al. 2020; Shahsavari et al. 2020) have demonstrated that part of the complexity of Pizzagate is its amalgamation of four separate narratives joined together using Podesta's hacked emails as a single connection point.[3]

There was more than enough fodder for the conspiracy once Wikileaks began daily releases of Podesta's hacked emails, which were quickly picked up and creatively interpreted by "internet sleuths." Where pizza and hot-dogs were mentioned in the emails, these campaign-stop catering decisions were interpreted as code for sexually abusing children (cheese = girl, pasta = boy, sauce = orgy). The logic behind this leap? The initials for cheese pizza are the same as child pornography.

As Robb noted, this process appears to be how the first verifiable person, Cynthia Campbell, posting on Facebook under the name Carmen Katz, presented the tale: "My NYPD source said it's much more vile and serious than classified material on Weiner's device.... The email DETAIL the trips made by Weiner, Bill and Hillary on ... the Lolita Express. Yup, Hillary has a well-documented predilection for underage girls.... We're talking an international child enslavement ring."[4] Robb meticulously traces how the post was amplified by a swarm of bot accounts (both Russian and domestic political operations) until it entered the right-wing media ecosystem through the conspiracy theorist Douglas Hagman's appearance on InfoWars. In this churn, Internet sleuths discovered an email invitation to

Podesta's brother that references performance artist Marina Abramovic's art series "Spirit Cooking." Her biographer James Westcott describes it as

> nothing but a little-known ... performance Abramovic did in an Italian gallery in 1996, in which she painted apparent instructions on the white wall with pigs blood. Instructions like: "with a sharp knife cut deeply into the middle finger of your left hand eat the pain." She also painted a small kind of icon in the corner with the blood too. It's pretty repulsive and rather luridly aims to shock but it's also clearly not serious [2017].

The "Satanic" elements of the piece dovetailed nicely with child sex rings because the audience was already nurtured to make this association from myriad legends and rumors during the Satanic Panics of the 1980s and 90s. Those roots march back a surprisingly long way. Collecting on QAnon began in March for us; video from Abramovic's various shows would routinely appear on Facebook and 4chan posts to buttress the still-circulating Clinton Satanic sex scandal, and fan the flames of more recent fantastic child trafficking tales.

Finally, it was revealed in the leaked emails that James Alefantis, the owner of Comet Ping Pong (the supposed favorite pizza place of Democrats) once dated David Brook, a Democratic fundraiser. As if the connection to cheese pizza wasn't enough to keep the story going, Jack Posobiec, an alt-right conspiracy theorist livestreamed his November 16, 2016, visit to Comet Ping Pong, claiming it was clearly a front that concealed hidden spaces for the child sex ring. An already popular conspiracy theory doubled its tweets after that. On December 4 of the same year, Edgar Maddison Welch, having spent days watching and reading about Pizzagate, walked visibly armed into Comet Ping Pong. As staff and customers fled, he shot at a locked door, and, having found no children nor even a basement where they were reportedly held, walked out and surrendered to police.

Even this horrific event did not end the narrative that a secret group of people acting in concert were imperiling the world's children. The legend smoldered, kept alive by right-wing conspiracy theorists like Alex Jones, David Seaman, and Mike Cernovich, who claimed that "every A-list actor in Hollywood were also pedophiles" (Stack 2017). Facebook users sharing content online also kept it alive; an ecosystem like Facebook rewards divisive and sensational stories. Such platforms provide conspiracy content to tens of millions of people (Legum and Zekeria 2020). It is not that QAnon revived the dead Pizzagate legend, more that it co-opted it. And as QAnon has grown so too has this conspiracy narrative.

There are several explanations for the expansion and proliferation of the Satanic child trafficking theme. There is a common hypothesis across a number of reports in which QAnon is just a continuation of Pizzagate, summed up in the pithy "Pizzagate on Bathsalts" (O'Hara 2018). As noted, Q's posts form a super-conspiracy, using Barkun's term (2013), and as such engulf a much wider set of narratives than just Pizzagate; in fact, there are remarkably few overt Q posts that promote anything like a child trafficking Satanic conspiracy, making it seem secondary to the larger Deep State narrative that appears to be QAnon's main focus. Of the 4,488 posts there are only 12 uses of Satan and its variants; one use of occult; and 21 uses of trafficking and its variants. All but two refer to mundane and generally international human trafficking rings (insofar as one can call any human trafficking "mundane"). Pedo or pedophile appear only 13 times, scattered throughout the years. The timing and frequency of Q posts, however, does suggest a purposeful exploitation and co-option of Pizzagate, since all but one post referring to Satanism occurs in 2017. The clearest exploitation may be the excerpt below; it appeared close to the one-year anniversary of the Pizzagate panic:

> Satan.
> Who follows?
> What political leaders worship Satan?
> What does an upside down cross represent?
> Who wears openly?
> Why?
> Who is she connected to?
> Why is this relevant?
> Spirit cooking.
> What does Spirit Cooking represent?
> Cult.
> What is a cult?
> Who is worshipped?
> Why is this relevant?
> Q [6 November 2017]

The clearest link to Pizzagate is the mention of "spirit cooking" which, although widely debunked, continues to actively circulate. An earlier post does link Satanists with child trafficking in a curiously specific manner: "The pedo networks are being dismantled. / The child abductions for Satanic rituals (i.e., Haiti and other 3rd world countries) are paused (not terminated until players in custody). / We pray every single day for God's guidance and direction as we are truly up against pure evil" (1 November 2017).

Haiti is repeated often in early Q drops where it corresponds with some current events but more importantly because it loops in the troubled post-earthquake relief efforts of 2010. That earthquake embroiled Hillary Clinton as Secretary of State and her family's charity, the Clinton Foundation (Charles 2020), in allegations of misdirected, misapplied, or just plain missing funds. No decent conspiracy theorist schooled in inductive reasoning would miss the specific connections, however, with orphans and needy children in Haiti. Linking Clinton to Haiti reinforces the Pizzagate assertion that Hillary Clinton is a pedophile bent on harming vulnerable children. The post also nods to the common assertion within the QAnon community that one of Trump's missions and greatest successes in his benevolent conspiracy against the Deep State is the destruction of human trafficking rings.

November 1 was a busy day for Q because, a few hours earlier, we got another question that later became central to pandemic QAnon storytelling: "Who exposed the pedo network within H wood? / You can't answer the above but will laugh once disclose details" (1 November 2017).

By the end of 2017 four elements to the Satanism narrative were in place; these later became the building blocks for the pandemic integration of the narratives that there are Satanists in government; Satanists operate international child trafficking rings; Satanists use children ritualistically; and a pedophile network exists in Hollywood. The beauty of this Celtic knot (or tetrad) of narratives is that it can present as four independent stories, or be combined in a vast array of possibilities. To be integrated into the pandemic only one further element needed to be added, the pandemic itself. A simple narrative soon explained that Trump was using the lockdown, especially travel restrictions, to prevent Satanic elites from escaping overseas before he could arrest them; and the stay at home order will protect citizens during mass military actions (Mantyla 2020). In other variations, the lockdowns provided cover for more complex military operations against the child traffickers.

If we begin with the Hollywood elite element of the tetrad, we get the story of them being under house arrest, wearing ankle monitors, awaiting swift justice, as in this Facebook post (Figure 7.1). The accusation that Hollywood is rife with deviants who imperil America and its values has been a key theme in right-wing conspiracy thinking since there has been a Hollywood. It appears in the anti–Semitic tradition of Jewish contamination of American popular culture (Byford 2011); during the communist witch hunt's of the McCarthy era, which contained no small element of anti–Semitism either (Vaughn 1996); and in the culture wars of the 1980s, best expressed in the work of the Parents Music Resource Center and their arguments that music and various types of popular culture threaten our children (Baddeley 2016).

The legend was extended to the Canadian Prime Minister, as Canadian anti-lockdown protesters and conspiracy theorists attempted to recontextualize the American narrative for the home team. Several different attempts were made including, linking Trudeau to sex trafficking via an anti-lockdown Facebook group post (May 15, 2020). The post used a *Daily*

Figure 7.1. Screenshot from a Facebook post suggesting Ellen DeGeneres, Oprah Winfrey, and Justin Trudeau are wearing house arrest monitoring equipment.

Mail headline "Drunk girl, 18, rushed from Canadian Prime Minister's home" (Farberov 2014). The poster must have assumed no one would click on it because it is pure misinformation. It is actually from April 23, 2014, and features the former Conservative Prime Minister, Stephen Harper. In the same Facebook group, a link was posted to an August 2019 YouTube video by April LaJune, a right-wing commentator, part-time conspiracist and QAnon adherent. She claimed Trudeau has ties to Jeffrey Epstein and the infamous Canadian mass-murderer of women, Robert Pickton.

Other Hollywood CTs followed, with or without accusations of sex trafficking children. In the reproduced Facebook post in Figure 7.1, "Elizabeth," the original poster, responded by sharing a YouTube video featuring Woody, the animated character from the 1995 film *Toy Story*, voiced by actor Tom Hanks (cirstenw 2020). The video narrates that Tom Hanks is either dead or has been subject to extraordinary rendition to Guantanamo Bay (Gazzo 2020).[5] Rumors about Oprah Winfrey eventually reached her; she tweeted on March 18, 2020: "Am being trolled for some awful FAKE thing. It's NOT TRUE. Haven't been raided, or arrested. Just sanitizing and self-distancing with the rest of the world. Stay safe everybody."

Adrenochrome

Where the four narratives of Satanic activity join up with elements from the virus origin narrative, we get the curious theory that the Hollywood elites are getting sick because of their tainted drug supply. Liz Crokin, a former Chicago newspaper columnist and early Pizzagate proponent, related one version of this narrative in a March 17, 2020, YouTube video:

> We have seen dozens and dozens, maybe hundreds of members of the cabal come out and say either they're either infected with the coronavirus or they're sick. We've know, like, Tom Hanks and his wife, ummm a lot of celebrities have said that they're not necessarily sick but they're self-quarantining. [...] There are two possibilities that are plausible. One is members of the elite that are self-quarantining and claiming that they have the coronavirus are possibly using this as an excuse to try and escape[...]. Number two is [...] The white hats[6] are allowing them to say this to keep people calm until all these military operations have been conducted. Third theory—actually I have three theories and, I'm just going to report and you decide if this is plausible or not, but there's a lot of anons that believe that the white hats tainted the elite's adrenochrome supply with the coronavirus and that's why so many members of the elites are getting the coronavirus. [...] Adrenochrome is a drug that the elites love. It comes from children. The drug is extracted from the pituitary gland of tortured children. It's sold on the black market. It's the drug of the elites. It's their favorite drug. It is beyond evil: it's demonic [transcription by John Bodner].

Adrenochrome is a real chemical compound but everything else about it is fiction, including that anyone wants to take it for longevity, personal beauty, or any other reason besides its main purpose: to promote open wound blood clotting. Adrenochrome features in QAnon CTs about child abuse because it must be harvested from children who are in pain. The origin of this concept is easily linked to Hunter S. Thomson's novels *Fear and Loathing in Las Vegas* (1972) and *Fear and Loathing on the Campaign Trail '72* (1973). Thomson's character Dr. Gonzo says adrenochrome has to come from "the adrenaline glands from a living human body." That the bodies are children is a QAnon addition.

According to "Google trends" searches of the term "adrenochrome" within America suddenly spiked in mid–March and continue at the time of this writing to be elevated, a trend which matches the ebb and flow of this conspiracy theory cycle we are investigating. The use of exotic or uncommon drugs by dangerous deviants is also a traditional element in several previous legend cycles and conspiracy theories of endangered children, from tainted Halloween candy, to the blue star acid temporary tattoo stories (Brunvand 2001). Even as a metaphor, a story depicting how elites prey upon and exploit the most vulnerable among us resonates in times of economic and social stagnation and increased wealth inequality.

Also, the idea of harvesting something life-enhancing from a living victim can be traced to the long and varied history of organ theft legends. These are often associated with Satanism (ritual sacrifice of hearts, etc.) as well as various xenophobic "enemy outsider" and even "enemy within" traditions. Given the Q drops focused on international trafficking rings, this legend subset reflects the findings of folklorists and legend/rumor experts Veronique Campion-Vincent (1997) and Gillian Bennett (2009):

> Campion-Vincent believes that it is possible to say that those involving the use of bodies as organ banks focused almost exclusively on children and more or less disappeared in late 1988 after a series of robust denials. Tales involving the theft of eyes followed; those involving kidneys evolved a little later, from about 1990. In 1997 stories of kidney thefts were the most dominant form of the legend in America and Western Europe. These stories more often featured adult males than children, though versions continued to appear featuring children who disappeared at Euro Disney or in central Paris. Since Campion-Vincent's book was written, very many more stories (rumors, legends, and factual accounts) about illicit organ sales and kidney thefts have begun to appear ... fears of eye and kidney thefts were rampant in South America, South Africa, and India in 1996–98. In 1999 Egypt's general prosecutor was reportedly investigating allegations that an organization north of Cairo charged with caring for homeless children was killing them and selling their body parts for profit [Bennett 2009:127].

A different narrative suggests Satanists are the abusers rather than Hollywood elites. The Satanists operate child abduction and trafficking operations. The sole instance of a Q Satanism post outside of 2017 says:

> We haven't started the drops re: human trafficking / sacrifices [yet][worst].
> Those [good] who know cannot sleep.
> Those [good] who know cannot find peace.
> Those [good] who know will not rest until those responsible are held accountable.
> Nobody can possibly imagine the pure evil and corruption out there.
> Those you trust are the most guilty of sin.
> Who are we taught to trust?
> If you are religious, PRAY.
> ...These people should be hanging [January 23, 2018].

Hollywood elites or Satanists: take your pick of enemy. QAnon's popular spread is likely because the conspiracy is so vast that micro-communities

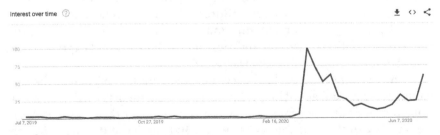

Figure 7.2. Google trends graph for "adrenochrome," July 1 2019–July 1 2020.

of interest emerge that lock onto one particular theme that interests them and reflects aspects of their worldview. This would explain the general ambivalence of, say the 8kun (and previously 4chan) community to the Satanism theme. The religious and supernatural elements embedded in the Satanic legends are not well suited to the rabidly atheist and nihilistic cultures of the chans/kuns so they do not become a focus—except once QAnon moved into more accessible formats like Facebook it was picked up by Q-Boomers, who do respond to these narratives.

It was child trafficking, coupled with Trump's (fictional) crackdown on these groups, that led to one of the most dramatic QAnon-related events of the pandemic. On April 2, 2020, Eduardo Moreno, age 44, crashed the train he was driving through a concrete barrier near the Port of Los Angeles in an attempt to purposefully crash near or ram the navy hospital ship USNS *Mercy*. It is somewhat unclear whether Moreno thought the ship contained trafficked children being taken away under cover of the pandemic, or something along the lines of malevolent armed forces coming to assist in locking down the United States. As reported by Meagan Flynn of the *Washington Post*, Moreno told the arresting officer: "You only get this chance once. The whole world is watching…. I had to. People don't know what's going on here. Now they will" (2020). It was reported that he told investigators he was "putting the pieces together … the ship is [not] what they say it's for." Flynn reports that Moreno believed "they are segregating us, and it needs to be put in the open," and he wanted to "draw the world's attention [so] … people could see for themselves [and] wake people up."[7] "Wake up" is one of the clarion cries of conspiracy theorists and, it was the Moreno event that interested some of this book's authors in the broader implications of conspiracy theories and real-world actions during the pandemic.

Later that month, on April 29, Jessica Prim was arrested on the New York pier near the *Intrepid*, a decommissioned aircraft carrier that Prim confused with U.S. navy hospital ship USNS *Comfort*, which had recently arrived to help the strained New York hospital system. On Facebook, Prim was live-streaming her multi-state trip to assassinate Joe Biden. In her videos she references several QAnon conspiracy theories, including the Comfort caring for the recently freed children who had been held beneath New York City in a Democrat pedophile, murder, and organ theft scheme. Prim was arrested without incident and faces many charges amid expressions of concerns for her mental health (Harris 2020).

The #savethechildren hashtag associated with this branch of the previous Pizzagate and sprawling QAnon conspiracy theory, tracing a similar trajectory for adrenochrome searches, exploded over the month of April, from daily mentions on Twitter of around 400 per day at the end of March, to 2069 on April 1, to over 38,000 for all of April and then dropping back down in May. The narrative was supported with various evidence, for example these screenshots from 4chan thread on Moreno's attempted "rescue" of April 2, 2020 (Figure 7.3; Figure 7.4).

April's imperiled children narrative integrated with news that the Samaritan's Purse field hospital had set up in Central Park on April 1. Around this time a fairly common traditional story of a massive bunker/secret city hidden beneath Central Park wove its way into the tale. Underground tunnels, rooms and passages have been common in conspiracy theories for decades.[8] In one narrative the passageways were reported to be filled with "mole children" who were recently freed "by the military" from the clutches of evil elites who had been using them as sex slaves and harvesting their organs. The narratives claimed alternatively that the field hospital was a disguise for the operation; and that the children were

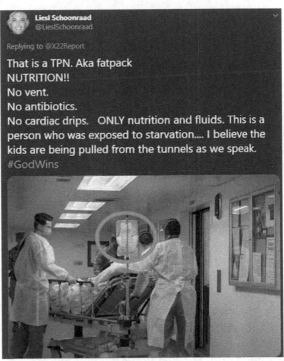

I HAD to tell you this. Please don't show my name if you send this to anyone

But my aunt is a nurse and one of her closest friends is also a nurse. She is working on the Navy ship docked in NY and confirmed they are bringing all the rescued children aboard currently that they've been saving. I've had goosebumps and chills for the last 15 minutes since I heard

Wow really I'll deff hide your face omg

Liesl Schoonraad
@LieslSchoonraad
Replying to @X22Report

That is a TPN. Aka fatpack
NUTRITION!!
No vent.
No antibiotics.
No cardiac drips.   ONLY nutrition and fluids. This is a person who was exposed to starvation.... I believe the kids are being pulled from the tunnels as we speak.
#GodWins

Figures 7.3 and 7.4: Screenshots from a 4chan thread on Moreno's "rescue" (2 April 2020).

being treated at the field hospital or on the USNS *Comfort*. In a competing narrative the USNS *Comfort* was in cahoots with the child traffickers.

Months later on July 3, 2020, Corey Hurren from the rural Manitoba town of Bowsman drove more than 1,200 miles to Ottawa to confront the Prime Minister Justin Trudeau. That morning Hurren drove into the pedestrian gate of Rideau Hall and stalked the grounds with several guns until cornered by police in a greenhouse and convinced to surrender. Rideau Hall with its 88 acre grounds is the site of the Governor General's residence (Government House) as well as the temporary home, in the building diminutively named Rideau Cottage of the Prime Minister and his family. No heads of state were present during the incursion. Later investigation of Hurren's business Instagram account turned up numerous posts of QAnon material (Lamoureax 2020). While his motives are still unclear, it is significant that two relatively well known Canadian QAnon proponents have uploaded YouTube videos of themselves approaching and rattling the same gate while accusing Trudeau of complicity in various crimes (Lamoureux 2020b).

QAnon as ostensive community

Legends and rumors allow their tellers to tacitly impel listeners to action; in conspiracy theory, the calls for action tend to be stated baldly and explicitly, particularly in QAnon's gamified version (Rosenberg 2019; Nicolaisen 1987; Tangherlini 2018). Nestled inside these narratives we find calls for individual action from the audience: to research, investigate, and monitor; to share your findings; to share this post, and so on. When they are absent from a specific post, suggestions will be supplied in comments from the audience in an act of communal creation. For example, the "hang Hillary" responses to the child sex trafficking stories shared on Facebook should be seen as part of the larger conspiracy theory itself. Likes and responses control and shape the story to reflect the shared cultural priorities and worldview of the group.

As we've seen in the examples of Edgar Maddison Welch, Eduardo Moreno, Jessica Prim, and Corey Hurren, calls for action translate into real world acts. This is a common process (sometimes called ostension— Ellis 1989b). In its simplest form ostension is the acting out of a legend narrative, sometimes called "legend tripping." Such acts as visiting a haunted house or saying the name "Bloody Mary" into a mirror three times are common examples. According to Bill Ellis, a scholar of legend and ostension,

> Through ostension, cultural traditions may function like a silent conspiracy that motivates similar acts in widely separated locations. That is, if a narrative is widely known through oral or media transmission, individuals may become involved in real-life

activities based on all or part of that narrative, even if there is no organization that is physically coordinating these people's actions [2000: xviii–xix].

QAnon didn't make anyone do anything. They just helped craft a narrative that people wanted to be a part of. And like all forms of legend tripping, you don't have to be a true believer. You can participate to disprove the ghost in the woods; you can do it to test the legend; you can do it for the enjoyment of time spent with friends or the delight of being scared; and you can do it because leading a group on a legend trip increases your value and social standing in your group or community. Why you are doing it doesn't matter, all that matters is that you are participating. We have seen this process in several other forms during the pandemic: criticizing people's use of personal protective equipment or tearing off of face masks; filming hospitals; hoarding of various types; some aspects of anti-vaccination protests. As we have seen some of these acts imperil the participants and people around them. Taken to extremes, rumor, legend and conspiracy theories can cause larger forms of ostension in the shape of rumor panics, "collective stress reaction in response to a belief in stories about immediately threatening circumstances" (Victor 1993:59), that threaten the lives and property of entire communities.

In the QAnon tetrad of child abuse CTs, the focus has shifted from enemies within to enemies above, a subtle but important change. This allows the communal rage demanded of the community beset by these horrors to hurl itself at specific political enemies instead of each other: namely, members of the Deep State. It is clear that QAnon has weaponized fears over Satanism and child harm and shoehorned them into conspiracy thinking associated with the Deep State.

At this point the resonance with the anti–Semitism of Chapters Three and Four is clear. If we march Satanism backwards through history, we see a much older set of deep stories, wherein enemies from below (Jews) steal Christian children and ritualistically murder them before Passover. The "Blood Libel" legend, whether overtly religious and supernatural or mundane and casting elites and A-List celebrities as the villains, operates on the same basic logic of scapegoating about how, if it weren't for THEM we could build a perfect place full of perfect people. Utopia is just a massacre away.

Eight

Waves of the Future or Waves of Oppression?

5G Fears

> People have been trying to warn us about 5G for years. Petitions, organizations, studies … what we're going through is the effects of radiations…. And to be clear, I'm saying there have been lots of studies & experiments that point to the possibility that the dangerous levels of electromagnetic radiation (5G) could be causing the contagious virus. —Keri Hilson

So far, the conspiracy theories that have emerged to explain the coronavirus and Covid-19 have some precedent in pre-existing conspiracy theories. Outside of the traditional rumor and conspiracy theories involving nefarious clandestine actors (either above, outside or within one's society) who are planning to enslave us, the biggest contender for an alternative explanation for the emergence of Covid-19 and its reshaping of everyday life is 5G technology.

Primer on 5G

Various beliefs and communities make up the anti–5G movement. Beginning in 2018, cellular companies began touting the benefits of 5G networks and working to roll them out around the world (Duffy 2020). The abbreviation 5G is used to identify the fifth generation of wireless networking technology for cellular devices, and what will replace the current 4G LTE (standing for "long term evolution") used across the globe (Hu 2018; Verizon 2019). The increased bandwidth and speed of 5G will allow for things like self-driving cars, smart city features, and electronically-run healthcare systems (Duffy 2020). Contrary to the conspiracy theories and technology legends, 5G uses three frequencies. The "low-band" is the same as 4G's 600–700 MHz; medium-band employs higher frequency for greater download/upload speed in the range of 2.5–3.7 GHz; high-band will use 25–39 GHz and because of its limited range will mainly be confined to cities. Implementing 5G involves installation of many "small cell" sites that are closer together, and in greater number, than current towers. Verizon and other telecommunication companies stated in 2018 that they would need to install roughly 300,000 new antennas to ensure that 5G would be available to most users, but pledged to try and use existing infrastructure to house them, in order to better hide them within communities (Dokoupil 2018). The camouflaging of the cells has become a significant theme in the current conspiracy theories surrounding 5G.

Implementation of the cells started in 2019 and has been steadily increasing throughout 2020, but anything like full coverage will be slow going in most countries. South Korea leads the world in 5G coverage with 85 cities, more than 75 percent of its main cities; China has coverage in more than 50 cities; excluding France, most European countries will have more than 25 major cities covered by the end of 2020; Canada has only six cities with 5G but the majority of the population lives in them. Stateside, 136 cities have been connected.

Rumor origins

How anti–5G conspiracies became linked to Covid-19 is a good example of the personal motivation of the conspiracy-minded to integrate new knowledge into their belief system, as well as the crisis and opportunity the pandemic presented to pre-existing CTs and their communities of believers.

Anti-5G groups date back to 2017 when the technology was first being tested. *Wired* reporter Sabrina Weiss (2019) noted a November 5, 2018, viral Facebook post claiming a recently installed 5G tower in the Netherlands had killed three hundred birds. The original report appeared on Health Nut News, a site which like the notorious Natural News[1] is a purveyor of various alternative health beliefs, rumors, legends and conspiracy theories including anti-vaxx, big pharma conspiracies, and a smattering of anti–5G and electromagnetic field (EMF) material since 2017. Researchers before and during the pandemic have identified sites and people associated with natural and alternative health theories as major vectors in transmitting misinformation, rumor and conspiracy theories (Breland 2020; Swire-Thompson and Lazer 2020). Weiss identified John Khules and his 2018 "Stop5G" Facebook group with being an early and influential disseminator.[2] As of this writing Khules has several Facebook groups (one boasting 35,000-plus members) and his webpage "Stop 5G Resistance Network" contains research links and reports as well as practical tips.[3]

Weiss also reports that "Since May 2018, RT America, the US arm of the Russian broadcaster has aired more than a dozen news segments warning of cancer, nosebleeds, and other health risks using sensationalist phrases such as '5G apocalypse' or 'an experiment on humanity,' telling viewers 5G 'might kill you'" (2019). Since the 2016 United States election it is never a bad idea to suspect a Russian disinformation campaign, which in this case seeks to create widespread distrust in American citizens toward elected officials and technology companies and, possibly to slow or disrupt the adoption of 5G.

Pre-pandemic health problems associated with 5G by conspiracists included cancer, infertility, autism, and Alzheimer's. This suite of diseases is notable not simply because they are widespread in the population and would be a general health concern to any large group of people. Each also has competing scientific and allopathic explanations as well as a large body of counter-knowledge[4] from alternative health practitioners and adherents. Alternate health beliefs like homeopathy and natural or osteopathic medical practices are not themselves conspiracy theories. Health beliefs are a complex topic involving cultural values, attitudes, social roles and economics, and systems of folk medicine, each one having their own logic, practices, histories and traditions.[5]

The WHO's announcement in 2011 that radiation from cellphones is "possibly carcinogenic" continues to be cited by critics (International Agency for Research on Cancer 2011) but no causal link has yet been found. Nevertheless, the study of negative health outcomes and electromagnetic fields continues. Findings for and against provide a constant drip of data that engages the anti–5G communities. In the early stages of the anti–5G movement there seemed to be only one strain of conspiracy: that governments, regulators, corporations, and scientists were covering up evidence of the dangers of 5G and other electromagnetic field (EMF) technologies.

New tech anxiety

As many researchers have pointed out, anti–5G is the latest example of narratives about recent technology and the anxiety it causes. Concerns over radiation and EMF lie at the heart of 5G. A general fear of radiation is over a century old; "radio-phobia" (fear of radiation) was featured in the *Los Angeles Times* back in 1903.[6] Today misunderstandings about radiation and EMF "leakage" continue to be central concerns (de Looper 2020). Since the nuclear age, radiation is considered "bad" and unfortunately the field of electromagnetic radiation contains the same term; yet the electromagnetic spectrum simply describes different waveforms from the longest (radio) to the shortest gamma radiation. Along that continuum is the visible spectrum that humans can see, among many other phenomena. Only the upper end of the electromagnetic spectrum is "ionizing," meaning they break apart molecular bonds and actually damage DNA. The rest of the spectrum is considered "non-ionizing," the wavelengths far too long to actually damage human cells (de Looper 2020). In fact, human skin will stop most of the next generation of 5G wavelengths (Triggs 2020).

Historic examples of government (willful) ignorance, like the famous viewing parties for atmospheric nuclear bomb testing in the 1950s and the horrific catalogue of researcher and technician death during the early days of x-rays, remain part of the skepticism that greets government and scientific reassurances of the safety regarding 5G. The electromagnetic field is a slightly separate concern. The term EMF is used haphazardly by general (as opposed to professional) anti–5G proponents (Sansare, Khanna, and Karjodkar 2011). All electricity and magnets (both natural and human made) produce EMF so technically the electronic age exposes us to hundreds or thousands of fields; some alternative health proponents label this electro-smog. The distinction between the two phenomena is largely one of movement: EMF are stable and stay put, while EMR (electromagnetic radiation) moves away from its source in an undulating wave.[7] A key feature—and a reputable rescarch question—remains on the effect of exposure to these fields and radiation over time, a gap in knowledge that fuels 5G skepticism.

The anti–5G discourse that engages directly with the science, like the anti-vaxx movement and other science-dubious predecessors, has created a counter knowledge and critique of EMF and EMR that uses and mimics scientific language to establish credibility. Rumors and legends about contemporary wireless technology have usually clustered their storytelling anxieties around cellphones. The 2008 viral hoax commonly titled "Cell Phone Radiation Pops Popcorn" showed a round table with five cell phones of various makes oriented in a circle around five kernels of popcorn; eventually one kernel pops (Figure 8.1). One version of the video has racked up more than 1.2 million views (osamesama 2008). In other tales, one or several cell phones cook an egg. The story was popular enough to generate a satirical video by stevejacko uploaded January 6, 2012, to YouTube entitled "my mobile phone cooked my eggs." The University of Southern California's folklore archive holds several tales of exploding cell phones or cell phones blowing up gas stations, a belief partially sparked by media reports from as far back as 1999 and still in circulation today (JudyTsai 2012). Cell phones were also said to cause breast cancer when kept in your upper pocket. There

Figure 8.1. Screenshot from "Cell Phone Radiation Pops Popcorn" (osamesama 2008).

was even a tale of a cell phone causing the death of a child in the hospital (to see these and other examples read DeVos 1996, 2012).

Cell phone legends follow concerns over other novel consumer products that use radiation technology, like microwave ovens. Everyone over a certain age knows a "poodle in the microwave" story, AKA "the microwaved pet." Before the microwave anxiety manifestations were worries about the electromagnetic field caused by large powerline corridors. The 1970s and early '80s media is littered with popular and scholarly reports of the potential dangers. Several careful studies have still not found any relationship between normal exposure to electromagnetic fields and cancer (NIH 2019a, 2019b).

As with most of the conspiracy theories covered in this book, some people have acted on them: avoiding cellphones, rejecting Wi-Fi for their homes, and refusing to live near cell towers. Writing in the *Atlantic*, Kaitlyn Tiffany provides some other examples: "In April 2019, Brussels stopped work on its 5G network, with the environmental minister of the region saying that citizens wouldn't be treated as guinea pigs.' A few cities and towns in Northern California have passed ordinances to curb 5G deployment, explicitly because of health concerns, and three members of Congress have written to Federal Communications Commission Chairman Ajit Pai about their constituents' worries over 5G safety" (2020). Others have gone a step further and sabotaged cell towers.

Contamination, coronavirus, and celebrity

Technology reporter Rebecca Heilweil (2020) traces some of the earliest examples of the integrations and realignment of anti–5G with the pandemic. She reports on the findings of John Gregory of *NewsGuard*, who noticed on January 20, 2020, a post on the French conspiracy website Les moutons enragés, claiming (in her words): "that the millimeter wave spectrum used by 5G technology and Covid-19, the disease caused by the novel coronavirus, could be related, pointing to reports about Wuhan installing 5G towers before the outbreak." This post may be related to a January 19 retweet of a *Russia Today* article that mentions the large number of 5G towers in Wuhan, but Heilweil says the retweet itself was only lightly engaged with at first. By March 20, however, there was enough chatter that it was picked up by Isobel Cockerell, who wrote a piece for the website *.coda*. On March 28 the *.coda* report was noted in a data dump about the pandemic on 4chan, where an anon who recovered from the infection posted, "But I was sick to the point that I remember thinking 'I wish this upon no one, no one deserves this.' I wondered at the time if it had something to do with 5G, general abundance of EMF radiation, or that it was part of something intentionally released, or a side effect of such a thing."

Cockerell reported that various conspiracy theories were rapidly proliferating on anti–5G Facebook groups in March, citing the following as a typical position: "'Do you Know the Corona virus is not a fuckin virus [two eye roll emojis] it's 5G that's actually killing people and not a 'virus,' wrote one Stop 5G UK member on March 10. The post was shared more than 1300 times."

Meanwhile, 5G rumors began actively circulating in Black American social media. In March of 2020, R&B singer Keri Hilson tweeted her thoughts on the root of the coronavirus breakout being linked to 5G networks. She implored followers to turn off 5G by disabling LTE on their phones and to go to her Instagram stories for more information, adding screenshots of articles to support her statements (Ransom 2020). She later deleted these posts, but informed her fans that her management had told her to do so (Cockerell 2020). In Hilson's tweets, she also cited Dr. Thomas Cowan's lecture linking 5G to the virus (Finley 2020). Hilson's posts were divisive, with a good portion of her fanbase questioning the songstress's beliefs. Others sided with Hilson in naming 5G a dangerous part of the Covid-19 pandemic (Cockerell 2020; Finley 2020).

Hilson had 4.2 million Twitter followers and 2.3 million Instagram followers at the time of her postings connecting 5G to the coronavirus, most of whom are Black (Finley 2020). Her thoughts seem to follow Patricia Turner's discussion of Black American rumor/conspiracy theories surrounding contamination concepts. Turner defines "contamination" as "any item in which the physical well-being of individual black bodies is being manipulated for racist reasons" and says the ultimate goal of the contamination no matter the method is to "curtail the growth of the black population" (1993:138). That might be through the (seemingly fanciful) rumors of the sterilizing agent in Church's Chicken; or HIV/AIDS being intentionally released to decimate first African and Haitian, then Black American populations (Manuel-Logan 2012c; Turner 1993:151–163), or the introduction of crack cocaine into Black neighborhoods of "in order to keep black people down" (Turner 1993:194). The Covid-19 contamination rumor emerged in the Black community through fears that 5G radiation waves either create or transmit the coronavirus, or weaken the immune systems so that fighting the virus will be more difficult (Ransom 2020). Those in power, the indeterminate *they*, contaminate Black people with radio waves emitting the coronavirus in order to harm them.

Yet Hilson was not the only Black or minority star to discuss these connections. Rapper Wiz Khalifa also addressed the controversy with a tweet that gained over 41,000 likes (Cockerell 2020). In addition, other artists of color including Black American rapper YG and British Sri Lankan rapper M.I.A. also supported theories linking 5G to the spread of Covid-19, or the complication of healing from Covid-19, to their followers (Bradley 2020; Threadcraft 2020). With a slightly different bent to his theoretical underpinnings, singer/Songwriter Teddy Riley discussed the connections with 5G (he referred to it as G5) during an Instagram interview with Charlamagne Tha God, host of the popular radio show "The Breakfast Club" (Cockerell 2020). Charlamagne referenced Riley's Instagram concert battle with singer/songwriter/producer Babyface Edwards and voiced concern that no one in Riley's entourage was seen on the Instagram Live feed wearing masks, although they were in close contact with each other.

Riley retorted that he wasn't concerned with Covid-19: "I just really feel like we're being bamboozled, you know what I'm saying? We're being made to believe so many things that are not the truth. It's not for me to say, I feel like my brothers and sisters need to know. The corona, everybody know by now what it really is. It's really about this new world order that they're trying to put in with these G5 connections" (Cockerell 2020; Finley

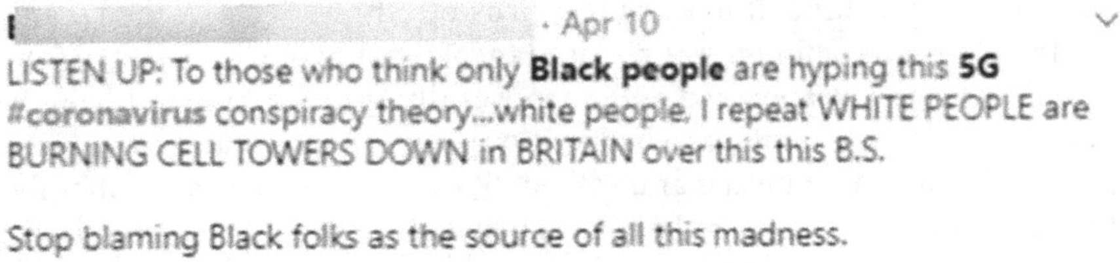

I · Apr 10

LISTEN UP: To those who think only **Black people** are hyping this **5G** #coronavirus conspiracy theory...white people. I repeat WHITE PEOPLE are BURNING CELL TOWERS DOWN in BRITAIN over this this B.S.

Stop blaming Black folks as the source of all this madness.

Figure 8.2. Twitter message describing the interracial nature of COVID 5G conspiratorial thoughts and actions.

2020). While Riley continued misinformation about any 5G connection to the coronavirus pandemic, he also brought in concerns about a New World Order, a concept more often associated with those concerned about End Times or totalitarian takeovers.

American actor Woody Harrelson, most recently starring in *The Hunger Games* film franchise, shared his theories linking the 5G network to the pandemic on his Instagram page to more than two million followers, and the post received 25,000+ likes (Brown 2020). In addition, actor John Cusack pushed the 5G theory to his Twitter following, stating that "5-G will be proven to be very very bad for people's health"; but he later chose to delete the tweet, calling individual followers who disagreed with his 5G concerns "just DUMB and fucking sheep" (Cockerell 2020).

A study released by the Oxford University Reuters Institute found that misinformation from prominent sources such as politicians, celebrities, and other public persona made up 20 percent of the claims they reviewed, yet accounted for 69 percent of the total social media engagements of the falsehoods (Brennen et al. 2020).

In early April side-by-side maps of American 5G and current Covid-19 outbreaks went viral online; they were quickly debunked but not without amplifying the CT (Lajka 2020). As we saw with the #savethechildren hashtag and its related conspiracy theories, 5G rumors spiked on social media in April (Heilweil 2020). In Canada anti–5G feelings got an unexpected boost during a rash of cell tower arsons in Quebec (see below). On May 6 it was reported that the chair of the Parliamentary Health Committee, Liberal MP Ron McKinnon, was sponsoring a petition to Parliament to restrict how close cell towers could be to schools and daycares. The Minister claimed to agree with the established science confirming the safety of 5G but was acting on behalf of his constituents on Vancouver Island (Chase 2020).

Throughout April, several competing theories about the relationship between 5G and the virus were in circulation: one, there is no virus and all the ill health is the result of 5G; two, 5G weakens the immune system, making it more difficult to ward the virus off; three, 5G at Wuhan transformed the virus before it was released (accidentally or on purpose); four, 5G activates the weaponized and purposefully spread virus; and five, the pandemic is cover—either as a hoax, an opportunity or a plan—to suppress protest through quarantines and roll out 5G all at once. It is in number five that 5G concerns become radically transformed and integrated into larger super-conspiracies warning of apocalyptic consequences as a conspiracy, rather than a simple alternative health belief or straightforward conspiracy about scientific cover ups. However, the integration of anti–5G into wider CTs is not straightforward or automatic. This example is from an April 20, 2020, post on an anti-lockdown Facebook group:

"A MUST LISTEN! stopthecrime.net

The correlation to this virus is BIG TELECOM 5G NETWORKS, IoT and Smart Micro Nano bots Sprayed of over Big Cities and Developed Rural areas now with Larger populations to, Same Spots as the COVID-19 hot Spots such as NY, CA, FL and Washington State are big COVID-19 HOTS same places that have rolled out 5G. The CDC, W.H.O. FCC, The Paysaurs, Rockefellers, the Rothschilds, and CIA, AMA, and the FDA. HAVE BECOME ONE.

ALL America Government health and Safety Agencies will be taken over this year. They all will become one with the UN SUSTAINABLE DEVELOPMENT GOALS of the NEW WORLD ORDER and THE RISE OF BEAST SYSTEM. 5G Emf Directed Energy weapons will be the ploy for us to become one with THE NOW EVIL AI.

WHICH THE MARK OF THE BEAST.

HENCE THE REASON TO LIFE TO IMAGE OF THE BEAST. BILL GATES OF HELL.

Economic downfall will happen

And control of food is exactly what they want.

This Covid-19 Plandemic is stage for a take over of all ECONOMIC, Spiritual, Physiological, and social life as we know it...."

Here 5G comprises just one small piece, added to the religious apocalypse version of a global totalitarianism society in which all buying and selling is controlled by participation with the Mark of the Beast. The post also directs people to a webpage and YouTube channel, where there are extensive opportunities to support the host through merchandise, donations or just consuming some advertising as you wait for the video to play.

In the first two weeks of May, a video supposedly made by a whistle blower working to install 5G went viral. A man wearing a high visibility vest, hard hat, and facemask faces the camera with a cell tower in the background. The man claims to be installing boards that cause Covid-19 and presents the board for us to view. Clearly visible is the mark "COV 19." Again we see the utility of the whistleblower persona in establishing authenticity in conspiracy narrative; this hoax (pseudo-ostension) was convincing enough to be shared widely on most social media platforms. Fact checkers eventually discovered that the board is part of a very old television circuit board that doesn't even have ports for mobile technology. The revealing of the hoax has done little to discredit the wider anti–5G belief, since supporters can easily dismiss this as a singular event and return to other sources of evidence. Moreover, the belief is durable because it already counts—as any conspiracy theory or research must—on bad data.

Figure 8.3. Screenshot (source unknown) showing close up of the COV–19 circuit.

On a Canadian Facebook group that began as anti–Trudeau but had transformed into an anti-lockdown page, a May 18 post linked to a YouTube video posted on April 18 (YTMostCensored 2020) shows 5G concerns expressed in a Canadian context.

> 5G BEING INSTALLED WHILE YOUR MASTERS TELL YOU TO STAY HOME
> This video is of a new 5G Cell Tower beside an elementary school in Calgary, Alberta. This 5G Tower was installed three weeks ago during the coronavirus lockdown. 5G uses radio waves in the form of microwaves and millimeter waves at super high frequency and with mass public exposure.... National Citizens Alliance is concerned about the health and privacy issues from 5G technology. We support a moratorium on the installation of 5G until independent scientists determine conclusively the health impact of 5G.

A sampling of replies includes:

> **FEMALE 1:** This is going to cause alot of medical problems. should not be aloud anywhere on this earth,
> **FEMALE 2:** Expect more people to become sick. We need a plan! Anyone.
> **UNKNOWN 1 (DIRECTLY FOLLOWING FEMALE 2):** they burned down 50 of them in the uk.
> **MALE:** Time to get back out and about no more staying home .get out and look around.

FEMALE 3: Funny, there are several documents stating that things are happening behind closed doors while we are TOLD to stay inside. New world!

MALE: [posts meme with the text]: If we dumped our PC's & Phones just thing the "powers To Be" couldn't install a chip (666) Bill Gates would go broke G5 would be a bingo call, Turdo [Trudeau] wouldn't get any attention & China would be back on the fence trying to make a dollar out of 15 cents.

UNKNOWN 1: There's only a handful of countries with 5g right now. However, there are numerous countries affected by covid 19. It's not a viable culprit.

MALE 2: replying to Unknown 2: Every single major outbreak area had 5G implanted, including both cruise ships. Countries without 5G haven't had major outbreaks. You can take ALL of Africa for example, barely any deaths! Or India, 1.3 billion people, less than 2000 deaths, no 5G. Or Vietnam, 100 million people, shares a border with China, no 5G, 0 CV deaths.

UNKNOWN 1 REPLYING TO MALE 2: um, no they haven't. You're wrong, lots of countries without 5g have had large outbreaks, and it has to do with the amount of citizens and the SIZE of the country as well.

QUIT SMOKING CRACK BOI

Here we see a fairly representative sample of people integrating whatever interpretation of 5G fits with their assessment of the pandemic. There is also the call for action to burn down towers, which started happening. On Facebook groups that are about the pandemic itself and not just 5G, a diversity of opinion exists in our sample on whether the 5G concerns were real; note Unknown 1 and his rebuttal to Male 2. The rebuttal is clearly based on common debunking information about the side-by-side maps, noting that they really just showed population density and that cities were getting hit hardest.

The group "National Citizens Alliance" (NCA) in the post is a far-right political party started in 2019 by Stephen Garvey, a conspiracist, racist and Islamophobe who disseminates "white replacement" and anti-globalist conspiracy theories (Boonstra 2019; Patil 2018). NCA have no policy position on technology in general or 5G specifically but are using the controversy to introduce themselves to potential members. In general, the pandemic has been a boon to fringe political parties and social movements who have used conspiracy theories as a Trojan horse to recruit new members and expand their networks. In fact, *Politico* discovered that 5G proponents were using their newfound fame among pandemic conspiracy theorists to recruit for their cause:

[R]esearchers warned that others are misusing widespread public fear of coronavirus to boost the spread of 5G conspiracies…. In late January, an invite-only Facebook group called "Coronavirus the real truth" was set up and quickly descended into spreading falsehoods and rumors about the global pandemic. Yet by late April, when almost 600 people had signed up, the group abruptly changed its name to "5G the real truth," and began spreading the theories linking COVID-19 to 5G, according to a review of these social media posts by POLITICO [Cerulus 2000].

At the time of this writing, while radiation and EMF remain the backbone of the anti–5G health beliefs, they have been completely sidelined and (temporarily?) replaced by pandemic related conspiracies. It is a process that reflects the way CTs are forced to adapt or die during a worldwide crisis. In this case anti–5G has greatly benefited from the pandemic, moving from its base in European alternative health belief communities to become a global force.

However, we cannot overestimate the adoption of the CT. Here is an example of one form of the 5G conspiracy re-posted May 24 on a large American based anti-lockdown Facebook group. The post tries to keep alive the fading "virus is a hoax" narrative which appeared early in the pandemic as well as directly address the anti-lockdown community's fears:

> 1st wave was a hoax/normal flu. They know that a small part of the population will see through it and minimize the pandemic threat vocally. Some people will also loudly protest the lockdown and social distancing.
>
> 2nd wave will be real, with lot of death. Through recently installed 5G which start 'beam-forming' on people's heads/chests preventing oxygen uptake (remember, 5G is 60ghz which is the frequency of oxygen hemoglobin uptake), which will produce respiratory distress identified as CV symptoms. People of all ages will be dying, even the young, since 5G has been installed in schools. This will (1) totally discredit truthers who questioned the seriousness of the "pandemic" (2) discredit lockdown protesters as irresponsible, destroying possibility of future protests (3) destroy the premise that only the old are vulnerable, and (4) cause a massive and harsh lockdown, worse than before, accompanied by internal border checkpoints....

The post was not successful given the flood of negative reactions:

> **MALE 1:** I'm afraid the 5G conspiracy is a load of shite. Absolutely nonsense
>
> **MALE 2:** Remember when people said this about 4G, and before that 3G, and before that cell phones in general? Oh, and remember when the model T was built, people thought the human body couldn't take the force of going faster than 35mph? Don't be so stupid and afraid of technology. Do be afraid of government!
>
> **FEMALE 1:** it's not the technology I'm afraid of—it's who's using it to gain power that terrifies me.
>
> **FEMALE 2:** And this is why no one listens to people who don't believe in the "devastation" of the virus. We all get lumped into the group of lunatic conspiracy theorists. If you want to believe this, there are places to post it. But we're trying to end the lockdown with actual facts and constitutional rights. This has no place here.
>
> **MALE 3:** The worst part about this 5G stuff is that it causes people to turn away from the real threats of government tyranny. People need to stop Alex jonesing and focus on one fight at a time. When we have our liberty back from this Covid-19 scare $hit then you can rant all you want about 5G, chemtrails, flat earth, whatever, stop conflating it with a real and present problem.

So while it appeared that the post was addressing real fears associated with the anti-lockdown group—fears of being discredited through dirty tricks (and science fiction machines)—the post is rejected because it doesn't fit the community's shared canon of anti-government conspiracies and practical political action of protesting, petitions, writing to elected officials, and prepping. In this example we can clearly see the way that conspiracy theories rely on meshing with people's pre-existing beliefs and systems for adjudicating evidence. Likewise, it is a good reminder that those who believe CTs are not gullible and credulous to a fault. They are using the same tools as everyone else to build and maintain theories of how the world works. And no one believes everything they are told. Well, almost no one. There's still QAnon.

Moral entrepreneurs and ostension by consumption

If the pandemic has been a boon to fringe elements of the Left and Right, attracting new adherents through a shared affinity of certain CTs, it has also been an opportunity for the entrepreneurial elements within conspiracy theory communities and/or those who are simply opportunistic. We defined "ostension" as acting out a legend narrative or acting on a conspiracy theory; this same process can take place through consumption and part of the power conspiracy theorists exploit is the desire to act out our narratives. This process is most clearly seen in 5G marketing.

Figure 8.4. Advertisement in a London pharmacy window (photograph by Giacinto Palmieri, used with permission).

In Figure 8.3 we have an echo of QAnon's #savethechildren but now we're saving them from radio waves instead of Hollywood celebrities. We can do this through "energydots" which the company explains is necessary because of the damage caused by EMF. On their Facebook page they note the number of studies that question the safety of wireless technology, cite the European Union precautionary principle, list some testimonials (essentially recreating the legend) and then explain just how their product works:

> The DOT itself is a low power magnet acting as a storage device. Magnets are often used to store information for example a video tape, tape cassette and magnetic stripe on a bank card all act as storage devices.

- energyDOTs are activated by Programmed Harmonic Interface Technology® (developed exclusively by Global EMF Solutions Ltd). This activation is similar to homeopathic medicine or other vibrational remedies, where an energy signature is stored in a solid substance.
- each energyDOT® is programmed with naturally occurring bio-energetic information signatures according to its purpose
- the powerful resonance held by energyDOTs® acts like a tuning fork on electromagnetic fields in its immediate environment.
- it re-tunes man-made EMFs to a natural harmonic by a process known as the "principal of entrainment"
- The human body's electrical sensors recognise the re-tuned emissions as being in harmony with its natural healthy state. The body no longer needs to react defensively to emissions from the "harmonised" device and electro-stress is relieved [EnergyDots 2016].

It should go without saying that there is no scientific basis for anything you have just read. There is, however, a precedent in traveling salesmen offering ultra-cheap bridges.

Another product was very publicly debunked and ridiculed online on May 28, 2020. Marketed by 5G BioShield they claimed to be "the first to market full-spectrum protection" of "proprietary holographic nano-layer catalyst technology" that promised "remediation from all harmful radiation, electro-smog & biohazard pollution." All of this in a device that looks like a USB stick and costs $416. The company suggests you wear it on your person or keep it close to whatever device you want shielded. The *BBC* reports that subsequent investigation revealed it is indistinguishable from a six-dollar USB device, except for the inclusion of a sticker (Cellen-Jones 2020).

Finally, the alternative health webpage mentioned earlier, Health Nut News, sells the xZubi. The landing page, featuring a Caucasian-presenting baby holding a cell phone, reports on the threats of EMF and various forms of radiation before claiming:

> The xZubi technology is a hologram made of three micro-thin layers of rare-earth, para-magnetic materials that absorb and neutralize man-made electro-magnetic radiation.
>
> The developers went through the highly rigorous process of obtaining a U.S. scientific patent. This involved 28 separate tests, including one exposing human DNA in a petri dish to a cell phone with—and then without—the technology.
>
> The proof is in the fact that this test resulted in those human cells 100% protected from the harmful effects of chaotic radiation.
>
> Other testing show that child and adult human brains are protected from stress by the xZubi device.
>
> To put it in very simplistic terms, it doesn't block all the radiation, or you wouldn't get cell phone reception! It blocks 84% of the negative effects of the radiation [Openshaw n.d.].

When a product reproduces a legend or conspiracy theory on their webpage, and the efficacy of the product is predicated on the same health belief systems and propositions that make up the legend itself, someone purchasing the product to use is participating in the legend through material objects and practices. It is ostension through consumption. Our examples above do just that. In some cases, this may cause little harm except some lost money. In others it could lead to people using the product instead of seeking professional medical assistance, like when televangelist Jim Bakker peddled "Silver Solution" or "Silver Sol" that he claimed "hasn't been tested on this strain of the coronavirus, but it has been tested on other strains of the coronavirus and has been able to eliminate it within 12 hours" (O'Kane 2020).

Many of the "snake oil" products peddled during the pandemic are not part of conspiracies, just scams that operate within the logic of various health belief systems. Where they shade near conspiracy is when they come in contact with discourses about suppressed cures by big pharma (usually pertaining to cancer). When hucksters exploit people who have insecure access to affordable and accessible health care; and when they exploit people's fears for themselves and their families to take money from those already financially harmed by the pandemic, these grifters are odious and beneath contempt.

The 5G towers and destructive ostension

A final and dramatic example of ostension involves the rash of cell tower arsons that followed the rise of anti–5G. Beginning in Europe in spring 2020, the arson attacks occurred across several countries (Chan,

Dupy, and Lajka 2020). The Associated Press reported in April 2020 that at least 50 fires targeting cell towers and equipment had been set in Britain (by May that number was up to 77), and telecom engineers were abused on the job at least 80 times in the United Kingdom (Chan, Dupy, and Lajka 2020). Sixteen towers had been torched in the Netherlands, and attacks were also reported in Ireland, Cyprus and Belgium (Chan, Dupy, and Lajka 2020).

Curiously, at the time of this writing there were no arsons in America but in one striking incidence that precedes the pandemic, a woman named Susan Moose fired on workers performing maintenance work on a tower near her home in Alexander County, North Carolina (Faherty 2019). Starting in May, American law enforcement bodies warned telecommunications companies to be prepared, but as of August arsons had not sprung up in the United States.

In Canada, on May 1 the first cell tower was set alight in a region north of Montreal in the Province of Quebec. Over the next week six more towers were torched before the couple blamed for most of them, Justin-Philippe Pauley, 28, and Jessica Kallas, 25, were arrested. According to Mack Lamoureaux the pair had no anti–5G material on their social media accounts. The only link between them and CTs on 5G was a brief quote from Pauley's mother stating that her son believed 5G was harmful (2020).

The close links between anti–5G and alternative health belief communities, coupled with its amplification by some elements in QAnon (Heilweil 2020), suggests that the novel evolutionary pressures that the pandemic brings to the anti–5G communities will continue to change the conspiracies and 5G conspiracies will also continue to affect the wider interpretation of the pandemic itself.

NINE

Drawing Lines
in Shifting Sand

The Covid-19 Cartoons of Ben Garrison

> Cartoons are not real drawings, because they are drawings intended to be read.—Chris Ware

So far in this book we have covered a host of conspiracy theories, some of them seemingly contradictory, some of them complementary. All along we have stressed that these theories do not appear in siloes: the individual person may draw on whatever they choose to make sense of their world. If all these conspiratorial ideas are like stars, we can point to patterns that have been drawn between a few that form a constellation (a specific theory); and then discern a few more until we have a zodiac; and then suggest how they interact until we have a horoscope, something that not only gives order to the stars but purpose. But while we participate in this astrology, we each nevertheless walk under the same sky, and reconcile the received wisdom as we gaze upwards from our front step.

This chapter tries to provide an overview of some of the themes in this book by examining how one person works through this reconciliation: how someone with an already established orientation towards conspiratorial thinking took in new information from the world around him and made sense of it. In this instance, as he went, he literally gave this process shape through the medium of cartoons.

Ben Garrison, rogue cartoonist

Ben Garrison has been described by *Wired* as the alt-right's favorite cartoonist (Grey Ellis 2017) and as someone who "has found significant success as a hero of 4chan, and is arguably one of the most recognizable [artists] of the alt-right movement" (Guy 2017:114). Following almost twenty years of newspaper industry experience as an illustrator (Taylor 2007) he started publishing his cartoons independently in 2009, "to protest the central banker bailout, bloated government and the slide toward tyranny" (Garrison 2017). He found a receptive audience among Tea Party Republicans and the alt-right that was blossoming during the first two terms of President Obama.

"Conspiracy theorist" is clearly a label one associates with someone else. Ben Garrison would not appreciate anyone labeling him such and certainly does not think of himself as one: "Doubters like me who aren't 'official' or 'reliable' journalists get called 'conspiracy theorists' because we doubt the official narratives created by the CIA and other 'authorities!'" (Garrison 2019a). His independence and lack of any one affiliation is his presumed strength, although he points out when his work has been shared by powerful entities, from right wing outlets like Breitbart and InfoWars to more mainstream sites like Slate and Politico (Garrison 2017). Nevertheless, his political cartoons often invoke conspiratorial themes, and the motives he ascribes to his antagonists and the all-encompassing nature of their perfidy aligns closely with how folklorists Gary Alan Fine and Bill Ellis noted that "conspiracy theories can explain large swaths of an otherwise ambiguous world; they are transcendent explanations, unlocking a closed world with a cleverly forged key" (2010:53). For Garrison it is a particular but not wholly unique lack of trust in virtually all entrenched and elite power, similar to how Mark Fenster describes what lies at the heart of conspiratorial thinking:

> The certainty of conspiracy theory, its eminent trustworthiness, lies in its utter lack of trust: the only thing of which one can truly be certain is the deception with which rulers rule. Paradoxically, the conspiracy theorist only "trusts" politics to be corrupt, or, more to the point, to be defined by secret plans for a global takeover. It is the extreme—indeed, ultimate—skepticism of the political sphere by a sector of the population that feels excluded [1999:71].

The Federal Reserve, the Deep State (Blanuša 2018), the Democratic Party, the United Nations, are all interrelated to Garrison, and as new situations arise each one is assessed, accounted for, reconciled with, and folded into this totalizing explanation of distrust.

Examining Garrison's cartoons and rants one can see conspiratorial thinking recalibrate in real time. The immediate and ephemeral nature of the political cartoon means it is best understood with a close read of the history at its reveal. The need for new content demands he express his thoughts at any given moment, and his outlook changes as the new present reality changes—such as the introduction of shelter-at-home policies and the economic shutdown—as well as the new interpretations—such as the emergence of the presumed contribution of 5G technology to the viral spread, and challenges to Fauci's integrity.

What follows is a study of the first one hundred days of Garrison's Covid-19 cartoons, from the earliest mention in late January, when it was an interesting piece of news trivia with implications for the stock market, to the end of April, six weeks into social distancing. While the complete history of the Covid-19 outbreak will undoubtedly be written, paying attention to what was emerging at the snapshot moment of each cartoon's coming into being helps to uncover how conspiracy theories are constructed over time.

Of cartoons and rants

Garrison's method is to publish a new drawing every few days, posting it to his Twitter feed and directing readers to his website. The tweet, as is the nature of the form, will briefly synopsize the contents of the self-named "rant" that accompanies each image on the site, along with hashtags and mentions. ("Beware the Deep State in a Crisis!" #SundayMorning BONUS #BenGarrisonCartoon for your #QuaratineLife Old Saying: "Give them an inch and they will take a mile." Great Ben Rant at https://grrrgraphics.com/beware-the-deep-state-in-a-crisis.) He has a large audience, with 214,000 Twitter followers (as of this writing) and similarly strong numbers on Facebook and Instagram; each new cartoon is shared, sometimes with commentary, broadly and enthusiastically across social media platforms. His work is also shared, sometimes ironically, outside of those networks as an example *in extremis* of the right's current state of mind. He also maintains an email list and will regularly retweet images with an invitation to subscribe.

Much of what can be said about the rant can be said about the political cartoon, although the latter is image and text, and the former is text alone. Ranting, perhaps best popularized as a genre of political comedy in the United States by Dennis Miller (Dunne 2000; Waisanen 2011) suggests that (a) the text should be considered more aligned with oral, performative, genres than literary, textual, ones, (b) it is emotive rather than calculated, (c) it employs humor, or at least the mechanics of humor, and (d) it is arguing from a specific perspective.[1] With his dual mediation, Ben Garrison's cartoons need to work on their own, independent from the rant, especially when the image is shared without sharing any of the original additional text. Conversely, the rant is a derivative of the cartoon, providing in essence what cannot be rendered in cartoon conventions. As Damian Rivers wrote of him, "providing an additional layer of participation, Garrison facilitates the meaning-making process through the provision of a textual commentary alongside his visual creations" (2019:253).

The two genres of political cartoon and rant both suggest using the mechanics of humor, such as exaggeration, metaphor, parallelism, to articulate with little ambiguity a particular targeted commentary. Political cartoons have a fuzzy relationship with humor. Clearly they often employ the mechanisms of the visual joke: they are "drawings in which an action, situation, or person is caricatured or symbolized, often in a satirical manner [...] mostly characterized by simple lines, exaggerated features, as well as sketch-like and simplified figures" (Samson and Huber 2007:1–2). As drawings, they are already one step removed from depiction toward representation: they are imaginary scenarios that become resolved with our understanding of what is real through recognizing the appropriateness of the metaphors employed.

> Political cartoons generally operate on two distinct levels: on one level, they tell an imaginary story about a make-believe world, while on a second, more abstract level, they refer to real-life events and characters. This relationship between the two levels of meaning is essentially metaphorical, inviting people to map properties from a more tangible area of reality onto one that is more abstract [El Refaie 2009:186].

Cartoons, like verbal jokes, delight their audience precisely because they are a way of seeing different connections between the ostensibly straightforward way the world is communicated to us in more serious ways of communicating. A pun works because it is an accident of history that some words sound like other words and yet their artistic juxtaposition or replacement of one for the other creates a surprising new possibility of meaning. Jokes and cartoons are not so much subjective as they are positional, because they assume some fluency with the world in which they circulate. Carl Rahkonen (1990) writes about viola jokes, which are exactly what you think they are: jokes about violas and violists told by orchestra musicians. As jokes they are not impenetrable to the non-musician, because they have certain formulas and motifs similar to jokes in other contexts and by virtue of being alive in North America one is likely to have a good understanding of joke structure. Yet they still might not be "funny" because they fail to resonate with how one lives in the world.

Similarly, as Leslie Newton notes about the cartoons in 20th-century urban elite magazines, "Because the *New Yorker* expected a level of intelligence and cultural aptitude from its readers, single-paneled cartoons often mocked the persons who are merely posturing smartness—and only the smart reader could distinguish the genuine wit from the ridiculous phony" (2012:69). In either instance, whether joke or cartoon, these things that are intended to delight are also communicating something to their audiences.

As such, they are useful ways of exploring themes within a culture. This also works well for jokes and cartoons that may not delight us, as external observers, not just when they are outside our frame of reference, as viola jokes may be, but when they are fully outside our norms. When one cannot accept the way one is asked to understand the world in order to find some joke amusing, even allowing for a certain latitude given for taboo violation within the play frame, the joke fails as an attempt at humor but is nevertheless a fruitful text of that world.

Political cartoons are all about the positions taken: they employ the mechanics of humor in the cartoon but their purpose is to communicate a point of view, an interpretation and—over the course of a cartoonist's career—a worldview. If they are found funny so be it, but the success of a political cartoon is measured not by whether it elicits laughter but whether it conveys the desired interpretation: "[Political] cartoons are not created simply for fun and innocent play. In general, they are representations of social phenomena and are guided by social and ideological intent" (Al-Momani, Badarneh and Migdadi 2017:65). Beyond the more simple interpretation of all humor as being subjective, the subordination of humor to the message of the political cartoon is summarized by a (vitriolic) take by Victor Raskin on humor's "political impotency," that "all political humor can do is to entertain and reward with a chuckle those who already hold the views that the joke assumes" (2008:27). As we will see, Garrison is "preaching to the converted" as Raskin suggests: although always looking to build his audience, he likewise knows what his established audience is looking for.

The political cartoon is an art form that depends on rapid mechanical reproduction: the thing to which the cartoonist applies their skill and originality is first and foremost intended to be majorly reproduced and disseminated. It is primarily the news of the day, the emergent first draft of consensus history. It is commentary: perspectival and interpretive as opposed to (ostensibly) objective and descriptive. Indeed, as Laurence Streicher observes, "the cult of objective reporting has to some degree precluded the discussion of probable consequences of the facts within the facts," and there is thus an argument to be made that the political cartoonist (Streicher prefers the term caricaturist) is an almost inevitable consequence, that "the presence of the caricaturist as a specialist in the production of meanings through image-making may well be associated with the value-neutrality of the news write-up" (1967:439). Timeliness is imperative, and as such it is not intended to be an enduring entity: particular cartoons may resonate and endure, anthologies may be created, and clippings may comprise a personal scrapbook or cubicle decoration, but these are secondary half-lives to its immediate, urgent initial performance.

With rare exceptions (Len Norris of the *Vancouver Sun*, Carl Giles of *The Daily Express*), cartoonists do not people their drawings with characters of their own creation but with historical persons represented as grotesques or with iconography of the surrounding culture: "metaphors in pictures capitalize on some pre-existing way of using pictures and make sense only if the metaphoric devices are understood as violations or modifications of another order" (Kennedy, Green and Vervaeke 1993: 251). They are discrete: because they are tied to the "historical now," to read one cartoon from a particular cartoonist does not require having previously read another. However, there is a professional and rhetorical advantage to developing a reputation for perspective and competency that frames audience expectations beyond the general expectations for the form to a particular cartoonist's work.[2]

Before the pandemic: January 25 to March 9

On Tuesday, January 21, the Centers for Disease Control and Prevention announced the first lab-confirmed North American case of what was then called 2019-nCoV, in Washington State (CDC 2020a) based on tests conducted the day before. The next day news broke that the Chinese government had closed off the city of Wuhan, a quarantine of unprecedented scale (Levenson 2020) that expanded to all of Hubei Province by January 24. President Trump, during an interview while at the World Economic Forum in Davos, opined that "It's one person coming in from China, and we have it under control" (Calia 2020). Also on January 24, two articles and a comment appeared in *The Lancet* outlining some of the initial findings: the first (Huang et al. 2020) examined the first cohort of 41 cases of lab-confirmed "2019-nCoV" infections as of January 2. Twenty-seven of these had exposure to the Huanan seafood market, a statistic that initiated a shutdown of the market on January 1 (497). Furthermore, the first fatal case had continuous exposure to the market, although his wife, with no known history of exposure there, also contracted it (500). In its concluding paragraph the authors correlated the emergent coronavirus with SARS and MERS: "Both SARS-CoV and MERS-CoV were believed to originate in bats, and these infections were transmitted directly to humans from market civets and dromedary camels, respectively. Extensive research on SARS-CoV and MERS-CoV has driven the discovery of many SARS-like and MERS-like coronaviruses in bats" (504).

In the comment, referring to Huang et al. directly, the authors made a critical qualification: "Exposure history to the Huanan Seafood Wholesale market served as an important clue at the early stage, yet its value has decreased as more secondary and tertiary cases have appeared" (Wang et al. 2020:471). This made explicit reference to the other article, a study of a family cluster that indicated person-to-person transmission (Chan et al. 2020). That article made frequent reference to the Huanan Seafood Market, including describing it once as "where game animals and meat were sold" (522). However, the description of that particular market is sourced to January 1 article in *ChinaDaily.Com.CN* reporting on its closure: "According to Red Star News, a netizen posted on Weibo that he or she has seen wild chickens, snakes and marmots killed for sale in the market. 'In addition to the seafood, the market also sold live cats, dogs, snakes and marmots,' the netizen said. 'There was even a signboard saying that they have live monkeys and deer for sale'" (Juan 2020).

A page one *New York Times* article by Beijing bureau chief Steven Lee Myers pointed attention towards indeterminate "food markets" in China, reiterating both the correlation between the early accounts of SARS and the novel coronavirus, and established tropes about Chinese food habits both as exotic delicacies and folk medicine: "Their consumption is driven as much by the desire to flaunt wealth as by a mix of superstition and belief about the health benefits of wildlife" (Myers 2020a). Arguably, from the onset of what was yet to become known as Covid-19, threads of preconceived ideas about a culture, often more anecdotal than ethnographic, have been presented as arguments not only by non-specialists but even by medical authorities for how we should assess risk.: *I do not eat those kinds of things, so my risk is less / so of course their risk is greater.*[3]

By the time cartoonist Ben Garrison published "Chinese Take Out" on January 25 (Figure 9.1), his first about the disease, it was early enough in the onset for public opinion and the mainstream press to consider it little more than SARS-Redux: a dangerous illness from China that with basic precautions should nevertheless be easily contained.[4] The cartoon comprises a red dragon with "China" written across its stomach and a napkin tied around its neck, sitting dejectedly and dyspeptically in a chair, with green bubbles of sickness floating from an open mouth still full of half-chewed, similarly green food. In the right hand a pair of chopsticks plucks a red virus-like object, with a very angry face, from a platter. The platter, held in the left hand, is piled high with animals: fish, pig, and chicken, but also cat, snake, rat, lizard, bear, turtle, and bat. On the table before him rests a teacup with an eyeball steeping inside, and an unfastened dog collar. "I wonder why I feel sick?" reads the dragon's thought bubble. On his website, Garrison provided an explanatory rant:

THIS WASN'T PART OF THE TRADE DEAL...

China's President Xi Jinping has warned that the "coronavirus" is spreading even faster than before. Millions are quarantined in several cities. Was it a bio-weapon

Figure 9.1. "Chinese Take Out." Cartoon by Ben Garrison, 25 January 2020. Used with permission. https://grrrgraphics.com/chinese-take-out

released by accident? Did it occur when the virus mutated and jumped among various animal species?

The Chinese eat a great variety of animals, which can be found in "wet meat" markets throughout the country. Various viruses can mutate and jump among species and then get transferred to humans. The Chinese authorities themselves say it could have originated at a seafood market where illegal transactions of wild animals were occurring.

Such wet markets offer a mix of a great many species including crocodiles, ostriches, donkeys, kangaroos, snakes, badgers, peacocks, camels, salamanders, wolves, koalas, dogs, cats, turtles and incredibly enough, bats! Apparently some people in China will eat just about anything. Worse, the animals involved are often mistreated or even tortured (to bring out the flavor). It's sick behavior and while it may not be scientific, there's a certain amount of karma involved when nature strikes back with viruses.

China is also well known for being one of the most polluted countries on Earth. The communist dictators have no respect for the freedom of their own people and certainly no respect for their own environment. Their disrespect toward nature has brought about the deadly coronavirus.

China also caters to some very weird and abusive superstitions and traditions such as "tiger penis soup," which is supposed to increase virility. Thankfully, the authorities in China have outlawed such an evil "harvest," but the black market remains.

Garrison is clearly articulating disgust at "some" people in China, along with the karma of nature—whether that means mistreated animals or the disrespected environment—striking back, and the seeming contradiction of calling out political leadership for having no respect for the freedom of its people while simultaneously praising it for outlawing certain practices. Only briefly is the suggestion of a "bio-weapon" made.

President Trump announced the formation of the coronavirus task force on January 29 and began implementing travel restrictions for non-citizens coming from China on February 2 (The White House 2020a, 2020b). For the next three weeks the President made few public statements, suggesting at a rally in Manchester that by April the warmer weather would make the problem disappear (Farhi and Martinez 2020).

Garrison's next cartoon about the virus was not until a month later, on February 25, the day after a thousand-point drop in the Dow Jones Industrial Average (Hajric and Ballentine 2020) and the White House request for $2.5 billion from Congress to aid in its response (Weiland, Cochrane and Haberman 2020). "The Stock Market Catches a Cold" reimagines the "Fearless Girl" statue on Wall Street (McLean 2017) with the head of a coronavirus; the bull she is confronting has fallen flat, lying with his legs splayed in a puddle of oil, green in the face with illness, as the plummeting graph line of the Dow index runs the length of his body to emerge like a tongue lolling out of his mouth. The cartoon reflects Garrison's indifference towards the markets as indicators of economic prosperity ever since the government bailouts of 2008. Consequently, China is invoked not for any direct purported role in the virus's origins but as a bad actor in trade partnerships. As he explains in his rant, "The virus also shows how much the globe has become reliant on the cheap labor and lax standards in China. The shutdowns due to the virus have wreaked havoc on production. It's a sure sign that we depend too much on a nation that's ruled by a backward clique of communist tyrants."

He returned to this theme on February 28 with "China in a Bull Shop," where a red dragon with the head of a coronavirus storms into a china shop wielding a baseball bat. The plates on display are marked with the stock ticker symbols of Fortune 500 companies. Behind the counter a fearful bull is desperately protecting his piles of cash earned from a bubbling stock market, as indicated on a graph shown on his laptop. The accompanying text makes no arguments about China, save for how "It took China's coronavirus to change all that," referring to the bubble. On March 9, "Black Monday I," when the Dow opened to selloffs so rapid that trading was suspended for fifteen minutes, he retweeted the china shop image, now referring to a "Wuhan Virus," and added more text to his post.

On either March 2 or 3 (in a since deleted original tweet), "Deep State Cures" was published, featuring an enormous coronavirus with the face of Bill Gates labeled "Eugenics," and several smaller ones labeled "Crisis,"

"Lies," "Get Trump," "Panic," "Fear," "Abuse," and "Power." While saying "It's the Law!" Gates injects a syringe labeled "The Swamp" into a nervous and masked Uncle Sam. The drawing is titled "The Cure Will Be Worse Than the Disease." Gates had published an article in the *New England Journal of Medicine* suggesting that Covid-19 was a once-in-a-century pandemic and proposed courses of action, namely to assist low- and middle-income countries in preparing for the burdens to be placed on their health care systems, to develop treatments and vaccines, and to invest in disease surveillance and data sharing internationally (Gates 2020a).

The rant begins with "Bill Gates, whose net worth is over $100 billion, once remarked that vaccines could reduce world population by 10 to 15%."[5] Garrison suggests that Gates is "vaccine-obsessed" but not worried about the current health crisis at all: "It's probably all going according to plan. One of Gates' allies will come up with a special vaccine that would cure it and who knows ... maybe lawmakers will make such a shot mandatory." Following a reprisal of much of the current anti-vaccination themes—causing autism, containing fetal tissue—he ends with what will become the dominant theme for much of the next two months, that the cause of Covid-19 is largely irrelevant: "It could be that the virus is a distraction—a crisis for us to focus on while they pull other shenanigans. The conspiracy theories are myriad, but I'm sure of one thing: The cure will be worse than the disease."

An hour after the repost of "China in a Bull Shop," Garrison posted his newest drawing, "Black Swan Event" (referring to Nassim Nicholas Taleb's 2007 term for highly improbable and unpredictable events with seismic consequences). The globe, with a terrified expression on its face and the torso and limbs of a man, is holding on desperately as he rides a black swan, labeled "Fear" and with the head of a coronavirus. The swan, with a sinister expression, tells the globe to "Hold on." They are just about to crest the edge of a waterfall, which is red (from ledger's ink) and labeled "Lake of Debt." In the text of the tweet Garrison refers to an "Overreaction stoked up by the fear merchants!" but on the web page, apart from Roosevelt's "Nothing to fear" quote as an epigram, fear is not invoked. The market plunge that should have happened in 2008 will happen now, and it will be global. "Debt is turning out the lights. There's a huge amount of debt everywhere in the system. Everyone got way too greedy and overextended including the ChiComs [China Communists]. Some conspiracy theorists are saying they released the virus intentionally to do away with a few hundred surplus workers. Their economy was due to crash and they know the virus is a good distraction from that."

In this initial phase, the origins of and subsequently the blame for Covid-19 were still with China and the Chinese, whether it be from their food habits or, potentially, from a lab. But Garrison's concern—indeed, his glee—appears to have stemmed from the corrective that coronavirus was bringing to the market. The economic fallout was fundamentally positive as it would initiate the death throes of an artificial bull market. There was also much that might seem fearful, but fear must not be the engine of our actions, especially if it becomes something that distracts us from our vigilance.

Fear parade: March 12 to March 21

On March 11, the World Health Organization officially classified the outbreak as a pandemic (Boseley 2020). With two Utah Jazz players (Rudy Gobert and Donovan Mitchell) testing positive, the National Basketball Association made the decision to suspend the rest of the season (Aschburner 2020), and in a televised speech from the Oval Office, the President announced a travel ban for Europe (Baker 2020). In the wake of more significant steps being taken, Garrison posted "Make America Well Again." It features a determined and trim Donald Trump in a doctor's coat and head mirror, with a stethoscope draped over his shoulders. He is using a tongue depressor on an anthropomorphized continental United States, green-faced and with green sick bubbles that vaguely resemble coronaviruses floating above. On the wall of the otherwise straightforwardly-depicted medical examination room a diploma reads "Dr. Trump" at the top and "POTUS" immediately below that. Scribbled lines represent a block of text (starting with a clearly rendered "Hereby") signed "Uncle Sam." The tweet tells us that "Doctor Trump is in the House and will #MakeAmericaWellAgain. Stay calm and wash your hands! Don't let the #Covid_19 fear peddlers scare you! Democrats will use crisis to enslave you" (@GrrGraphics 2020d).

The rant builds on the theme: in addition to praising the President for the "[calm] suggestions" of hand washing, limiting travel, and social distancing, and comparing coronavirus with the flu, Garrison notes that "Panic is in the air," citing the NBA season suspension and the closing of school districts. He reiterates (for what will be the last time for a while) the arguments of "China in a Bull Shop" and "Black Swan Event": "The stock market has succumbed to the fear, but it was in a bull market bubble for far too long anyway." Ultimately, after reiterating how warmer temperatures will cause it to "eventually evaporate," Garrison makes his main argument: "The globalists love a good crisis. They use them to undermine our freedom as well as our health." He retweets it later that day (after edits to the original post with the latest statistic of 37 dead) and once more the following day, then again on March 14 in celebration of the President testing negative for

Covid-19 (Karni and Haberman 2020). Within a week (19 March) the image was turned into a repeating animation and was regularly retweeted alongside encouragement to sign up for Garrison's email list.

On March 12, a spokesman for the Chinese Foreign Ministry floated the idea that the coronavirus might have been brought to Wuhan by the American military during their participation in the World Military Games held there in October 2019 (Zhao 2020: see Myers 2020b). With this news breaking, two days later Garrison posted "The Blame Game," featuring a tennis match between an athletic President Trump and President Xi of China, the latter depicted as Winnie the Pooh[6] and with his name across his shirt—on a court where the sections between the service and base lines are emblazoned with the Chinese flag at one end and an American blue rectangle with "USA" in the upper left corner. The faces of six skulls emerge out of the weaving of the net. Instead of a ball, a coronavirus is hurtling towards a scrambling Xi. He cries out "Fault!" but the President intones "No, it's your fault!" Bill Gates sits in the umpire's chair, laughing, although neither the tweet nor the website mentions Gates; presumably he is content either way, as the virus is an opportunity whichever its source. Instead, in the midst of describing the godlessness of the communist state, Garrison mentions how "The current Chinese Communists are lying about the release of a bioweapon from one of their labs in Wuhan. The ChiComs must present themselves as incapable of error, so they're now blaming the United States military for the virus."

For his March 16 cartoon "Fear Parade" (Figure 9.2), Garrison brought back the theme of fear first suggested in "Deep State Cures" and then expanded in "Black Swan Event." The image itself is labeled "The Hegelian Parade," and labels the participants "Problem Reaction Solution," a way that Hegel's dialectic has been adapted within conspiracy theorist language (Drinkwater et al. 2018). "Problem" is the drum major, with the globe for a head and a coronavirus at the tip of its mace. Problem looks back with a smirk at "Reaction," a trumpeter blaring "Fear" in red capital letters. At the end of the parade "Solution" beats a bass drum labeled "Tyranny" and wears full military riot gear, replete with assault rifle, mask, and jackboots. Beginning with a misquote of Rahm Emanuel's "Never let a crisis go to waste" aphorism (Joni 2008; Rosenthal 2009), Garrison writes, "Whether or not the US had anything to do with the creation and release of the COVID 19 virus, it is sadly predictable that our government will use the situation to further increase its power by lessening our freedom." He suggests that the attacks of 11 September 2001 were also state-sponsored with the specific objective of initiating the Patriot Act, and that because the lockdown of Boston in the immediate aftermath of the marathon bombings of 15 April 2013 aided in capturing the suspects, the looming shutdown

Figure 9.2. "Fear Parade." Cartoon by Ben Garrison, 16 March 2020. Used with permission. https://grrrgraphics.com/the-fear-parade

is more an excuse in exercising power, and they will initiate lockdowns for mandatory vaccinations and confiscating firearms. "Only government will have the official word along with the CDC and World Health Organization. By the way, Bill Gates helped fund the WHO and I also heard he was part 'owner' of the virus patent. Last week he suddenly resigned from Microsoft's board. Perhaps he knows he's partially responsible in some manner and is heading to a private location to avoid a hemp necktie." Garrison again turns to conspiracy theory explicitly, and names his favorite: "I've read all the conspiracy theories regarding the reason for the release of the virus. One of the most believable contentions is the virus is a distraction from 5G, which is dangerous to humans. Ironically, Wuhan is big on 5G. 4G is fast enough, but 5G is necessary for the globalist power freaks (such as Bill Gates) who desire 'smart cities' that monitor everything citizens might do."

 For the next few cartoons, the message was consistent. Garrison's wife, Tina, contributes the occasional cartoon, and on 17 March "The Fear Channels" showed a frightened couple sitting in front of a television while coronavirus talking heads yelled terrifying headlines: "The Worst is Ahead!" "Recession!" "Trump is Killing Everyone!" In the rant, it is affirmed that "The coronavirus is real and should be taken seriously," but "Stay calm and use common sense. Don't panic. Panic begets fear and fear leads to control and tyranny." The next day, after Vice President Joe Biden won the Arizona, Florida, and Illinois primaries (Epstein, Lerer and Kaplan 2020), Garrison produced "Social Distancing," It featured Biden outpacing an exhausted Senator Bernie Sanders on a running track, while a runner with a coronavirus head races past in the background. In the rant it is suggested that Sanders will stay in the race and thus "endanger lives by helping expose people to the coronavirus by forcing people to show up at voting stations," while Biden, among his listed faults, is described as "more worried about climate change than the virus."

On 19 March the cartoon "Trump Ready to Help Americans" shows the President flying a gold helicopter (with the Trump T emblazoned on the front and POTUS along the tail boom) giving a thumbs up to his passenger, Andrew Yang, the former Democratic contender who had touted a universal basic income policy, AKA the "Freedom Dividend" (T. Alberta 2020). Money is streaming from the helicopter as "$2,000 to Each American" is spread over a cityscape, evoking the contemporaneous rumors of helicopters spraying disinfectant (Arkhipova and Brodie 2020). In "Spare a Square?" (20 March) Tina depicts the bears from the Charmin toilet paper ad campaign enjoying the piles of cash resulting from panic buying.

At this stage in the response to the pandemic Garrison reaffirms that the coronavirus is a real threat, with murky but perhaps at this point irrelevant origins: however, while precautions should be taken, part of being vigilant is also not giving in to fear-based pressures to go beyond what is being asked. How that pressure will manifest and why, emerges over the next two weeks.

Plannedemic: March 22 to April 7

Democratic House Whip James Clyburn was reported to have said, while on an 18 March conference call to the caucus in preparation for a stimulus bill, that "This is a tremendous opportunity to restructure things to fit our vision" (Lillis and Wong 2020). Senate Majority Leader Mitch McConnell, in a floor speech on March 21, cited it when warning Democrats not to use the stimulus as a political opportunity (Ferrechio 2020). The next day, Garrison published "Beware the Deep State in a Crisis." The Capitol Building, green-tinged and with the American flag upside-down and in tatters, is depicted as an angry and many-tentacled beast, reminiscent of the use of the octopus in anti–Semitic cartoons of previous centuries (Lenepveu 1899; Seppla 1938). The tentacled beast also resembles Alfred Owen Crozier's 1912 cartoon criticizing the Aldrich Plan (a precursor to the Federal Reserve) and appears as a frequent motif in Garrison's cartoons (Garrison 2018). On the pediment is a list of initials and abbreviations: CFR (Council on Foreign Relations); FBI; CIA; IRS; Big Pharma; CDC; WHO; TSA; BATF (Bureau of Alcohol, Tobacco, and Firearms); and "Fed. Res."

The capitol is menacing a group of citizens marooned on a minuscule desert island, saying, "I'm the government and I'm here to help." This paraphrases Ronald Reagan's infamous "I think you all know that I've always felt the nine most terrifying words in the English language are: I'm from the Government, and I'm here to help" (1986). Each tentacle holds a labeled object: a riot policeman saying, "Your papers, bitte!" (labeled "Martial Law"); a syringe containing vaccine ("Mandatory"); a 5G tower ("'Smart' Tyranny"); a drinking glass emblazoned with a skull ("Fluoride"); a bomb ("Endless war"); a money-bag destined "to the IRS" ("Tax theft"); an airplane leaving "Chemtrails"; the Statue of Liberty (itself labeled "Freedom") snapped in half ("Patriot Act"); a bowl full of Frankenstein's monsters heads ("GMO Food"); and a padlock ("Lock down"). The beast is a distillation of the all-encompassing nature of conspiracy thinking, that not only do conspiracies happen, but that they are interrelated: As Jovan Byford put it, "[Conspiratorial] narrative gradually slides towards a view of society and history as coherent and predictable, but at the same time deceptive. It establishes connections between diverse historical events and assumes that conspirators are ubiquitous and omnipresent, active in every part of the world and unaffected by logistical constraints" (2011:37). The rant continues the theme, beginning with the Clyburn quote and making specific mention of social distancing and lockdown guidelines with "Our freedom of assembly is gone. POOF!"

> We The People had better darn well shut up and do as we're told! Lives are at stake! You don't want anyone to die, do you? Of course you don't! Therefore, you WILL stay in your home and watch the fear porn channels each day. Start begging for still yet another government safety net. Demand that government receives more power and authority! Demand martial law and the mobilization of the troops! Demand Bill Gates release his vaccine antidote—you know, the one that comes with a handy-dandy microchip that can be scanned at government checkpoints to make sure you got your shot.

"Beware the Deep State in a Crisis" sets the tone for the next few cartoons in which Democrat obstructionism is a regular feature; it completes the "Fear Parade" argument by providing evidence of a desire to use the current situation as a tactic for a larger agenda; it folds the coronavirus into the established network of a totalizing conspiracy; and, in addition to explicitly name-checking such ideas as vaccines proven to cause autism and the ills of fluoridation, it adds another theme of the Bill Gates coronavirus conspiracy, namely that there is an antidote that is associated with mandatory microchipping.

Following an opinion essay in the *Washington Post* suggesting that the President's daily briefings on the unfolding crisis should not be aired live (Sullivan 2012), Tina produced "The Visible Enemy" (March 23). It contrasts a microscopic coronavirus with "the corrupt, China loving propagandists of the Fake News Media," represented by reporters from news outlets presumed critical of the administration. Two days later, a cartoon by Ben used classic tropes to respond to the "partisan bickering [and] progressive virtue signaling" of Democrat delays in the passage of the stimulus package (Halon 2020; Lipton and Vogel 2020). "Pelosi Hates America" shows a hopping-mad Mitch McConnell with the relief bill in his hand while two ostriches labeled Pelosi and Schumer have their heads buried, the latter in the sand and the former up her own rear end. "You're doing it wrong, Nancy!" says Schumer.

With "The Plannedemic" on March 28, Garrison returned to a host of themes that had been building in the previous month.[7] Bill Gates (unlabeled, yet named in the tweet and the rant) is wearing a skull lapel pin, a scroll laid out in front of him, oriented for the viewer to see. It is a six stage plan: (1) Fear, illustrated by a coronavirus hovering over an homage to Edvard Munch's "The Scream"; (2) Information control and censorship, as

Figure 9.3. "The Plannedemic." Cartoon by Ben Garrison, 28 March 2020. Used with permission. https://grrrgraphics.com/the-plannedemic

a startled man at a computer sees his screen filled with a stop sign (and the screen of his smart phone an exclamation point); (3) Shutdown and social distancing, with a switch flipped to off over a man gesturing to a woman to keep her distance; (4) Blame President Trump; (5) Martial law and checkpoints, illustrated by a policeman in full tactical gear, and (666) Mandatory vaccine rollout. Gates is pointing to "Blame President Trump" and says, "We are here." In the rant Garrison notes how Gates' past warnings of a possible pandemic were "Conditioning us. Getting us used to the idea." The vaccine-antidote with microchip mentioned in "Beware the Deep State in a Crisis" is absent, but the rant's claims of his father being a eugenicist and his support of GMO foods and vaccines in general intimate that Gates' plan is to use the crisis as an opportunity for population control. Even social distancing is framed as part of the plan: "We now have social distancing to further divide the human race—as if we were all some sort of disease in need of eradication." Ultimately, the cartoon emphasizes the "Problem Reaction Solution" model from "The Fear Parade": "Things are going according to plan. They can't control us physically, but he can control us mentally through fear drummed into our brains 24/7 by mass media."

After "Plannedemic," Garrison didn't produce a cartoon for almost a week, while Tina put out two. Nancy Pelosi appeared on television and said that "As the President fiddles, people are dying" (Cohen 2020): the day after, Tina's "Pelosi the Fiddler" (March 30) features the Speaker of the House playing a skull-shaped violin as the United States is in flames, while the rant lists ways that Pelosi has stalled the government's response. "My Country" (1 April) is a tribute to Mike Lindell, of the MyPillow company, who switched 75 percent of his manufacturing to the production of face masks for medical personnel but whose announcement of this at the White House was widely mocked by commentators: "Lindell then launched into a short infomercial for his company, followed by a eulogy to Trump as the man who had rescued a nation that had 'turned its back on God'" (Collins 2020).

Garrison returned on 4 April with "Bill Gates Medical Fascist." Gates is shown in front of a Nazi flag where the swastika is made of four hypodermic needles. He is wearing a uniform modeled on the SS: his cap has an insignia comprising a caduceus, a needle, and skull and crossbones; on each epaulet is a blue circle with lines of latitude and longitude; and there is a coronavirus on one lapel and the Microsoft Windows insignia on the other. He is holding a baby-blue armband with a digital green checkmark, and he says to the reader, "You must wear a <u>Bluetooth armband</u> to prove you received the COVID-19 vaccination!" Behind him a computer is running Windows "5G Edition." The rant begins with a common quote misattributed to Benjamin Rush, a signer of the Declaration of Independence and Surgeon General of the Continental Army. The quote suggested that, were medical freedom not enshrined in the Constitution, "medicine will organize into an undercover dictatorship and force people who wish doctors and treatment of their own choice to submit to only what the dictating outfit offers."

After disparaging Dr. Anthony Fauci as "a top medical 'authority' who is also good friends with Hillary Clinton and the Deep State," Garrison emphasizes how the lockdown and social distancing are backed up by brute force: "The [American Medical Association], the [World Health Organization], the [Centers for Disease Control and Prevention] and the rest of the medical authorities are corrupt and in league with the globalist Deep State. None of them care if our constitutional rights are violated. Our federal government doesn't care about us, either. Our rights be damned. They think we can be bought off with a paltry thousand bucks or so." But he holds his greatest vitriol for Gates, repeating the claims of eugenics, and introducing the idea of digital tracking: "With each vaccine, Bill wants to add a tiny, digital element which will provide biometric identification. If this isn't the 'mark of the beast,' I don't know what is." Garrison had employed the 666 motif in "The Plannedemic," but now makes the Mark of the Beast allusion explicit.

On April 7, "Free Our Economy" shows a somber Uncle Sam behind prison bars formed from the red stripes of the American flag, with the stars replaced with padlocks. The tweet demands that we "Protect the vulnerable—let the healthy go back to work!" In the rant Garrison continues to recognize the legitimate threat of coronavirus but, citing tuberculosis at one time killing one in seven Americans and repeating a comparison of Covid-19 to the flu, "there have always been diseases and death. It's part of life." He calls statistics into question, repeating a rumor in active circulation that "All flu cases are now considered to be 'Covid-19.' Hospitals are changing the cause of death to the coronavirus even when it's not the case." Dr. Fauci is identified as "a Bill Gates man," running a script to ensure fear and obedience. "George Soros, Bill Gates, Henry Kissinger, and the rest at the very top of the pyramid […] want to shut down our economy and deindustrialize us. They want socialism and serfdom. Then we will become more dependent on government—a government they control." A cashless digital economy that they control will cut off free speech as no one would risk losing access to credit. With little ambiguity, he maintains that "They are evil and they're using their corporate mass media pound out a steady drumbeat of fear while offering their high-tech enslavement as a way to make the fear go away. […] NEVER take Bill Gates' vaccine."

By this point the threat of Covid-19 to personal and collective health was being weighed against the threat to civil liberties: according to Garrison, Bill Gates and the Deep State were taking advantage of the fear to introduce a new form of order. China is no longer mentioned, and it is time to cast doubt on the very idea of the disease itself and the recommended actions to combat it.

Mark of the Beast: April 8 to April 28

The context of Covid-19 allowed for a few cartoons that were more disease-adjacent than specific. Tina produced "Face Mask Fashion Democrat Style" (April 8) when photos circulated of both Schumer and Congresswoman Sheila Jackson Lee wearing protective masks that weren't covering their noses. Contemptible Democrats, by name or by type, wore theirs in ridiculous manners, in explicit contrast with "Anyone who has ever sanded wood, groomed a dog or cleaned out a dusty attic knows the proper way to wear a mask." On April 10 Garrison released "What deficit?" after it was reported that former Federal Reserve Chair Janet Yellen had said that inflation would not be a long-term issue with its current response to the crisis, thus returning him to one of his main concerns. He even began his post on the website with "Warning: Classic Ben Rant."

But April 11 saw "Fire Fauci." The day before, Dr. Fauci had appeared on CNN and said that "Now is no time to back off" (Borter and Hampton 2020). In the cartoon, President Trump is in the back seat of a car, while Fauci drives and Dr. Deborah Birx, Coronavirus Response Coordinator, sits in the passenger seat. A "Gates Foundation" badge decorates her lapel, featuring a smiling Gates holding an enormous syringe. Trump asks, "Are we there yet?" and Fauci slyly responds, "In a few more months! … Maybe." In the rant Garrison suggests that Trump made a huge mistake putting Fauci "in the driver's seat," and that both Fauci and Birx are "owned" by Bill Gates. Garrison says Gates wants the lockdown to be dragged out as long as possible so that when Gates rolls out his vaccine he will be hailed as a savior. Needing the vaccine to fulfill Gates' plan is why Fauci has denied the use of hydroxychloroquine. Garrison also starts to suggest how the digital tracing element of the vaccination is not an armband or card but somehow in the vaccine itself: "They think the citizens will insist on getting the shot. Yes, the same shot with digital elements. A vaccine 'tattoo,' or mark of the beast. In some states it will become mandatory. In California, vaccines are already mandatory. We're losing our ability to decide what goes into our bodies. It's the ultimate in Orwellian tyranny and Bill Gates is Big Brother."

This line of thought is continued in "Big Brother Bill" (April 13) depicting Gates's face on an enormous screen in a city square with "COVID-1984" emblazoned over top. Gates says, "Time for your next vaccine!" to the crowd depicted in silhouette below. They in turn respond with "We will obey!," "Bill Gates has <u>saved</u> us!," "We have our digital tattoos!" and "We love you Big Brother!" The rant repeats much of what has been said about him already, with such additional points as "Gates has many medical and pharmacological stooges working for him—including the diminutive Fauci, who helped make sure American taxpayer money went to fund the coronavirus research in Wuhan."

From here Garrison pivots to a theme that will emerge over the next month but had so far been largely absent in his discussions of Covid-19: the failure of Globalist ecofascism and how climate change was a manufactured crisis that failed. "The virus is working much better for them than their climate change bunk. They want to portray humans as a virus infecting the planet." And while social distancing is again suggested as a tool for limiting protest, specific emphasis is placed on the closing of churches: "Churches have been targeted. They want faith directed at Gates, not God."[8] This last point is echoed four days later in "Signs of the Times" (April 17): a path is clear to the open liquor store and abortion clinic, but the church is closed and blocked off with a police barricade.

His rant suggests that Democrats have become the anti–Christian party because "Christians do not like abortion. The Democrats love abortion with an almost religious fervor. They worship it. They want to harass anyone who disagrees with them." The "scamdemic" (a new coinage he does not return to) provides the opportunity to prevent free association and practice of religion. "The elite want complete obedience to global government rule. They want people to be dependent on government and God interferes with that. The Illuminati want everyone around the globe to worship Big Brother government—not God."

The President announced his intention to cease subsidies to the WHO on April 15 (Klein and Hansler 2020), precipitating the six-hour "One World: Together at Home" streaming fundraiser in support of the WHO April 18 (Pareles 2020). Tina then produced "Horton Defunds the WHO" (April 20) featuring the Dr. Seuss character transformed with the President's blond bouffant hair and red necktie, shaking money from the little clover as tiny voices say "Don't blame China!" and "Millions will die!" and "Because corruption is corruption, no matter how small." The rant reiterates how the WHO "is a corrupt relic dedicated to covering up China's mistakes," and that it was a complicit partner in China's early mishandling and potentially intentional misinformation. When a tweet (quickly deleted and thus drawing attention to itself) from Congresswoman Alexandria Ocasio-Cortez seemed to celebrate the price of oil falling to a negative number, Garrison released "Oil Crash" (April 21). Under the words "Oilrona Virus" a polished oil barrel with a dollar sign is identified as the "Before," with the "After" being a weathered steel trash can with oil seeping out and coronavirus-shaped bubbles floating above. Ever opposed to market intervention, he nevertheless seems torn by the free-fall price of a major American commodity, yet resolute that fear stemming from neither Covid-19 directly nor the economic uncertainty it has caused should make one any less opposed to the Green New Deal initiatives.

This tension becomes resolved in part in the next cartoon, "Give Me Safety AND Death" (April 22). The left half of the cartoon is under the title "Then," and shows a parchment-colored faux-woodcut of Patrick Henry declaiming "Give me liberty or give me death!" The right half ("Now") has Garrison's standard depiction of a male liberal (purple shirt, scruffy beard, gauged earlobes, and glasses, wearing rubber gloves, a face mask, albeit pulled down to show his full panicked expression) and a badge with a cartoon kitten that reads "Safety first." He cries out "Give me safety!" Standing behind him, Bill Gates holds an enormous syringe and thinks "…and then death." Garrison's suggestion that the current crisis is a more successful attempt at instilling fear that climate change is now a dominant theme: "For years they pushed fear via the 'climate change' narrative, but it never really caught on. People had more important things to worry about than the weather. Most were too busy working and trying to pay the bills. Nobody wanted the globalist 'green new deal,' which would shut down the oil industry, our economy, and cost everyone their jobs. Now the Deep state has found something that works for them—a scary man-made virus. Oil has collapsed and people have lost their jobs. Just what they wanted—the destruction of America!" The very fact that quarantine and the economic slowdown has meant more time to listen to the "drums of fear" perpetuated in mass media is suggested as part of the plan. If fear is the reaction to the problem, safety is the purported end point of the suggested solutions of the limitations on personal liberties. "They'll tell us it's for our safety—that hypnotic word that allows Big Government to do whatever it likes to us. 'Stay home, stay safe!' To hell with their safety! I want my freedom! I especially don't want Bill Gates' Satanic 'mark of the beast' vaccine."

Two days later came "The Evolution of Bill Gates." As a drawing it could have been in a file for years, as it is not Covid-19 specific, yet clearly for Garrison's purposes apt and timely. A recent Microsoft ad featuring the artist Marina Abramovic had to be pulled after conspiracy theorists brought up old stories about her alleged Satanism that emerged at the time of Pizzagate (Marshall 2020). This only helped to refract the increasing mentions of the "Mark of the Beast" vaccine. Parodying the "March of Progress" illustration (Shelley 2001), Gates is shown at four stages of life: as an infant he shakes a blue globe rattle while "stink lines" emanate from his diaper; as a child he holds a slide rule and picks his nose; as a middle-aged man he wears a business suit and clutches a briefcase with the Microsoft

Windows logo in one hand and a money bag in the other. But in the present he is a demon, in a ragged hooded black cloak like the Grim Reaper, with red skin, taloned feet and a devil's pointed tail. Instead of a blade his scythe has a syringe labeled "Mandatory," and a snake wraps around the handle like the Rod of Asclepius. In the crook of his harm he carries a picnic basket labeled "GMO," with an ear of corn sticking out.

The rant reaffirms most of the salient talking points—eugenics, not elected, not a medical expert, Fauci is his henchman—but with increasingly strident language. The looming threat is "whatever vaccine he will roll out. […] such a vaccine will accustom us to what Gates really wants us to get—an implanted identity chip that will allow us to buy and sell in a cashless society. If that happens, it's game over. Bill Gates and his pedophile Satanists will win." Were the point not clear, he ends definitively: "Bill Gates is murdering monster that must be resisted at all cost. Do not take his mark of the beast vaccine!"

As April drew to a close, Garrison extended the mark of the beast imagery to "Fauci the Blue Demon" (April 28). This cartoon adapted the WHO logo of a Rod of Asclepius over an azimuthal map of the world wreathed in olive branches, their tips ending in syringes and Fauci's head atop the serpent. Fauci spouts horns and a serpent's forked tongue as he tells the reader to "TRUSsssT USsss!" The rant is brief, with little new to say, and perhaps occasioned by Brad Pitt having portrayed Fauci on *Saturday Night Live* on April 25 (Itzkoff 2020). Garrison devotes a paragraph to this performance. "Fauci and Gates want worldwide vaccination with the 'mark of the beast,' tagging technology. They both want medical tyranny. […] Gates is an arch eugenicist. Fauci is one of his demons—and since he's in the medical field, let's make him a blue one."

April 28 also marked one hundred days since the first U.S. case of Covid-19 was detected. It was one day short of the one millionth case and by then more than 56,000 Americans had died. The next months would see lockdown protests followed by protests reacting to the murder of George Floyd by a former Minneapolis police officer. Garrison shared his strong opinions about that murder.

Urgency of the messages

In folklore studies we occasionally refer to the "when" of extraordinary narratives, what Bill Ellis (1989a) called the "half-lives of the legend." Something happens that we know pushes against the limits of how we understand the world to normally operate: often this experience is of a kind with other extraordinary happenings and so the group we live among has a potential *name* for it and we apply that name to that experience. As I try to tell you about it I use the names to *translate* it into some kind of narrative (whether that's an actual story with characters and motivations doing actions in sequence, or the implied story that a cartoon suggests), and it might not be pretty but hopefully it is effective: it is important that I tell you about this, the aesthetics be damned.

After this initial communication I might retell it, and you might retell it, more aware of the conventions of effective communication, turning it into something more *finished*, more polished: a "good" story. After a while, when everyone knows the story, it doesn't bear much retelling, except when someone new enters the group. Then it can be told again to an uninitiated audience; otherwise, it is merely referred to in passing, a *metonym* or kernel narrative that can be invoked as a parallel example and additional supporting evidence when the next extraordinary experience is articulated without having to be told in full again. Finally, and what is often the only thing the folklorist has access to, comes the *report*, where, absent any context, someone (and typically someone else, external to the group) has summarized the event, more as data and plot than as communicative event: "These people believe...."

The fact that Garrison earns his living as a self-employed (or, his term of choice, rogue) cartoonist is both relevant and beside the point. A professional requirement to be regularly generating content encourages support through his Patreon, traffic directed to his online store, click-throughs on ads on his website, appearance fees, and all the ways that people earn in the contemporary webcomics economy when one's product is essentially free (Misemer 2019; Plamondon 2018). Such income is established largely by developing a reputation for competency and fluency, which in Garrison's case is a distillation of an immediate response to current events that simultaneously informs and reaffirms his audience's particular worldview. Because he expresses this worldview well, creating images that evocatively communicate how a moment in time ought to be interpreted, his expressions are in turn sought out in an ongoing cyclic relationship of cartoonist and audience. He speaks *to* his audience because he speaks *for* them.

A cynic could point to shifting ideas in Garrison's presentation of the Covid-19 crisis as a sign of inconsistency and thus of intellectual vacuity. How can he praise the relief payments in "Trump Ready to Help Americans" on March 19 and say "They think we can be bought off with a paltry thousand bucks or so" on April 4 in "Bill Gates Medical Fascist"? But new facts emerge, new policies are enacted, and new opinions are expressed that all require immediate response. Garrison can only reflect on what he knows through both the mainstream outlets he routinely derides, and those channels more in keeping with his worldview: if one wishes to apologize for his inconsistencies, they derive from information emerging in real time.

As one plots the trajectory of Garrison's cartoons over the first four months of Covid-19, the inconsistencies and contradictions from cartoon to cartoon are far outweighed by the overall consistency of worldview. We know the way the world operates, who are the bad actors, and what is at stake: now, how is it manifested at this moment? And, given the call to action implicit and often explicit in conspiracy theory messaging (Tangherlini 2018), what is to be done about it? It is not simply important to Garrison that we know what his opinion is, it is urgent that we do something. Through the genres of the political cartoon and the rant, with all the ambiguity that humor allows, Ben Garrison provides a first and very public effort at articulating and interpreting the historical now for a like-minded audience who will in turn redistribute and amplify his interpretation because they could not have put it better themselves.

TEN

When All Is Said—or Done

Examining Ourselves, Talking to Others

> People think that stories are shaped by people. In fact, it's the other way around. Stories exist independently of their players. If you know that, the knowledge is power.—Terry Pratchett

During Covid-19 many conspiracy theories emerged from shadowy corners of social media into public consciousness to negatively affect the way people saw the pandemic—and those working to stop it. It may never be possible to quantify the effects of conspiracy thinking and theory on this epoch of world history, particularly in the hands of those who headed governments. Online and in conversation, misinformation, intentional disinformation and conspiracy theory twisted together throughout the pandemic, and there are few indications this could change. The social, economic, and health crises brought on by Covid-19 were exacerbated by conspiracy theory exploitation, amplification, astroturfing, and proselytizing from true believers.

Take the harm caused by the #filmyourhospital hashtag, which began March 28 and was most active in April (Gruzd and Mai 2020). The theory was that hospitals were complicit in a mass deception, exacerbating or even making up case counts. A common meme shared at the time showed two seemingly identical pictures depicting an emergency ward in Italy and another in New York City. Accompanying text read, "Top photo was shared last week from an ICU in Italy. Bottom photo was shared of an ICU in New York this week. Notice the difference??? THERE ISN'T ONE!! And this is your mainstream media ladies & gents … wake up, you are being fed lies! Careful where you get your info because unfortunately you can't trust much anymore." Videos of hospital parking lots and entrance areas went online, supposedly proving that there was no pandemic. This practice became increasingly caustic as anti-lockdown supporters attacked doctors and nurses online and in person, blaming them for everything from covering up empty emergency rooms, murdering the elderly, and faking the cause of death to inflate Covid-19 numbers (White 2020; McEvoy 2020).

As Gruzd and Mai have pointed out, these attacks were part of a larger disinformation campaign to erode trust in experts and sites of independent knowledge production. Such disruption is part of a wider and long-running politicization of conspiracy thinking in populist movements. #Filmyourhospital hurt people who were trying to help others during the pandemic, and as the idea of the pandemic being completely faked failed under new evidence, it morphed into being conflated—still an attack on knowledge centers and expertise. Conspiracy theories that predated Covid-19 morphed and recombined to encompass the pandemic in many ways, fading and advancing in new forms with added ammunition as facts about the virus emerged. We should expect they will continue to do so. And these CTs will continue to cause harm atop a crisis already fraught with economic and social peril.

Many of us have heard the stories explained throughout this book in some form from friends and family, leading to our ultimate question in this final chapter: how can we debunk them? Can we gently prod people we care about toward more accurate information? Should we? How much are we in charge of making other people think "correctly?" As dangerous as some of these CTs have turned out to be, isn't trying to censor others an equally dangerous proposition?

Aye, there's the rub.

Most of us have a "Cousin Tim" sending endless updates roaring across social media, ranging from the mild to the wild. If you too have a beloved conspiracy theorist in your life, you've probably tried to convince them to give up a favorite theory to no avail. Before we discuss some ideas to help in that effort, let us pause to differentiate between talking someone we love out of potentially self-harmful or just plain irritating behavior at family gatherings, and engaging in useless fact-flinging on the Internet. We are not suggesting anyone set themself up as The Truthteller in situations with strangers—least of all online. It does no good, and as we shall see shortly, it can do actual harm. Advice here is confined to how to handle friends and family you already know, when they want to talk about things you don't. Or when you are concerned about their level of isolation, a key factor in identifying when a CT has gotten too far inside someone's lifestyle. If you think someone you love is in too deep, you might want to visit online forums where those who have quit those groups and thought patterns support each other.

We aren't listing specifics in every category, but for QAnon the Reddit forum "QanonCasualties" can be instructive. For militias that edge into hate groups, the Anti-Defamation League and Integrity First for America are good starting points. A quick Google search will reveal other resources with little difficulty. And we remind everyone that, at the end of the day, thought is free. Taking charge of what other people are allowed to think is not a job any of us need to have. Influencing those we love to be part of the solution, not the problem, is different from trying to tell them what they should think. Keep that in mind. We need to show the respect we want to receive.

Of stones and glass houses

Because the painful truth is, most of us hold some conspiracy theories in our heads, and we think they are true conspiracies. People suffering genuine harm from the questionable actions of pharmaceutical companies, in actions that have been objectively proven through our institutions of trust like the press and the courts (Welch 2020), will not find the idea of big pharma testing vaccines on minimum-wage "expendable/essential" workers far-fetched. When systemic racism is real and forever palpable, the targeting of Black communities through 5G falls within rational and necessary cautions of reason; don't be naive about false positives versus false negatives when your life is on the line. Even the rejection of a plot as too fanciful may be conditioned by, "Well, I can see why people might believe that, because…." You may not believe in the conspiracy theory about Hollywood child abduction for purposes of harvesting adrenochrome, but you might not think fondly of the culture of privilege and licensed excess flaunted by celebrities either.

Conversation with our more conspiracy-minded friends often ends with Hufford's famous words about belief; the things we believe are sane and the things they believe are not. But your loved one thinks the same of you. So, before bugging your friends and family about their conspiracy beliefs, it's worth spending some time poking around in the dusty corners of your own mind to see which things you believe that might sound like a conspiracy to others. In a 2015 study, researchers found 55 percent of people believed at least one political conspiracy theory and most believed more than one (Oliver and Wood 2014). Odds are you at least have an affinity towards one of the CTs in this book, because we all want the comfort of a human-caused event or action to explain the bizarre circumstances that fell upon us so swiftly in early 2020.

The question then becomes, why that one? What about your favored explanation makes you feel better? Which element of the story attracts you? Does it hand over a clear villain to blame, and you didn't like that person or institution in the first place? Dissect something inexplicable or utterly unfair? What fear does it comfort? Thinking about your own thinking isn't always easy, but it does help to see the places where you just want that story to be true. Odds are good your friend feels the same way about a different idea.

Examining our own biases, values, and preferred narratives is also an exercise in being critical yet respectful, first with ourselves and then extending that care out to others in our lives. Thinking about our own thinking requires a deep dive into why something appeals to us. Conspiracy theories create order from events that sometimes have no coherent explanation— large crises come from small and unconnected actions, and that disconnect is frustrating to everyone watching them unfold. Human nature abhors the vacuum of uncertainty. While the move from not knowing to knowing is of fundamental importance to human minds, answers that satisfy should not therefore be allowed to take precedence over answers that are real, particularly when that satisfaction is based on confirming our biases, grievances, or divisions. Understanding how our own thinking predisposes us toward a specific conspiracy theory can help us empathize with others.

When you start to examine your own way of viewing a CT, you find biases. Most of these have names. We have talked about confirmation bias quite a bit in this book (looking for data that affirms your sense of the world) but many more cognitive biases exist, shared by most of us. In health and statistics, entire classes focus on detecting, removing, and avoiding bias in research and writing. They exist because everyone is subject to multiple predilections of explanation or interpretation that prevent us seeing a clear picture of the world around us. We're humans; we interpret more than observe. Some of these biases even have fun names like "availability cascade" in which the repetition of a narrative in public creates the illusion of truth by sheer volume, regardless of whether the story is actually true. (This is where amplification by journalists can be inadvertent; in an attempt to cover all sides of a story, including the non-credible one, they may repeat a CT and become part of an availability cascade.) In simple terms, repeat a lie often enough and people will believe it just because it's everywhere. Examples of these narratives reach personification in the form of the "Welfare Queen" (Mould 2016), the "Halloween Sadist" (Best and Horiuchi 1985), and the "Polish Plumber" (Noyes 2018): their stories are told so often that we believe the bad actors are walking in our midst.

Many of the biases around numbers extend to the rest of life. "Clustering bias" is the tendency to see patterns in numbers that aren't there, whether while gambling or just looking at phone numbers. Clustering bias extends well past numbers, into events, time lines, and stories; it sits side by side with the idea that nothing happens by accident—not even a novel coronavirus. Other cognitive errors covered earlier include conjunction error and problem-reaction-solution. For those interested in further exploration, Malcolm Gladwell's *Blink* is a good introduction to the many ways human thinking is not nearly as logical as we like to believe. We can all improve our ability to see our own biases by thinking about our own thinking and watching for the moments we see patterns or explanations that we want to be true but probably aren't. Understanding our own biases and how they form our thinking doesn't just reduce our tendency to take conspiracy theories as given, it also helps us think through our own decisions and improve the ways we make them in the future.

How to (fact) check yourself

So you've examined your own thinking and realized you too hold some beliefs that veer into conspiracy theory territory (as we all do) and looked at how your own biases contribute to your beliefs. As you've seen throughout this work, many conspiracies start from a small grain of truth and expand over time into endless forms and stories: that famous snowball storytelling effect. How do you figure out what parts are fact and which are fiction? If you have the Internet at your fingertips, your first steps are pretty easy. (Yes, that's ironic given how fast the Internet can spread misinformation, but the Internet is a tool, like fire. You can burn or warm yourself, depending on how you use it.) Let us begin the exercise by imagining the latest forwarded link from Cousin Tim arriving in your inbox, along with his interpretation about why you need to take it seriously.

Consider the source: As we said at the beginning, always pay attention to where information is coming from and the voice in which it is offered. If you cannot see a source or do not recognize it (a la the YouTube video on contact tracing put up by FreedomLover1977) then dig down. It doesn't take long to either find the person, or discover that one cannot find the person. In the first case, evaluate this person's agenda. Are they trying to convince you of something? What groups are they a part of? How credible is your beloved cousin? In the second case, a hidden source is a big red flag. Are you being astroturfed? Why doesn't the source want to be known? And again, always look for multiple sources, preferably from different angles and different people.

Also, consider the tone of the voice. Is it gleeful about some pandemic mishaps? Is it centering one argument at the exclusion of others? Look for dispassion in news reports. Passion belongs to testimonials. Disinformation runs on emotion.

Read past the headline: This sounds like freshman college student advice, but consider two things. First, the sheer volume of information available to us actually encourages us to use less of it; when we are bombarded with information we skim, and TV or radio reports we half-listen to in the background as we multi-task. Doomscrolling is not research. Neither is looking for headlines that confirm what we already think, and just reading those articles.

Second, it is easy to fool people with sneaky headlines or outdated information. How often in recent days have you seen a news report on Facebook that, although true, was from 2018? Taken out of context, the report means something else, but it still gets assigned meaning unless one checks past the headline. Likewise, those writing professional or social media news content know that they have one chance to grab your attention, let alone approval. Especially in intentional disinformation campaigns, headlines try to incite agreement more than represent research.

Who is being cited? It is always worth thinking about whether an article or website references experts in a field. In a discussion of the origins of Covid-19, are the speakers virologists or politicians? If it's about healthcare, are they medical doctors? You can usually find a person's academic background through some quick searching. Infectious disease is a very specialized field, so make sure the coronavirus articles you read are citing people who know what they're talking about. Look for articles that cite more than one person and tell you why they're citing those people. Remember that an attack on "experts" is often sold to "we the people" as liberation from elites who want to tell you how to run your life; in reality this ploy is trying to keep you from accepting verifiable expertise as a viable source. The experience of public health science and policy during the pandemic, and prior hostility towards climate change scientists, is eerily similar and equally troubling.

Quotes and misquotes: A popular meme tells us that Abraham Lincoln once said, "Don't believe everything you read on the Internet." The attribution of advice or of an entire story to an authority or trustworthy voice is usually evident in a conspiracy theory; it lends credence to the story because it is used in non-conspiratorial thinking as well. While some quotes are entirely fictitious (like the Lincoln quote above), many quotes are much harder to call "fake." If you see quotes that look like a public personality has been caught saying something truly explosive, make sure you're seeing the entire quote. It's very easy to take part of a sentence out to change its meaning. If you say "I understand you feel the sky is purple, but I doubt that" an unscrupulous content producer can extract "The sky is purple!" and make you sound ridiculous, with the defense that those words are 100 percent attributable to you. Many fact checking websites are particularly focused on checking quotes for this reason.

Debatable data: Numbers and graphs can seem like solid information to trust in any article: objective, quantitative and, when shaped into a chart, quickly grasped as an image. But manipulating them is relatively easy if you're good at math. While peer-reviewed journals carefully review graphs and statistics to make sure they mean what the author says they mean, numbers on the Internet are often pulled out of context. Always check the source of the data to find out what the article actually said and where they got their information. For example, if a study is performed on ten people, if one of them had a health condition, the study could tell you 10 percent of people had that condition. If the study involved a hundred or a thousand people, one person would probably be statistically insignificant, while finding ten in a hundred with a specific condition would more realistically represent 10 percent. Check study sizes, and how the statistics are being interpreted.

Look for other news sources and reliable articles: Issues of confirmation bias will tend to lead people to sites that reinforce their preconceived ideas. Philips and Milner (2020) and many other scholars have attempted to document and provide people with tools to avoid the trap of closed media ecosystems. One of the most consistent things in collecting and analyzing sources used in a particular conspiracy theory community is that they come from a very small subset of places, and most of them will reference each other. Trying to get either yourself or someone else to move beyond this bubble can be difficult, especially when information itself has been politicized and attacked by authoritarian regimes across the world. The erosion of trust in mainstream media as well as other sources of information production like colleges and universities, scientists, research organizations, etc., is itself part of conspiratorial thinking as well as the weaponization of CTs.

Many conspiracies, particularly about Covid-19, have shown up somewhere in the news or relate to a news story. Look for a news story about the topic besides the one that incited your interest, and make sure it is from another source. See what they have in common and what's different. Has the story been posted in multiple places? If it has, do they all have the same political or ideological bias? If not, how does the story differ between sources? (Bad news: almost every source has bias; the trick is to be mindful of them and temper your reaction accordingly.) "The Interactive Media Bias Chart" produced by Ad Fontus media (www.adfontesmedia.com) has become an invaluable tool in assessing news organizations, the reliability of their reporting, and their implicit or explicit biases.

What are the facts? It's always worth looking on fact-checking websites as well. Snopes (www.snopes.com) is the most famous, but its successes at pointing out inaccuracies has made it a target; it is often dismissed as "too liberal." If you are wishing not only to fact-check but to marshal evidence for Cousin Tim, consider: *USA Today*'s Fact Check (www.usatoday.com/news/factcheck/); *Politifact* from the Poynter Institute: (www.politifact.com/): for the United Kingdom *Full Fact* (https://fullfact.org/); for Europe the European Journalism Training Association's *EUFact* (https://eufactcheck.eu/); and for Africa the independent *Africacheck* (https://africacheck.org/). All of these sites have sections devoted to Covid-19: for sites devoted solely to Covid-19, consider Poynter Institute–hosted *#CoronaVirusFacts Alliance* (www.poynter.org/coronavirusfactsalliance/) and Ryerson University's *Misinformation Watch* (https://COVID-19misinfo.org/).

Hold your ground: Even those who are not conspiratorially minded know that one must be guarded when dealing with a news story. A somewhat exhausting sense of responsibility exists that, if you are not forever vigilant, you and in turn your community could be vulnerable. The solution for this exhaustion is to establish sources that you trust and outsource the vigilance to them, which is more or less precisely how the idea of a fourth estate (the media) arose.

In fact, conspiracy thinking is a lot like public health; the best treatment to avoid contamination is actually prevention. In public health, we avoid getting sick by vaccination (unless we're anti-vaxxers). The way to avoid a conspiracy theory is to have trusted sources of news you have reliably come to believe in for specific reasons. We don't mean "*The Post* was good enough for Grandad, so it's good enough for me," but actual fact-checking sufficient to build trust. It is a natural human tendency to trust a news source that affirms our innate beliefs, rather than one that challenges us. Where do you get your news, and why? When (hopefully not if) that source publishes something you disagree with, how do you respond?

Once you have a fact-checked source, if someone says you are being duped, you can roll out your due diligence; they won't believe the same sources as you because of that, and indeed that placement of trust leaves us open to accusations of living in a bubble and being complicit in the power of the elites. To a conspiracy theorist, the choice appears to be a world of citizen journalists or a world of sheeple. Such binaries do not exist, and when challenged, you will be able to say why you believe one source, but not another, and leave it at that. You don't have to reinvent the wheel, even if your friend wants you to. Creating communities of trust helps ease the burden.

Also, this response tends to bring you into proximity with people who also fact-check what they believe. Some of the most fascinating conversations two honest humans can have lie in the moments when those willing to do the research for credible sourcing reach different conclusions, and explain why to each other. The goal of dialogue becomes, not persuasion, but a free exchange of ideas. This is still possible, even in so divided a country as the United States of America.

Conversations, conflicts, and questions

When discussing conspiracy beliefs with people we care about, it is so often tempting to aggressively debunk them, providing a flood of facts that "prove" them wrong, or to simply state that only "crazy people" think like QAnon (for example). If any of those tactics worked, conspiracy theories would have disappeared long ago, and definitely would not thrive in the age of Google and fact-checking websites. Keep in mind the cautionary tale of Ong's Hat; even when the creator owned up to the whole story being entirely his creation, people didn't believe him and continued searching for a non-existent portal in space-time. A complete constellation of facts don't matter when you're in deep conspiracy thinking.

Particularly around health issues like Covid-19, asking people to change beliefs that seem instinctively believable is complicated. As Deborah T said in the chapter on vaccination, doctors who simply tell their patients they are wrong don't make much headway. In fact, patients often find another physician who will reinforce their beliefs, or at least not challenge them. As one physician said, "If I were to challenge [my patients] on their beliefs, it wouldn't be surprising if they accused me of being the one who hadn't done my due diligence in researching Covid-19" (Kim 2020). In so many ways, this is the trap to watch for, whether we are supporting or debating a conspiracy belief.

The authors in this work have tried to be sympathetic to those who espouse conspiracy theories. As much as they can be malignant and lead to genuine, real world harm, those who share CTs are often coming from positions lacking power or security. The comfort of a conspiracy theory is a tempting respite from the caution of science or even the compromise of governance.

But that does not mean that by listening to understand we must withhold judgment. As Kitta put it while studying anti-vaccination communities:

> Just as the formation of narratives and their use is a complex process; so is dismantling narratives. There is no simple or quick solution to this process, but we can begin by acknowledging and being critical of these types of stories, no matter who tells them. Folk voices are not sacrosanct, and folklorists can be fair to their participants by trying to understand them and the stories they tell. However, not all traditions are worth studying (or maintaining). Not all social norms are in the best interest of all members of the folk group [2019:135–136].

Conspiracy theories are told because it is truly and deeply important for the teller that you know this thing. It is important to listen to them, truly and deeply, but to learn about the teller rather than the plot. If you want to talk to a friend about a conspiracy theory, focus on the friend, not the facts that refute their position.

Motivational interviewing

In both counseling and in health, a technique called "motivational interviewing" uses compassionate questioning about someone's beliefs to help them check their own thinking. In fact, the questions we asked you to ask yourself above are a version of this method. Motivational interviewing is a way to express empathy through reflective listening, or saying back to the person what they said to you, not always in their own words, but what you understood them to say. The interviewer (which may sound formal, but can mean you talking to your mother) reflects what the person says, avoiding argument or confrontation. When the other person expresses resistance to something you've said, you adjust your wording. This doesn't mean you agree. Also, motivational interviewing focuses on the person, not the CT they hold.

For instance, your mother might say, "You sound like you think QAnon is crazy." You could respond with something along the lines of "I'm more interested in what you think about it," or "Did I? Tell me more about the Hollywood elites." Don't use a version of "you got that right, Mom" or other combative, conversation-stopping banter.

Then look for the places where your conversation partner's goals and values belie their current beliefs or behavior. For instance, say your mother ran the church nursery and you knew she had gotten an abused child removed from a dangerous household. Ask her how she identified children who were not having good home lives, and how easy it was to pick such a kid out from others. Slowly you point out to her, *by getting her to say it herself*, that the systematic kind of abuse being described by QAnon is not feasible to keep hidden, even in a powerful system like Hollywood, any more than it was in a faith community where people were complicit in protecting members of their own family. Yes, bad people exist, and want to keep things quiet, but they can't at the scale spoken of in QAnon.

You could also ask about your mother's experience as a mandated reporter, or any other element that leads to affirmation that she is someone who cares deeply about children, and why this is a good thing. Then differentiate between caring deeply and borrowing trouble; there are enough endangered children in the world without adding to their woes by rushing to help those who don't need it and ignoring those who do. Does QAnon divert empathy and support for children who really need it by focusing on something more salacious, for instance?

Affirmative dismissal

Besides motivational interviewing, you have the option of affirmative dismissal. Again, both techniques focus on the person who holds the conspiracy theory rather than its content. Affirmative dismissal is a behavior that many women who grew up in church environments will recognize, but the terms describing it differ widely. We chose "affirmative dismissal" because it is so descriptive of the core values behind the technique; it could also be described as assertive sidestepping.

Someone you love says to you, "I totally believe Bill Gates is going to use his vaccine to microchip us all and track our movements. It's gonna be the Mark of the Beast." You could fire back facts, but instead you search for the core fear or belief in that person's kernel narrative. (Remember those, when the CT is boiled down to a mere sentence or concept as a shorthand for the whole piece?) If you know this person well, odds are good you already know the core of the fear or need expressed. You hug the person (assuming they are a member of your communal household and therefore following safe quarantine practices) and say, "I totally believe your life is awesome and worth having. I totally believe there will be a Mark of the Beast someday. I don't believe Gates is setting it up. Our lives are exciting enough to track, but other people's aren't so why would he?"

This method sometimes leaves threads a person can pull on, but it also leaves relationships intact. And dialogue open. Your beloved mom, Cousin Tim, Aunt Sue, whomever: they have been affirmed that you heard what they said. You have put down a marker that you do not agree with them. You have offered one piece of information for why, but not in a combative way, or with dismissive humor. As two of the authors can affirm, women have used this for generations to avoid fights at family dinners. An added benefit of this assertive sidestepping is how often a loved one will later reopen the conversation voluntarily. When the CT-holder asks for factual information, it is a different dynamic than when you try to offer it unsolicited. This is a positive benefit of affirmative dismissal.

Starve them out

Not every situation requires affirmative dismissal, but the technique does add to a larger approach we should all keep in mind. We can help to starve out the narratives that depend on repetition and emotional responses for their life. Throughout the pandemic, professional coverage of a conspiracy theory on mainstream platforms accidentally bestowed a level of legitimacy that invited belief. "It must be true if even CNN and FOX are discussing it." Repetition creates casual acceptance without mindful awareness. In interpersonal communication we may sometimes choose to avoid arguments about CTs because strong negative emotions help to reinforce the notions of persecution and isolation some conspiracy theories rely on. These stories don't just feed on air time; they feed on human emotions. It requires knowing when to know which technique to use, but sometimes refusing to feed the ego or attention needs of the teller can be the best way to dampen enthusiasm for a CT.

"Look how angry she got when I told her she was wrong! She's been brainwashed!" may be the response you want to direct at your Aunt Sue, but it is also what Aunt Sue is thinking about you. Divert. Refuse to engage. Starve the stories. Even though one of the tenets of conspiracy thinking is that mainstream refusal to cover it proves its dangerous truth, over the long haul, starving them of attention may kill CTs, as a fire dies for lack of oxygen. The trick, as we advised early in this chapter, is to stay engaged with an individual without reinforcing their CT beliefs.

Similar advice is common on the Internet: don't feed the trolls. While much of our advice will be more difficult in online environments it is still important to recognize where and when shared social bonds allow you to engage with people and when you are just reinforcing and amplifying CTs by yelling at strangers. Also, social media does not provide private conversation unless you make it one. Where you and your loved one have a few thousand spectators watching your argument develop, people will jump in and divert energy. It is also way too tempting to both the spectators and yourselves to devolve into a "who's winning" space. If you get 37 likes and Cousin Tim gets 12, you have not "won" anything, but you have pushed away Cousin Tim. Motivational interviewing, affirmative dismissal, and starving the emotions out of the moment can all work online, but don't use them with strangers. For posts that have actual factual inaccuracies, report them. For posts that say mean things, remember that disinformation runs on emotion. In fact, how often have you shared a meme because you knew it was false? That's not helping.

To engage on the Internet with a stranger is to fling facts at a person who (1) does not know you; (2) has no reason to trust you (especially if you say, "I'm a doctor/nurse/academic who studies conspiracy theories"); (3) can easily dismiss you as something beyond the bounds of their world (an elite, a Democrat/Republican, a misogynist; it is easy to call names on the Net); and (4) will use you as further proof that they are correct. You will in fact reinforce the thing you wish to counteract, unless you do so in a positive, motivational, non-personal way. And even then, if you don't know the person, you have nothing to trade on. Be cautious where you expend energy online; you don't want to be part of the problem as an inadvertent reinforcer. If you must engage with strangers online, remember the pan-religious Golden Rule: treat others the way you want to be treated. And remember that disinformation feeds on emotion. Don't go there.

Connection over isolation

Isolation results from conspiracy thinking, and those who share specific narratives tend to come together in a defensive community. Sometimes people are less wholehearted believers in the idea, for instance, that the virus began deliberately in a Wuhan laboratory, but their spouse says so, all their friends say so, and they just keep quiet. That could be your loved one, or it could be you. In either case, examining what being a member of a group means to you or your loved one again focuses on the theorist, not the conspiracy theory. What is Cousin Tim getting out of being the one to sends out so many conspiracy posts every day: attention, affirmation, feeling like the big guy on campus? Why is Aunt Sue silent when her husband starts talking about the horrors of the Deep State? Likely Aunt Sue isn't in as deep as Cousin Tim, yet both need affirmation that they are not alone.

"You and I don't agree with everyone else in the family about this QAnon stuff, do we?" might be a good starting point for Aunt Sue. "You do so much research!" affirms that Cousin Tim is smart. Send him a guide on standards of excellence for lab results, or how to form and test an unbiased hypothesis, and see if he can guide himself into a different kind of approval. Telling him that same information in a "you're doing it wrong" talk will not work; there's no guarantee that handing over a guide will, either, but it plays to his strengths and leads him in a productive direction. It's up to him to walk it.

As it is all of us. We live in strange times. It is natural to seek comforting answers to the hard circumstances engendered by the pandemic. The conspiracy theories we have covered in this book will continue to morph and change and more CTs will emerge as the consequences of the pandemic with its illness, deaths, economic challenges, social distancing, lockdowns and childcare issues stretch over the following months and years. Diligence is required to accurately assess threats, risk, information, and knowledge production. And these processes will be different depending on individual contexts but what will remain is that conspiracy theories that falsely identify people or groups as dangerous others, whether healthcare workers, members of a racialized community, peaceful protesters or public health officials, must be resisted. They are intellectual and emotional cul-de-sacs.

A world where utopia is just a massacre away is not one we want to live in. If we want to live in a world where people aren't looking for excuses to hate each other, we have to help tell the stories that unite rather than divide us.

Acknowledgments

This work benefited from many experts freely offering time, knowledge, and insights. We appreciate the input of the following:

Dale Orton for the cover design concept; Computer specialist "K"; Dr. P, MD; Daniel Ray, PhD; Aileen Harris, executive director of AHEC NOVA; Katina Michael, PhD; members of Vaccine Talk; Crystal Rose, MLIS who whisked the citations and bibliography into order and created the index; Amy Spitalnick, executive director of Integrity First for America; Marcie Timmerman, executive director of Mental Health for America, Kentucky chapter; Ken. J. Purscell; Esther Vincent, Johnston Miller and Andrea Harrington for providing primary texts; Beth O'Connor at the Virginia Rural Health Association for podcasting with contributors on Rural Health Voice; all the excellent investigative reporters who documented the early rumors, legends and conspiracies for us and those who come after; and Dr. Andrea Kitta for commenting on early chapter drafts.

Author Biographies

John Bodner, PhD, is an associate professor of folklore in the Social/Cultural Studies Programme at Grenfell Campus of Memorial University of Newfoundland. He has written on conspiracy theory's close cousin, contemporary legend, in his papers "Cherry Beach Express: Rumour and Contemporary Legend Among a Homeless Youth Community in Downtown Toronto." (2006) and "'Once I'm There I Can Find Out Where I Am': Place Making and the Homeless Geographies of a Downtown Toronto Street Kid Community" (2014). He has conducted fieldwork among tree planters, street kids and illegal marijuana growers to document the relationship between marginalized communities, work, identity, crime, and tradition.

Ian Brodie, PhD, is an associate professor of folklore at Cape Breton University. He is the author of *A Vulgar Art: A New Approach to Stand-up Comedy* (Mississippi 2014) and *Old Trout Funnies: The Comic Origins of the Cape Breton Liberation Army* (CBU Press 2015). President-elect of the International Society for Contemporary Legend Research, he has served as president of the Folklore Studies Association of Canada. He is currently working, with Jodi McDavid, on a manuscript tentatively titled *You Meddling Kids*, about the depiction of the supernatural and legend material in children's television.

Donald Leech, PhD, is an associate professor of history at the University of Virginia's College at Wise. He has published several articles on the changes in the English urban society and economy in the 15th and 16th centuries as the Middle Ages merged into the modern era. He also wrote about the early process of enclosing and privatizing common lands as part of the same changes. Donald enjoys teaching at the college, and has been recognized with an *Outstanding Teacher of the Year* award on two occasions.

Ashley Marshall, JD, MPA, is completing her PhD in public administration and policy while serving as chief executive officer of a nonprofit. Through her work tackling systemic racism, oppression, and justice she has fought the impacts of conspiracy thinking, rumor, and legend that continue to perpetuate inequalities.

Anna Muldoon, MPH, is a former science policy advisor for the U.S. Department of Health and Human Services and is currently completing her PhD in Human and Social Dimensions of Science and Technology at Arizona State University. Her work focuses on social responses to infectious disease, ranging from conspiracy narratives to religious history to fashion and fiction. She has published on a number of issues around infectious disease, including law, history, and disease surveillance.

Wendy Welch, PhD, MPH, is the author or editor of six books and lives in Wytheville, Virginia. Her memoir *The Little Bookstore of Big Stone* was translated into five languages and named Book of the Year in Korea. She won the Pearl Buck Writing for Social Justice Award in March 2019 and published her first fiction (*Bad Boy in the Bookstore*) in March 2020. Her most recent edited anthology with McFarland is *From the Front Lines of the Appalachian Addiction Crisis*, a compilation of healthcare providers discussing patients and policies in substance use disorder. Welch runs the Graduate Medical Education Consortium of Southwest Virginia. Visit her website at wendy-welch.com.

Chapter Notes

Chapter One

1. Major counter-theories to the official interpretation of the pandemic include: Anti–vaxx, QAnon, 5G, and the themes of enemies from outside, enemies from above (elites, government) and enemies from within (Shahsavari, Holur, Tangherlini and Roychowdhury 2020). We appreciate the work of folklorist Tim Tangherlini and a team of big data computer engineers in identifying these same themes.

2. Conspiracy theories may be told as entertainment by non-believers: "Have you heard of this? They say..." is a common enough way to turn someone else's belief into whimsy. In such instances, the arguments for coherence and validity invoked by the believer are replaced with a belittling critique.

3. "Black" is used in order to be more inclusive. African-American or Canadian could be considered too restrictive due to immigration from Africa and the Caribbean (Simms, 2018). More recent immigrants have different experiences from individuals in the United States who are descendants of slaves. The term "Black" is more inclusive of all historical roots, while continuing to acknowledge that systemic and structural racism will negatively impact any person considered Black (*Ibid.*). Unless differentiated, the term should be assumed to represent Canadians and Americans.

4. "Deep State" references the belief that powerful actors within and outside the government control the actual mechanisms of the administration. The belief has some elements in common with traditional American conspiracy theory but came to America in 2017 from Turkey (*derin devlet*) where

academic researchers were using the term some 20 years ago. See the QAnon chapter for more details.

5. Barkun bases this categorization on Jesse Walker's *The United States of Paranoia: A Conspiracy Theory* (2013).

6. Michael Barkun identifies two types of New World Order beliefs. One centers around the Christian and Muslim beliefs in a Second Coming and Armageddon/The Last Day, and will involve supernatural actors, demonic influence, and a satanic overlord identified as the Antichrist. The second is more a political interpretation (reflected in contemporary libertarian or right-wing militia beliefs) that secret societies rule the world. The two may overlap and borrow from each other among conspiracy theorists, but are not synonymous in how they function (2013:40).

7. The 1980s and 1990s in America, Canada, and parts of Europe saw many people, particularly educators and caregivers of school age children, accused of ritual physical and sexual abuse of their charges. The belief coalesced around the abuse being a form of Satan worship, and resulted in trials and convictions. Those interested in this historic epoch of conspiracy theories' influence should read Bill Ellis' *Raising the Devil* (2000) and *Lucifer Ascending* (2004) as the Satanic Panic will not be discussed in depth here.

8. The communal creation of narrative cluster through the success or failure of collective experimentation is not unique to conspiracy thinking nor indeed to digital culture. What distinguishes digital culture from analogue is not the process but that, because the Internet is essentially an infinite archive, we see a record of all experiments

and their immediate evaluations, including the failures: the ephemerality of oral tradition leaves only the successful.

9. The John Birch Society is best remembered for its rabid anti-communism and influence on the Republican Party. But it cannot be reduced to a communist conspiracy theory since it became the clearing house for a wide assortment of anti-government conspiracy thinking. The Society fought against fluoride (a communist mind control plot); the United Nations and any other global institutions (making Welch the father of the modern anti-globalists; the JFK assassination (alternative theory that he was murdered by a communist); and later became obsessive about the Illuminati. The John Birch Society is alive and well today. A list of populists who trade in conspiracy would be lengthy, but a short list of significant figures who have engaged well-documented conspiratorial scapegoating includes: Recep Tayyip Erdogan of Turkey (PM 2003–2014; president 2014 to present); Viktor Orban of Hungary (prime minister 2010); Andrzej Duda of Poland (president 2015); and the sole left wing example of this selective list, Nicolas Maduro of Venezuela (president 2013).

10. This is known as the fertility-income paradox and the demographic-economic paradox, where fertility rates appear partially correlated to the Human Development Index (Conceição 2019; World Bank 2020)

11. The National Highway Traffic Safety Administration (NHTSA) states that 90.7% of American reported wearing seatbelts in 2019, while 37,133 people killed by crashes in 2017 included 47% not wearing seat belts. An estimated 14,955 people were saved by wearing seat belts, and 2,549 more could have been if they had worn their belts.

12. *Plandemic* was a video that began circulating May 4 via YouTube, giving bad medical advice about washing one's hands, wearing masks, and visiting the beach during quarantine. The high-production quality short film featured a PhD who presented test results linking vaccination to a mouse coronavirus that led to Chronic Fatigue Syndrome. The doctor's work was later discredited, along with her assertion that animal viruses in vaccinations caused multiple human illnesses, because her lab results could not be replicated by other researchers. The 26-minute video became an almost immediate hit (more than 1.5 million views in its first week).

13. BIPOC stands for "Black, Indigenous, People Of Color." The term centers on Black and Indigenous persons due to the common erasure of both groups, but is commonly thought to include Latinx and Asian persons as well under the "people of color" inclusion. There are disputes as to how the term was created, or if the term should be used versus naming out all who are represented under the acronym (Garcia 2020). It is being used here as a more nuanced version of "people/persons of color." Specific race and ethnicity will be used when discussing only one race or ethnicity.

14. In 2017, the *Merriam-Webster* dictionary added this popular insult, defining it as "people who are docile, compliant, or easily influenced" (Daileda 2017). It was first used in March 1945 by British writer W. R. Anderson in his "Round About Radio" column of the *Musical Times*, to describe people mindless obeying their government (1945:84).

Chapter Two

1. On the power of the body and its contamination by various forces in legend see Bennett 2009.

2. Originally the term was "Patient O" as in "patient outside of California" during the early days of the AIDS crisis. The letter was confused with the number and through popular reporting the term and the practice of identifying "the first person" entered the general population (McKay 2014).

3. *The Epoch Times* is the media wing of the Falun Gong religious movement which agitates against the Chinese communist regime while promoting many right-wing conspiracy theories. The paper is based in the United States and uses English as its primary language.

4. Geographic quarantine is the blockading of a specific area and preventing movement in or out to prevent disease spread. During Covid-19, this was the method attempted around Wuhan, China.

5. "Biosafety Level 4 (BSL-4) laboratories investigate the most dangerous pathogens and have the maximum biocontainment levels. Microbes contained in BSL-4 laboratories pose a significant risk for transmission

and are frequently fatal; most have no reliable cure. The BSL-4 laboratories provide a safe environment in which laboratory staff can work with and study these highly pathogenic microbes" (Xia et al. 2019).

6. The following and subsequent reproduced online conversations are edited for clarity by randomly assigning aliases to the six-digit identification numbers associated with each participant and rendering in as plain a format as possible the direction of the threaded conversation.

7. Here, Chinese Communist Party, although the more generally accepted abbreviation is CPC (Communist Party of China).

8. The idea that theory has been decoupled from conspiracy is presented in Nancy L. Rosenblum and Russell Muirhead's *A Lot of People Are Saying* (2019). Their central thesis misunderstands the formal features and folk production of conspiracy theories because they rely on the textual record. Conspiracy theories in their earliest state are, like rumors, proto-narratives that emerge out of group storytelling (Tangherlini 2020).

9. Parts of the conspiracy that the Chinese plot was to depress asset prices in a pandemic and go on a global buying spree, were cited in various Canadian Facebook pages when it was reported that Shandong Gold Mining Co. Ltd. was purchasing TMAC Resources Inc., whose operations concentrated on Nunavut, on May 8, 2020 (McGee 2020).

10. Ben Garrison illustrates the concept in his cartoon "The Fear Parade," discussed in chapter 9 (Figure 9.2).

11. For a brief synopsis of the ban see Burki 2018.

12. Critique of China at the level of national politics is not confined to America; Australia is calling for an international inquiry into the origins of the virus and in Canada a former justice minister is calling for the use of the Magnitsky Act which allows for the sanctioning of specific individuals of a foreign regime deemed culpable for crimes against Canada/Canadians (Chase and Fife 2020). Several right-wing newspapers in Canada have also called for a more aggressive response to China (Lilley 2020; Glavin 2020).

13. Jakob and Lili Segal's *AIDS: USA Home-Made Evil* (1986) is a primary text. For academic treatment of the phenomenon see Goldstein 2004:91–94; and Sabatier 1988.

14. For a broader discussion of contemporary legend, conspiracy theory and Black communities, see Fine and Turner 2001.

Chapter Three

1. For general surveys of the Black Death see Zieger 1969; Gottfried 1983.

2. The following sections on the rise of anti-Semitism and persecutions of Jews are based on Goodich 1998; Moore 1987; Nirenberg 1996.

3. There is a considerable body of work on "Whiteness." Good examples are Allen 1994 and 1997; Painter 2010; and Roediger 2007.

4. The Milbank article mentions that some politicians follow Friedrich Hayek's extreme "free market" ideology. Medieval thinkers may have one up on them, as they thought more in terms of a Moral Economy, which put fairness ahead of personal profit. Selfish "free market" fundamentalism is very modern.

5. In July 2020 in the midst of the Covid-19 pandemic a fresh outbreak of bubonic plague hit the headlines, causing momentary consternation when two cases were reported in Mongolia and a rodent tested positive in Colorado (Ramzy 2020). However, this was actually a typical event as a few cases per year occur in areas where it is endemic. If caught in time the disease is easily treated with antibiotics.

6. At the time of writing the exact numbers were still in flux. A mortality rate approximately 10 times that of flu and a rate of contagion at least double seem likely.

7. These categories are identified in *ADL* 2020c.

8. Infamous Nazi propaganda depicted Jews as rats—a racist caricature which Art Speigelman documents in his primary source material for his graphic novel *Maus*, entitled *MetaMaus* (2011).

9. InfoWars is a website founded and controlled by Alex Jones. It promotes right-wing conspiracy theories and fake news while selling survivalist supplies. It is based in Austin, Texas.

10. The term comes from a 1984 film called *Breakin' 2: Electric Boogaloo*, which was almost a carbon copy of *Breakin',* its predecessor from only seven months earlier. "Electric Boogaloo" became a standard

reference for any unnecessary sequel or replica, and the boogaloo movement arose from "Civil War 2: Electric Boogaloo" (Allam 2020). Big Igloo, Big Luau, and Ice House became rhyming slang derivations for the original term to avoid platform censors. Ironically, the term boogaloo was originally associated with a musical style mixing Latin and Black influences.

Chapter Four

1. The link to the *Zambian Observer* article on the native website was removed, but it could be located using the Internet Wayback Machine. An animated gif meme featuring a celebratory dance was created by happykesha and published on ifunny.co on April 17, 2020 continuing to illuminate the feelings of Black people when they believed they were immune. https://ifunny.co/video/hon-2020-just-got-a-whole-lot-better-zambianobserver-chinese-r6DTqVUa7

2. We try to provide examples related to conspiracy theories in Canada, home to two of the authors. In this instance no data exist because Canadian provinces do not collect race/ethnic information as part of health-care demographic information. This policy is being reviewed in light of the pandemic (Nasser 2020).

3. Eric Garner was murdered by New York City Police over allegations of selling loose cigarettes on the street. Ahmaud Arbery was murdered by civilians who erroneously believed that he had stolen items from a vacant house weeks prior to his murder (Coleman 2020).

4. For example, the U.S. Government twice captured such narratives through rumor clinics and hotlines, in order to mine out more information about possible truths within the rumors and legends. Black soldiers in World War II told stories about being assigned dangerous missions due to their expendability as Black persons; and during the Civil Rights Movement, communities shared stories of violence perpetrated by White supremacists to suppress the movement towards equality (Turner 1993:1; 73).

5. A "diss track" per the *Urban Dictionary* is "a track [song] made by one artist to insult another artist." https://www.urbandictionary.com/define.php?term=diss%20track (accessed June 28, 2020).

6. Mr. Irving later recanted his belief in flat earth theory as "just trolling" (Ruiz 2017).

7. In fact, participants drafted into the military were the subjects of covert attempts to prevent their access to syphilis treatment or prevention under Army care (CDC [n.d.]).

8. In 1947, the Nuremburg Code was established to provide basic ethical principles for medical research involving human subjects as a result of the Nazi physicians' forcible testing of prisoners in concentration camps during World War II (Nix 2017). One of those basic principles was that a test subject must give informed consent prior to participating in an experiment (Nix 2017). At the time that the Tuskegee Study was revealed as unethical, this was the only regulation that covered human subject research (Jarmusik 2019).

9. Militias are not all White or about White power; some are solely anti-government, as with the boogaloo movement. Virginia Knights invites Black members into their anti-government militia. Since 2017 there has been an increase in activity by Black nationalists, whose extremism is born out of Black American oppression, but is nevertheless still extremism. Such groups include the New Black Liberation Militia (NBLM) which was formed in 2009 and is based in Atlanta, Georgia (Johnson 2017), as well as the NFAC (Not Fu##king Around Coalition) which began after the extrajudicial murder of Ahmaud Arbery by former law-enforcement officers in Georgia (Creekmur 2020; Krayewski 2020).

10. Where White power groups also identify with Christianity, recognition of how recycled this trope is rarely reaches cognitive awareness. Churches in America can be sympathetic to Israel, but this is a complicated topic beyond the Covid conspiracies we examine here. Those interested in the difference between anti-Semitism and pro–Israel sentiment, and in the blindness of many churchgoers to the anti-Semitism hidden within extra-biblical End Times conspiracy theory, should visit the websites of the Anti-Defamation League (https://www.adl.org/) and Integrity First for America (https://www.integrityfirstforamerica.org/).

11. "Antifa" refers to groups and individuals who consider themselves anti-fascist. Rather than having a centralized organiza-

tion (as media narratives sometimes suggest), they comprise a diverse collection of ideologies ranging from left-wing politics to anarchism. Most antifa groups focus on direct action, rather than political organizing.

12. Native American communities and Latinx populations also have been disproportionately ravaged by Covid-19 (Branigin 2020). In early April 2020 the Navajo nation was hit with 20 Covid-19 deaths, which at the time was more than had occurred in the entire state of New Mexico (Romero 2020). In New York City, 34 percent of the Covid-19 patients who died between March and June 2020 were Latinx despite the fact they make up only 29 percent of the city's population (Dwyer 2020).

13. In March 2020, the Southern Poverty Law Center reported that the number of White nationalist groups increased 55 percent since 2017, which marks a second consecutive year of increases (Southern Poverty Law Center 2020).

Chapter Five

1. Joseph Needham (1980) notes that "according to persistent (and, as we believe, rather trustworthy) Chinese tradition" smallpox inoculation dates back to about 1000 CE, and "came out from the shadows of secrecy and began to be written about in Chinese medical books" in the early 16th century (1980:28).

2. For a timeline spanning significant anti–vaccination events from 1796 to 2014, see Dubé, Vivion and MacDonald 2015.

3. Interested readers are encouraged to visit VT for deeper context into the Covid-19 vaccination discussion, and for a list of their administrative rules. The group can be found at https://www.facebook.com/groups/vaccinetalkforum/

4. Locht's employer, Inserm, took to Twitter and stated that the interview was taken out of context and that it was "#Fake-News" (Rosman 2020).

5. Non-profit director Bekka Ross runs a children's home in Tanzania and is a colleague to one of the authors. In discussion on this topic via private message, she said, "Artemisinin is the main ingredient in ALu, the main treatment for malaria that has taken over from drugs like hydroxychloroquine and other quinine-based drugs. It would not surprise me at all to find that artemisinin is an effective treatment. Anecdotally, we don't know anyone in Tanzania who had malaria who got COVID-19" (June 1, private message). Madagascar's President Andry Rajoelina (who has something of a reputation for enjoying conspiracy theories) touted the benefits of artemisinin repeatedly. On May 15, 2020, the World Health Organization (WHO) put out a statement that this claim was as yet unfounded. Hirsch contacted "the respected Max Planck Institute of Colloids and Interfaces in Germany, which is currently conducting clinical trials on a different breed of the same plant, in this case grown in Kentucky. This specially grown, more potent variety of sweet wormwood is being tested on cells to determine its effectiveness in fighting coronavirus infections and the results so far, the institute's director, Prof Peter Seeberger, told me, are 'very interesting.' Human clinical trials are likely to follow" (Hirsch 2020).

6. While traditional vaccines are made of pieces of a virus that have been inactivated in some way, RNA vaccines harness the human cell's ability to produce molecules to activate the immune system. They are relatively new and have been the subject of several conspiracy theories around what else they could tell cells to do. RNA vaccines are easier and faster to produce and, so far, appear to have fewer side effects than traditional vaccines.

7. The idea of a microchip inserted into a vaccine predated the pandemic, at least in satire: two years prior, the satirical online site *The Onion* even ran the headline, "Flu Vaccine Recalled due to Defective Government Tracking Chips" (2018). For more on the misinterpretation of satire as "real" news, see Brodie 2018.

8. Joyce first wrote about the issue in August 2017 for the *Pacific Standard*. Interest in Gates and the vaccine issues surrounding Covid-19 brought the story back to public awareness in 2020.

Chapter Six

1. Hadith are collections of sayings attributed to Muhammad that help interpret Quranic principles or prophecy. Hadith are extra-canonical, and Sunni and Shia differ

on which to give preference. The minority Shia (15 percent of all Muslims) stick more to those attributed to the Prophet's close circle and do not take much stock in Sahīh Muslim, the Hadith from which much of the Great Massacre teachings are drawn.

2. In the recurring theme of the Blood Libel, several legends and conspiracy theories from this time period are preserved that document tales of Jewish cannibalism of murdered children among other stereotypes of sexual deviance and uncleanliness (Wagemakers 2010).

3. This biblical plague has come up during most of the recent infectious disease events, including Covid-19. Zika, Ebola, H1N1, and smallpox (the threat of its release) have all been identified as the biblical plague, though none show the specific symptoms mentioned.

4. Bible quotes are from the *New International Version*.

5. When not limited to English language use, the phrase appears earlier; George Johnson links it to the 1806–1826 plots of Filippo Buonarotti while in exile in Geneva and establishing international revolutionary secret societies (1983:65).

6. While the phrase may sound derisive, moral entrepreneurs (and crisis entrepreneurs) can be true believers as well as those seeking to make a name and/or a fortune by placing themselves to the fore of an issue; think of the Komen Foundation or Mothers Against Drunk Driving.

7. The Illuminati panic of 1797–1802 (or so) was a political weapon wielded first by one side and then the other in the nascent political party system of America. It set the tone for centuries of conspiracy thinking (Johnson 1983:56–63). This "enemy outside" sub-genre of conspiracy would be nurtured in American isolationism, anti-communist projects, and radical leftist publications, eventually forming a loose coalition around the name "anti-globalist."

8. Keller (1996) repositions the Apocalypse as a transformational opportunity, not a crisis ending in tragedy for many. She also suggests that apocalyptic thinking saturates entertainment, politics and religious culture in America, influencing both Frykholm (2004) and Radosh (2008).

9. There are other entertainment works: the novel *Scars* (Prence 2010) stars a young protagonist living through the Great Tribu-

lation amidst her own teen angst; *At the End of All Things* (Graves 2011) adds zombies to the Great Tribulation; and *The Second Coming: A Love Story* (Pinsker 2014) features two men who each claim to be Jesus returned. In other media, Comedy Central's *Black Jesus* (McGruder and Clattenburg 2014--), shows a returned Jesus living in modern-day California.

10. In fact, at least one author of this book stubbornly clings to a small conspiracy narrative of their own: a junior clerk who knew their Bible said "Hey y'all, watch this" and pushed the bill up or down a few places in the stack waiting to be assigned consecutive numbers, just to be ornery.

11. Both the Bill and Melinda Gates Foundation and Soros' Open Society Foundations are Foundation Partners in Partners in Health, alongside the Hiltons, the Ford Foundation, the Hemsleys, the Kelloggs, Roald Dahl Charitable Trust, Ronald MacDonald House, and many others. Chelsea Clinton serves on the Board of Trustees (pih.org). PIH is providing contact tracing services in several states.

12. Another example of this trope is a real nurse, Erin Marie Olszewski who claims in a YouTube video and book to expose the lies of the pandemic from within the New York City Elmhurst Hospital (Journeyman Pictures 2020; Olszewski 2020). An antivaxxer, her claims have been systematically debunked but she remains a hero to the anti-lockdown proponents.

13. We would like to thank K-- for her work tracking down several leads surrounding this video.

14. Suspicion of contact tracing apps is also widespread in anti-surveillance communities, who express similar fears without NWO concerns.

Chapter Seven

1. Trump was interviewed by Jones for InfoWars in December 2015 and Jones brags that he calls Trump regularly.

2. The antecedent of creating mysterious and fake books is H. P. Lovecraft's famous *The Necronomicon*, first mentioned in the 1922 short story "The Hound."

3. The emails were released during October and November of 2016 by Wikileaks.

4. The "Lolita Express" is the nickname

given to Epstein's private jet by locals on the Virgin Islands near his own private island (Whalen 2019).

5. Celebrity legends are a common subcategory of contemporary legend, the most famous of which is probably "Paul is Dead" which explains that Paul McCartney died on November 6, 1965, and was replaced with a double. The motif of a "double" is part of one version of the "Tom Hanks is missing" legend/conspiracy.

6. "White hats" refer to a benevolent QAnon counter-conspiracy, "good forces at play, men and women working within the government to thwart the Deep State" (*ADL* [n.d.]).

7. The original affidavit can be found at www.courthousenews.com/wp-content/up loads/2020/04/MercyTrain-CRAffadavit.pdf

8. The infamous case of McMartin Preschool in Manhattan Beach, California, involved allegations of secret tunnels where children were abused.

Chapter Eight

1. Because of spreading misinformation and peddling dubious health products for sale, Natural News had over 100,000 pages delisted from Google search engines in 2017 and Facebook shut down the site on the platform in June 2019 (Novak 2017; Mole 2019).

2. Prior to his anti-5G work Khules was an active UFO researcher. This information is not given to disparage Khules but to note that conspiratorial thinking becomes an interpretive frame that can be used across a broad range of phenomena. Both the UFO tradition and anti-5G share some common health beliefs in the ailments and deaths following alien abduction/surveillance, or the illnesses that can be caused by the Men in Black (Rojcewic 1987).

3. Another influential proponent who slightly predates Khules is Reza Ganjavi, who started "Stop5G International" in 2017.

4. This is Damian Thompson's term for misinformation but it works well in relation to health beliefs because it denotes that groups and individuals are presenting alternative knowledge (facts or entire systems) to generally agreed upon facts and theories (2008).

5. For an overview of this topic see Brady 2001.

6. As we've seen in other examples, early excesses and a general lack of care in using x-ray technologies did cause various problems, including cancer. These real events are used to question current practices, especially where the science might be inconclusive.

7. A more precise definition: EMR can be a wave or a particle in form, and EMF is a description of the space that is altered by EMR, or the path that EMR takes/creates.

Chapter Nine

1. "[Humorous ranting] is an impulsive, incessant oral expression of heightened emotions of or related to anger—an emotive oral tradition wherein the orator devotes a relentless amount of time to denigrating subject x due to their heightened feelings regarding x, but spends perhaps less time than is necessary accurately articulating their rage in a calm, methodical manner" (Gabriele 2016:96)

2. This process is similar to that of the stand-up comedian who works to develop a reputation for competency, which in turn builds an audience who seeks them out specifically, a topic explored at length in an earlier work (Brodie 2014).

3. Diane E. Goldstein describes this "social constructionist" argument in her discussion of how scientific efforts to explain "African AIDS"—i.e., the seemingly disproportionate rates of HIV infection on the African continent—used "ethnographic information to foreground aspects of traditional culture, emphasizing the failure of Africans to adjust to the conditions of Western civilization. Heavily stereotyped and abstracted from social, historical, or cultural context, these studies condemn traditional culture through an emphasis on the risks intrinsic to such practices as blood brotherhood, ritual scarification, and traditional healing techniques" (2001:131).

4. For ease, cartoons will be cited in the text just by their name. Full citations to Ben and Tina Garrison's cartoons, including links for both the web page and the twitter feed, are listed in the works cited.

5. As discussed in an earlier chapter, a decline in the world population would not be through genocide but through lowering birthrates: "Parents choose to have enough kids to give them a high chance that several

will survive to support them as they grow old. As the number of kids who survive to adulthood goes up, parents can achieve this goal without having as many children" (Gates 2009).

6. "*Why is Xi portrayed as Winnie The Pooh in my cartoon?* Because dissidents in China were using the rotund cartoon bear as a symbol of Xi. He was promptly banned in China to prevent further mocking. Xi wants his own Mao-like cult of personality. He wants to be worshipped. The fat little bear interferes with that. Therefore, Xi must be associated with Winnie at every turn" (Garrison 2019b). For context, see McDonell 2017.

7. The viral video of virtually the same name ("Plandemic") was not released until 4 May 2020 (Frenkel, Decker and Alba 2020).

8. On April 14 Garrison published "Real Science Defenders" in conjunction with the publication of *Plague of Corruption* by Judy Mikovits and Kent Heckenlively. Mikovits was the most prominent voice in the "Plandemic" video that was released in early May (see note 12), and the book depicts Anthony Fauci as having a pattern of undermining research in order to personally profit from potential patents. In addition to giving the space for the rant over to Heckenlively, Garrison provided a blurb for the book. The cartoon depicts four superheroes: Mikovits, Heckenlively, Andrew Wakefield, the principal author of the since-discredited and withdrawn study that linked the MMR vaccine to autism (Kitta 2012:32–33), and Robert F. Kennedy Jr., who also maintained a causal link between MMR and autism (*Ibid.* 69). They are apprehending a monster with a pill bottle head, a seven-pointed tail with a syringe at each point, with a lab rat in a cage in one hand and in the other a syringe filled with something made in part from fetal tissue. Peeking out from the pill bottle is a terrified Francis Collins, head of the National Institutes of Health, while Fauci runs at his feet, clutching a money bag. A serpent identified as California Governor Gavin Newsom emerges from the sewer and, while holding yet another syringe, says "It's the law."

References Cited

Aberth, John, ed. 2005. *The Black Death: The Great Mortality of 1348–1350: A Brief History with Documents*. New York: Palgrave Macmillan.

Abramson, Dustin, Derrick Fu, and Joseph Edwin Johnson. 2020a. Cryptocurrency System Using Body Activity Data. U.S. Patent Application 16/138,518 (filed 26 March).

_____. 2020b. Cryptocurrency System Using Body Activity Data. International Patent Application PCT/US2019/038084 (filed 26 March).

Ackerman, Daniel. 2020. Before Face Masks, Americans Went to War Against Seat Belts. *Business Insider* 26 May. https://www.businessinsider.com/when-americans-went-to-war-against-seat-belts-2020-5

Adams, Jerome. 2020. Exclusive Interview: U.S. Surgeon General Jerome Adams on COVID-19's Disproportionate Impact on Black America. By Madison Gray. *BET.Com* 8 April. https://www.bet.com/news/national/2020/04/08/surgeon-general-jerome-adams-cororonavirus-black-americans.html

ADL (Anti-Defamation League). 2020a. ADL Calls for Platforms to Take Action to Address Hate Online During Pandemic. 8 May. https://www.adl.org/blog/adl-calls-for-platforms-to-take-action-to-address-hate-online-during-pandemic

_____. 2020b. ADL's Audit of Anti-Semitic Incidents: 2019 Year in Review. 12 March. https://www.adl.org/2019-audit-h

_____. 2020c. Coronavirus: Anti-Semitism. 22 April. https://www.adl.org/blog/coronavirus-antisemitism

_____. 2020d. Coronavirus Crisis Elevates Anti-Semitic, Racist Tropes. 17 March. https://www.adl.org/blog/coronavirus-crisis-elevates-antisemitic-racist-tropes

_____. 2020e. On Social Media, Haredi and Orthodox Jewish Communities are Scapegoated and Blamed for COVID-19. 29 April. https://www.adl.org/blog/on-social-media-haredi-and-orthodox-jewish-communities-are-scapegoated-and-blamed-for-covid-19

_____. 2020f. With Hate in Their Hearts: The State of White Supremacy in the United States. https://www.adl.org/education/resources/reports/state-of-white-supremacy

Africa Daily Mail. 2020. The Black African Student Escaped Corona Virus. 13 February. (Removed from website). Archived at https://perma.cc/JA5Q-7XL4

Agência Angola Press. 2020. Italian Man Becomes Nigeria's First Case of Coronavirus—Minister. *ANGOP* 28 February. http://www.angop.ao/angola/en_us/noticias/africa/2020/1/9/Italian-man-becomes-Nigeria-first-case-coronavirus-minister,2a0a2308-159b-48ca-b097-cd460ed3ea3f.html

Akenson, Donald Harman. 2018. *Exporting the Rapture: John Nelson Darby and the Victorian Conquest of North American Evangelicalism*. Montreal: McGill-Queen's University Press.

Al Jazeera. 2020. Iran Leader Refuses US Help; Cites Coronavirus Conspiracy Theory. *Al Jazeera* 23 March. https://www.aljazeera.com/news/2020/03/iran-leader-refuses-cites-coronavirus-conspiracy-theory-200322145122752.html

Alberta, Tim. 2020. Republicans Adopt Andrew Yang's Cause. He Isn't Celebrating. *Politico* 17 March. https://www.politico.com/news/magazine/2020/03/17/coronavirus-universal-basic-income-andrew-yang-134922

Aleem, Zeeshan. 2020. Covid-19 Conspiracy Theories Are Being Fed by Institutions Meant to Inform the Public. *Vox* 26 July. https://www.vox.com/2020/7/26/21338174/coronavirus-conspiracy-theories-fauci-sinclair-plandemic?fbclid=IwAR1nDq_70szRAOSI5i4EQlM-P2MxDV5QdEkvOBFs9fghB4RzCVmSKaCSL6Q

Al-Momani, Kawakib, Muhammad A. Badarneh, and Fathi Migdadi. 2017. A Semiotic Analysis of Political Cartoons in Jordan in Light of the Arab Spring. *Humor* 30.1: 63–95. doi: https://doi.org/10.1515/humor-2016-0033

Anderson, Jessica. 2020. Baltimore Police Officer Appears to Cough on Purpose at Public Housing Complex Residents, Video Shows. *Baltimore Sun* 7 April. https://www.baltimoresun.com/coronavirus/bs-md-baltimore-officer-coughing-video-20200407-wupouuyyzbagjcloujvv56zgeu-story.html

Angley, Ernest. 1950. *Raptured.* Wilmington, NC: Carolina Press.

Anna, Cara. 2020. Protest against Africa's 1st COVID-19 Vaccine Test Shows Fear. *PBS NewsHour* 1 July. https://www.pbs.org/newshour/world/protest-against-africas-1st-covid-19-vaccine-test-shows-fear

AP-NORC. 2020. Expectations for a COVID-19 Vaccine. *The Associated Press-NORC Center for Public Affairs Research* May. http://www.apnorc.org/projects/Pages/Expectations-for-a-COVID-19-Vaccine.aspx

Arendt, Hannah. 1951. *The Origins of Totalitarianism.* New York: Schocken.

Arkhipova, Alexandra, and Ian Brodie. 2020. When Rumours Fly Like Helicopters: An International Conspiracy "Language" for the New Reality? *Social Anthropology/ Anthropologie Sociale* 28. doi:10.1111/1469–8676.12826.

Aschburner, Steve. 2020. Coronavirus Pandemic Causes NBA to Suspend Season After Player Tests Positive. *NBA.com* 12 March. https://www.nba.com/article/2020/03/11/coronavirus-pandemic-causes-nba-suspend-season

Aubrey, Allison. 2020. Who's Hit Hardest by COVID-19? Why Obesity, Stress and Race All Matter. *NPR (National Public Radio)* 18 April. https://www.npr.org/sections/health-shots/2020/04/18/835563340/whos-hit-hardest-by-covid-19-why-obesity-stress-and-race-all-matter

Bacon-Smith, Camille. 1992. *Enterprising Women: Television Fandom and the Creation of Popular Myth.* Philadelphia: University of Pennsylvania Press.

Baddeley, Gavin. 2016. *Lucifer Rising: A Book of Sin, Devil Worship and Rock and Roll.* Medford, NJ: Plexus Publishing.

Baker, Peter. 2020. U.S. to Suspend Most Travel from Europe as World Scrambles to Fight Pandemic. *New York Times* 11 March. https://www.nytimes.com/2020/03/11/us/politics/anthony-fauci-coronavirus.html

Barkun, Michael. 2013. *Culture of Conspiracy: Apocalyptic Visions in Contemporary America.* Berkeley: University of California Press.

Baumgartner, Emily, and James Rainey. 2020. Trump Administration Ended Pandemic Early-Warning Program to Detect Coronaviruses. *Los Angeles Times* 2 April. https://www.latimes.com/science/story/2020-04-02/coronavirus-trump-pandemic-program-viruses-detection

BBC News. 2020. Africa Will Not Be Test Ground for Vaccine—WHO. 6 April. https://www.bbc.com/news/world-africa-52192184

Beck, Glenn. 2010. *Glenn Beck.* Episode aired 9 November, on *Fox News.*

Becker, Howard S. 1966. *Outsiders: Studies in the Sociology of Deviance.* New York: Free Press.

Belew, Kathleen. 2018a. *Bring the War Home: The White Power Movement and Paramilitary America.* Cambridge: Harvard University Press.

Bellah, Robert N. 1967. Civil Religion in America. *Daedalus* 96: 1–21. https://www.jstor.org/stable/20027022

Bennett, Gillian. 2009. *Bodies: Sex, Violence and Disease and Death in Contemporary Legend.* Jackson: University Press of Mississippi.

Bennett, Gillian, and Paul Smith. 1993. *Contemporary Legend: A Folklore Bibliography.* New York: Garland Publishing.

Bergmann, Eirikur Einarsson. 2018. *Conspiracy and Populism.* New York: Palgrave Macmillan.

Berlet, Chip, and Matthew N. Lyons. 2000. *Right-Wing Populism in America: Too Close for Comfort.* New York: Guilford Press.

Berry, Peter. (Writer). 2008. *The Last Enemy.* 5 episodes. Aired 17 February, 24 February, 2 March, 9 March, and 16 March, on *BBC.*

Best, Joel, and Gerald T. Horiuchi. 1985. The Razor Blade in the Apple: The Social Construction of Urban Legends. *Social Problems* 32.5: 488–499.

Bevege, Alison. 2020. Inside the Australian Factory Packed with Coronavirus Supplies Being Sent to China in "Disgraceful" Operation that "Will Cost Lives"—As Doctors Here are Forced to Buy Painting Masks from BUNNINGS. *Daily Mail* 30 March. https://www.dailymail.co.uk/news/article-8167869/Inside-Australian-factory-packed-coronavirus-supplies-sent-CHINA.html

Bicks, Emily. 2020. Dr. Fauci Confirms Coronavirus "Disproportionately" Affecting African Americans. *Heavy.Com* (blog) 7 April. https://heavy.com/news/2020/04/dr-fauci-coronavirus-african-americans/

Binder, Matt. 2018. Why Some Baby Boomers Are Eating Up the QAnon Conspiracy. *Mashable* 7 August. https://mashable.com/article/qanon-conspiracy-baby-boomers-4chan/

Blank, Trevor J., and Lynne S. MacNeill, eds. 2018. *Slender Man Is Coming: Creepypasta and Contemporary Legends on the Internet.* Logan, UT: Utah State University Press.

Blanuša, Nebojša. 2018. The Deep State Between the (Un)Warranted Conspiracy Theory and Structural Element of Political Regimes? *Media, Conspiracies, and Propaganda in the Post-Cold War World.* Special issue of *Critique and Humanism* 49.1: 369–384.

Bligh, Annabel. 2020. Expert Guide to Conspiracy Theories Part 2: Who Believes Them and Why? *The Anthill* (podcast) 23 March. https://www.stitcher.com/podcast/the-conversation/the-anthill/e/68228382

Bodner, John. 2019. Introduction. *Crime and Folklore,* special issue of *Ethnologies* 41.1: 3–70. https://doi.org/10.7202/1069846ar

Boonstra, Olivia, and the Canadian Anti-Hate Network. 2019. Hate Groups Find Foothold on East Coast. *AntiHate.ca* 29 July. https://www.antihate.ca/tags/national_citizens_alliance

Borger, Julian. 2020. Mike Pompeo: "Enormous Evidence" Coronavirus Came from Chinese Lab. *The Guardian* 3 May. https://www.theguardian.com/world/2020/may/03/mike-pompeo-donald-trump-coronavirus-chinese-laboratory

Borter, Gabriella, and Liz Hampton. 2020. Empty Churches, Food Drive Mark Start of Easter Weekend in Coronavirus-Hit U.S. *Reuters* 10 April. https://uk.reuters.com/article/uk-health-coronavirus-usa/empty-churches-food-drive-mark-start-of-easter-weekend-in-coronavirus-hit-u-s-idUKKCN21S17B

Boseley, Sarah. 2020. WHO Declares Coronavirus Pandemic. *The Guardian* 11 March. https://www.theguardian.com/world/2020/mar/11/who-declares-coronavirus-pandemic

Bowcott, Owen. 2019. China is Harvesting Organs from Detainees, Tribunal Concludes. *The Guardian* 17 June. https://www.theguardian.com/world/2019/jun/17/china-is-harvesting-organs-from-detainees-uk-tribunal-concludes

Boxwell, Robert. 2020. How China's Fake News Machine Is Rewriting the History of Covid-19, Even as the Pandemic Unfolds. *Politico* 4 April. https://www.politico.com/news/magazine/2020/04/04/china-fake-news-coronavirus-164652

Bradley, Laura. 2020. Celebrities Are Spreading a Wacky Coronavirus 5G Conspiracy and They Need to Stop. *The Daily Beast* 6 April. https://www.thedailybeast.com/celebrities-are-spreading-a-wacky-coronavirus-5g-conspiracy-and-they-need-to-stop-4

Branigin, Anne. 2020. Surgeon General Jerome Adams Tells Black People to Lay Off Alcohol, Tobacco, and Drugs to Prevent COVID-19 Deaths: "Do It for Your Big Mama." *The Root* 10 April. https://www.theroot.com/surgeon-general-jerome-adams-tells-black-people-to-lay-1842797456.

Breland, Ali. 2020. Wellness Influencers Are Spreading QAnon Conspiracies About the Coronavirus. *Mother Jones* 15 April. https://www.motherjones.com/politics/2020/04/wellness-qanon-coronavirus/

Brennen, J. Scott, Felix Simon, Phillip N. Howard, and Rasmus Kleis Neilsen. 2020. Types, Sources, and Claims of COVID-19 Misinformation. *Reuters Institute for the Study of Journalism* 7 April. https://reutersinstitute.politics.ox.ac.uk/types-sources-and-claims-covid-19-misinformation

Breslow, Jason. 2020. Why Misinformation and Distrust Are Making COVID-19 More

Dangerous for Black America. *NPR (National Public Radio)* 10 April. https://www.npr.org/sections/coronavirus-live-updates/2020/04/10/832039813/why-misinformation-and-distrust-is-making-covid-19-more-dangerous-for-black-amer.

Briggs, Charles. 1988. *Competence in Performance: The Creativity of Tradition in Mexicano Verbal Art.* Philadelphia: University of Pennsylvania Press.

Brown, Lee. 2020. Woody Harrelson Among Stars Sharing Coronavirus Conspiracy Theories Tied to 5G. *New York Post* 6 April. https://nypost.com/2020/04/05/woody-harrelson-sharing-coronavirus-conspiracy-theory-tied-to-5g/

Brunvand, Jan Harold. 2001. *Encyclopedia of Urban Legends.* New York: Norton Paperbacks.

BuzzFeedVideo. 2016. I Put a Payment Chip in My Hand to Replace My Wallet. *YouTube* 21 May. https://youtu.be/hTBJ6OIGkzc

Byford, Jovan. 2011. *Conspiracy Theories: A Critical Introduction.* London: Palgrave.

Cacioli, Lucas. 2020. Bill Gates' COVID Conspiracy Grows in Italian Parliament, Allegations of Population Control by Political Anti-Vaxxer. *Blockchain News* 20 May. https://blockchain.news/news/bill-gates-covid-conspiracy-grows-in-italian-parliamentallegations-of-population-control-by-political-anti-vaxxer

Calia, Mike. 2020. Full interview: President Trump Discusses Trade, Impeachment, Boeing and Elon Musk with *CNBC* in Davos. Interview by Joe Kernen. *CNBC* 22 January. https://www.cnbc.com/2020/01/22/davos-2020-cnbcs-full-interview-with-president-trump.html

Campion-Vincent, Véronique. 1997. Organ Theft Narratives. *Western Folklore* 56: 1–37.

Carpio, Myla Vicenti. 2004. The Lost Generation: American Indian Women and Sterilization Abuse. *Native Women and State Violence,* special issue of *Social Justice* 31.4: 40–53.

Casper, Jayson. 2016. Who Awaits the Messiah Most? Muslims. *Christianity Today* 30 December. https://www.christianitytoday.com/ct/2017/january-february/who-awaits-messiah-most-muslims-isis-dabiq-eschatology.html

CBS News. 2020. Know Your Privacy Rights as Coronavirus Contact Tracing Ramps Up. *YouTube* 21 May. https://www.youtube.com/watch?v=rmht8z3_TlU

CDC (Centers for Disease Control and Prevention). n.d. The Tuskegee Timeline. U.S. Public Health Service Syphilis Study at Tuskegee. https://www.cdc.gov/tuskegee/timeline.htm

_____. 2020a. First Travel-related Case of 2019 Novel Coronavirus Detected in United States. (Press release). 21 January. https://www.cdc.gov/media/releases/2020/p0121-novel-coronavirus-travel-case.html

_____. 2020b. COVID-19 Case Investigation and Contact Tracing for Health Departments. 27 May. https://www.cdc.gov/coronavirus/2019-ncov/downloads/php/principles-contact-tracing-booklet.pdf

Cellen-Jones, Rory. 2020. Trading Standards Squad Targets Anti-5G USB Stick. *BBC* 28 May. https://www.bbc.com/news/technology-52810220

Cerulus, Laurens. 2020. How Anti-5G Anger Sparked a Wave of Arson Attacks. *Politico* 2 May. https://www.politico.eu/article/coronavirus-5g-arson-attacks-online-theories/

Chan, Jasper Fuk-Woo, Shuofeng Yuan, Kin-Hang Kok, Kelvin Kai-Wang To, Hin Chu, Jin Yang, Fanfan Xing, Jieling Liu, Cyril Chik-Yan Yip, Rosana Wing-Shan Poon, Hoi-Wah Tsoi, Simon Kam-Fai Lo, Kwok-Hung Chan, Vincent Kwok-Man Poon, Wan-Mui Chan, Jonathan Daniel Ip, Jian-Piao Cai, Vincent Chi-Chung Cheng, Honglin Chen, Christopher Kim-Ming Hui, and Kwok-Yung Yuen. 2020. A Familial Cluster of Pneumonia Associated With the 2019 Novel Coronavirus Indicating -to-Person Transmission: A Study of a Family Cluster. *Lancet* 395: 514–523. https://doi.org/10.1016/S0140-6736(20)30154-9

Chan, Kelvin, Beatrice Dupy, and Arijeta Lajka. 2020. Conspiracy Theorists Burn 5G Towers Claiming Link to Virus. *AP News.* 21 April. https://apnews.com/4ac3679b6f39e8bd2561c1c8eeafd855.

Chappell, Bill. 2010. Bush Says West's Attack Was Low Point of His Presidency. *NPR* (National Public Radio) 3 November. https://www.npr.org/sections/thetwo-way/2010/11/03/131052717/bush-says-kanye-west-s-attack-was-low-point-of-his-presidency.

Charles, Jacqueline. 2020. Bill Clinton Once Enjoyed a Bright Legacy in Haiti. Then the 2010 Earthquake Struck. *Miami Herald* 10 January. https://www.miamiherald.com/ news/nation-world/world/americas/haiti/article238480993.html

Chase, Steven. 2020. Liberal Health-Committee Chair Sponsors Petition That Says Cell Towers Can Pose Danger to Children. *Globe and Mail* 6 May. https://www.theglobeandmail.com/canada/article-liberal-health-committee-chair-sponsors-petition-that-says-cell-towers/

Chase, Steven, and Robert Fife. 2020. Former Liberal Justice Minister Urges Sanctions Against Chinese Officials Who Covered Up Early COVID-19 Outbreak. *Globe and Mail* 20 April. https://www.theglobeandmail.com/canada/article-former-liberal-justice-minister-urges-sanctions-against-chinese/

Chitsamba, Misso. 2020. Doctors Reveals Why African Skin Resists Coronavirus. *Face of Malawi* (blog) 13 March. https://www.faceofmalawi.com/2020/02/doctors-reveals-why-african-skin-resists-coronavirus/

Chiu, Allyson. 2020. A High-Risk Florida Teen Who Died from Covid-19 Attended a Huge Church Party, Then Was Given Hydroxychloroquine by Her Parents, Report Says. *Washington Post* 7 July. https://www.washingtonpost.com/nation/2020/07/07/florida-carsyn-davis-coronavirus/

Chomsky, Noam. 2002. *Media Control: The Spectacular Achievements of Propaganda*. New York: Seven Stories Press.

Christopher, Nilesh, 2020. India Made Its Contact Tracing App Mandatory. Now People Are Angry. *Wired* [UK] 14 May. https://www.wired.co.uk/article/india-contact-tracing-app-mandatory-arogya-setu

@cirstenw. 2020. Gene Decode #11 Exclusive Germany and Italy. *YouTube* 22 April. https://youtu.be/wl5C3ggMYKc

Clark, Alexis. 2019. How "The Birth of a Nation" Revived the Ku Klux Klan. *History* 29 July. https://www.history.com/news/kkk-birth-of-a-nation-film.

Clark, Doug Bock. 2020. Inside the Nightmare Voyage of the Diamond Princess. *GQ* 30 April. https://www.gq.com/story/inside-diamond-princess-cruise-ship-nightmare-voyage.

Clarke, Steve. 2002. Conspiracy Theories and Conspiracy Theorizing. *Philosophy of the Social Sciences* 32: 131–150. doi:10.1177/004931032002001.

Cockerell, Isobel. 2020. Meet the Celebrities Pushing 5G Coronavirus Conspiracies to Millions of Fans. *Coda Story* (blog) 14 April. https://www.codastory.com/waronscience/celebrities-5g-conspiracies/

Cohen, Stanley. 1972. *The Folk Devil and Moral Panics: The Creation of the Mods and the Rockers*. London: MacGibbon and Kee.

Coleman, Aaron Ross. 2020. Black Bodies Are Still Treated as Expendable. *Vox* 5 June. https://www.vox.com/2020/6/5/21277938/ahmaud-arbery-george-floyd-breonna-taylor-covid

Collins, Gail. 2020. Well, at Least Trump Hasn't… *New York Times* 1 April. https://www.nytimes.com/2020/04/01/opinion/trump-coronavirus.html

Collinson, Stephen, with Caitlin Hu. 2020. America's Mask Resistance Is Just the Latest Example of a Perennial Struggle. *CNN: Meanwhile in America* 23 June. https://www.cnn.com/2020/06/23/world/meanwhile-in-america-june-23-intl/index.html

Corp, Casey. 2020. Is There a Religious Left? *The New Yorker* June 11. https://www.newyorker.com/books/under-review/is-there-a-religious-left

Crokin, Liz. 2020. Coronavirus Cover for Mass Arrests? Part II. *YouTube* 17 March. https://youtu.be/mSHqb9ctRGk

The Crossover (@TheCrossover). 2017. Uh Oh: Draymond Is a Flat Earth/Kyrie Truther. *Twitter*, 18 February, 2:37 p.m. https://twitter.com/thecrossover/status/833014995583643649

Crozier, Alfred Owen. 1912. The Coming Money Trust (illustration). In *U.S. Money Vs. Corporation Currency*. Cincinnati: The Magnet Company.

Csillag, Ron. 2018. The Secret of Chabad's Global Expansion. *Canadian Jewish News* 23 May. https://www.cjnews.com/living-jewish/the-secrets-of-chabads-global-expansion

CST (Community Security Trust). 2020. *Coronavirus and the Plague of Antisemitism*. Research Briefing. April. London: Community Security Trust. https://cst.org.uk/data/file/d/9/Coronavirus%20and%20the%20plague%20of%20antisemi tism.1586276450.pdf

Dale, Rodney. 1978. *The Tumour in the Whale: A Collection of Modern Myths*. London: Duckworth.

Davis, James, Geoffrey Wetherell, and P.J. Henry. 2018. Social Devaluation of African Americans and Race-Related Conspiracy Theories. *European Journal of Social Psychology* 48.7: 999–1010. https://doi.org/10.1002/ejsp.2531

Davis, John. 2016. The Flat Earth Society Welcomes B.o.B. *The Flat Earth Society* 28 July. https://www.theflatearthsociety.org/home/index.php/blog/bob-bobby-ray-simmons-jr-flat-earth-society.

_____. 2012. *What Happens Next: Contemporary Urban Legends and Popular Culture*. Santa Barbara: Libraries Unlimited.

de Blasio, Bill (@NYCMayor). 2020. My message to the Jewish community. *Twitter*, 28 April, 11:05 p.m. https://twitter.com/NYCMayor/status/1255309615883063297

de Looper, Christian. 2020. The Wildest 5G Conspiracy Theories Explained—and Debunked. *Digital Trends* 8 April. https://www.digitaltrends.com/news/5g-conspiracy-theories-debunked/

Dennis, David. 2016. Why Black People Need Conspiracy Theories. *Complex* 6 October. https://www.complex.com/life/2016/10/black-conspiracy-theories

de Senneville, and Loup Besmond. 2016. Dans le Monde, un Chrétien sur Quatre est Évangélique. *La Croix* 25 January. https://www.la-croix.com/Religion/Monde/Dans-monde-chretien-quatre-evangelique-2016-01-25-1200735150

de Vos, Gail. 1996. *Tales, Rumor, and Gossip: Exploring Contemporary Folk Literature in Grades 7–12*. Englewood: Libraries Unlimited.

DHS (Department of Homeland Security). 2019. DHS Strategic Framework for Countering Terrorism and Targeted Violence. 13 December. https://www.dhs.gov/publication/dhs-strategic-framework-countering-terrorism-and-targeted-violence

DiResta, Renee. 2020. For China, the "USA Virus" is a Geopolitical Ploy. *The Atlantic* 11 April. https://www.theatlantic.com/ideas/archive/2020/04/chinas-covid-19-conspiracy-theories/609772/

"Dr. P." 2020. Personal interview with Wendy Welch. 1 May.

Dokoupil, Tony. 2018. 5G Service Is Coming—and So Are Health Concerns Over the Towers That Support It. *CBS This Morning* 29 May. https://www.cbsnews.com/news/5g-network-cell-towers-raise-health-concerns-for-some-residents/

Dolan, Eric W. 2018. Feelings of Social Devaluation Among African Americans' Linked to Belief in Conspiracy Theories. *PsyPost* (blog). 21 August. https://www.psypost.org/2018/08/feelings-of-social-devaluation-among-african-americans-linked-to-belief-in-conspiracy-theories-51992

Douglas, Karen M., and Ana C. Leite. 2017. Suspicion in the Workplace: Organizational Conspiracy Theories and Work-Related Outcomes. *British Journal of Psychology* 108: 486–506. doi:10.1111/bjop.12212

Douglas, Karen M., Robbie M. Sutton, and Aleksandra Cichocka. 2017. The Psychology of Conspiracy Theories. *Current Directions in Psychological Science* 26.6: 538–42. doi:10.1177/0963721417718261.

Drauluns, Dirk. 2020. "Finally, a Virus Got me." Scientist Who Fought Ebola and HIV Reflects on Facing Death from COVID-19. *Science* 8 May. https://www.sciencemag.org/news/2020/05/finally-virus-got-me-scientist-who-fought-ebola-and-hiv-reflects-facing-death-covid-19

Drinkwater, Kenneth, Neil Dagnall, Andrew Denovan, Andrew Parker, and Peter Clough. 2018. Predictors and Associates of Problem–Reaction–Solution: Statistical Bias, Emotion-Based Reasoning, and Belief in the Paranormal. *SAGE Open* 8.1. doi:10.1177/2158244018762999.

Druke, Galen, and Maggie Koerth. 2020. Politics Podcast: Can COVID-19 Conspiracy Theories Be Stopped? (podcast) *Fivethirtyeight* 14 May. https://fivethirtyeight.com/features/politics-podcast-can-covid-19-conspiracy-theories-be-stopped/

Dubé, Eve, Maryline Vivion and Noni E. MacDonald. 2015. Vaccine Hesitancy, Vaccine Refusal and the Anti-Vaccine Movement: Influence, Impact and Implications. *Expert Review of Vaccines* 14.1: 99–117. DOI: 10.1586/14760584.2015.964212

Ducharme, Jamie. 2020. Melinda Gates Lays Out Her Biggest Concern for the Next Phase of the COVID-19 Pandemic. *Time* 4 June. https://time.com/5847483/melinda-gates-covid-19/

Duff, Gordon. 2020. Documentary Proof: University of North Carolina Generated COVID-19. *Veterans' Today Network* 29 April. https://www.veteranstodaynetwork.com/2020/04/29/documentary-proof-university-of-north-carolina-generated-covid-19/

Duffy, Clare. 2020. 5G Explained: What It Is, Who Has 5G, and How Much Faster Is It Really? *CNN Business* 6 March. https://www.cnn.com/interactive/2020/03/business/what-is-5g/

Dundes, Alan. 1997. Why Is the Jew "Dirty"? A Psychoanalytic Study of Anti-Semitic Folklore.

In *From Game to War: Psychoanalytic Essays on Folklore,* 92–119. Lexington: University of Kentucky Press.

Dunne, Michael. 2000. Dennis Miller: The Po-Mo Comic. *Humor* 13.1: 77–90. https://doi.org/10.1515/humr.2000.13.1.77

El Refaie, Elisabeth. 2009. Multiliteracies: How Readers Interpret Political Cartoons. *Visual Communication* 8.2: 181–205.

Elba, Idris (@idriselba). 2020. Live stream video. *Twitter,* 17 March, 4:50 p.m. https://twitter.com/idriselba/status/1239995118154702848

Ellis, Bill. 1989a. When Is a Legend? An Essay in Legend Morphology. In *The Questing Beast: Perspectives on Contemporary Legend IV,* edited by Gillian Bennett and Paul Smith, 31–53. Sheffield: Sheffield Academic Press.

_____. 1989b. Death by Folklore: Ostension, Contemporary Legend, and Murder. *Western Folklore* 48.3: 201–220. doi 10.2307/1499739

_____. 2000. *Raising the Devil: Satanism, New Religions, and the Media.* Lexington: University of Kentucky Press.

_____. 2001. *Aliens, Ghosts, and Cults: Legends We Live.* Jackson: University Press of Mississippi.

EnergyDots (@EnergyDotsMauritius). 2016. How Do EnergyDots Work? *Facebook* 16 June. https://www.facebook.com/EnergyDotsMauritius/posts/589354347935703

Epstein, Reid J., Lisa Lerer and Thomas Kaplan. 2020. Joe Biden Wins Primaries in Florida, Illinois and Arizona: Highlights. *New York Times* 17 March. https://www.nytimes.com/2020/03/17/us/politics/march-17-democratic-primary.html

Espinoza, Joshua. 2020. Idris Elba Blasts Conspiracy Theory That Black People Can't Get Coronavirus. *Complex* 17 March. https://www.complex.com/pop-culture/2020/03/idris-elba-blasts-conspiracy-theory-black-people-cant-get-coronavirus

Evans, Robert, and Jason Wilson. 2020. The Boogaloo Movement Is Not What You Think. *Bellingcat* 27 May https://www.bellingcat.com/news/2020/05/27/the-boogaloo-movement-is-not-what-you-think/

Evelyn, Kenya. 2020a. Georgia's Covid-19 Reopening Pits White Governor Against Black Mayors. *The Guardian* 22 April. https://www.theguardian.com/us-news/2020/apr/22/georgia-reopening-kemp-governor-mayors .

_____. 2020b. "We're Expendable": Black Americans Pay the Price as States Lift Lockdowns. *The Guardian* 25 May. https://www.theguardian.com/world/2020/may/25/covid-19-lockdowns-african-americans-essential-workers .

Express Tribune. 2015. Plan to Track Fourth Schedule Suspects Using Chip Implants Meets Scathing Criticism. *Express Tribune* 14 March. https://tribune.com.pk/story/852977/plan-to-track-fourth-schedule-suspects-using-chip-implants-meets-scathing-criticism/

Faherty, Dave. 2019. Woman Opens Fire on Cell Tower Workers Hundreds of Feet in the Air. *WSOC TV* 26 November. https://www.wsoctv.com/news/local/woman-opens-fire-on-cell-tower-workers-hundreds-of-feet-in-the-air-sheriff-says/1012483719/

Farberov, Snejana. 2014. Drunk Girl, 18, Rushed from Canadian Prime Minister's Home. *Daily Mail* 23 April. https://www.dailymail.co.uk/news/article-2611817/Drunken-girl-18-rushed-Canadian-Prime-Ministers-mansion-middle-night-alcohol-poisoning-attending-teenage-sons-birthday-party.html

Farhi, Arden, and Peter Martinez. 2020. Trump Urges Independents to Vote for the "Weakest Democrat" on the Eve of New Hampshire Primaries. *CBS News* 10 February. https://www.cbsnews.com/news/trump-rally-manchester-today-2020-02-10/

Fears, Darryl. 2005. Study: Many Blacks Cite AIDS Conspiracy. *Washington Post* 25 January. https://www.washingtonpost.com/wp-dyn/articles/A33695-2005Jan24.html

Fenn, Elizabeth A. 2000. Biological Warfare in Eighteenth-Century North America: Beyond Jeffery Amherst. *The Journal of American History* 86.4: 1552–1580. DOI: 10.2307/2567577.

Fenster, Mark. 1999. *Conspiracy Theories: Secrecy and Power in American Culture.* Minneapolis: University of Minnesota Press.

Ferrechio, Susan. 2020. McConnell Warns Democrats Against Politicizing Relief Package Negotiations. *Washington Examiner* 21 March. https://www.washingtonexaminer.com/news/congress/mcconnell-warns-democrats-against-politicizing-relief-package-negotiations

Fine, Gary Alan, and Bill Ellis. 2010. *The Global Grapevine: Why Rumors of Terrorism, Immigration, and Trade Matter.* Oxford and New York: Oxford University Press.

Finley, Taryn. 2020. No, Keri Hilson, 5G Did Not Cause Coronavirus [Update]. *Huffington Post* 16 March. https://www.huffpost.com/entry/keri-hilson-5g-did-not-cause-coronavirus_n_5e6f8ba7c5b6dda30fce0348.

Flynn, Meagan. 2020. Engineer Intentionally Crashes Train Near Hospital Ship Mercy, Believing In Weird Coronavirus Conspiracy, Feds Say. *Washington Post* 2 April. https://www.washingtonpost.com/nation/2020/04/02/train-derails-usns-mercy-coronavirus/

Fordham, Evie. 2020. China "Still Lying" About Coronavirus Outbreak: Sen. Tom Cotton. *Fox Business* 24 February. https://www.foxbusiness.com/politics/coronavirus-covid-outbreak-tom-cotton

France 24. 2020. With Only Three Official Cases, Africa's Low Coronavirus Rate Puzzles Health Experts. *France 24* 1 March. https://www.france24.com/en/20200301-with-only-three-official-cases-africa-s-low-coronavirus-rate-puzzles-health-experts.

@FreedomLover1977. 2020. Contact Tracing Scarier than you Imagined. *Vimeo* 22 May. https://vimeo.com/421657568

Freeman, Daniel, Felicity Waite, Laina Rosebrock, Ariane Petit, Chiara Causier, Anna East, Lucy Jenner, Ashley-Louise Teale, Lydia Carr, Sophie Mulhall, Emily Bold, and Sinead Lambe. 2020. Coronavirus Conspiracy Beliefs, Mistrust, and Compliance With Government Guidelines in England. *Psychological Medicine* 1–13. doi:10.1017/S0033291720001890

Garrison, Ben. 2017. About. *Grrr Graphics.* https://grrrgraphics.com/about

_____. 2018. The Deep State Hydra Attacks (blog post). *Grrr Graphics.* 20 July. https://grrrgraphics.com/the-deep-state-attacks

_____. 2019a. The Ginsburg Sighting (blog post). *Grrr Graphics.* 25 January. https://grrrgraphics.com/the-ginsburg-sighting

Gartland, Dan, and Extra Mustard. 2017. Kyrie Irving Is a Flat-Earth Truther. *Sports Illustrated* 17 February. https://www.si.com/extra-mustard/2017/02/17/cavaliers-kyrie-irving-flat-earth

Gates, Bill. 2010. Innovating to Zero. *TED Talks,* February. https://www.ted.com/talks/bill_gates_innovating_to_zero

_____. 2020a. Responding to Covid-19—A Once-in-a-Century Pandemic? *New England Journal of Medicine* 382:1677–1679. DOI: 10.1056/NEJMp2003762

_____. 2020b. I'm Bill Gates, Co-chair of the Bill & Melinda Gates Foundation. AMA about COVID-19. *Reddit* 18 March. https://www.reddit.com/r/Coronavirus/comments/fksnbf/im_bill_gates_cochair_of_the_bill_melinda_gates/

Gazzo, Jane. 2020. Why Does Twitter Think Tom Hanks Is Dead? *The Brag* 15 June. https://thebrag.com/why-does-twitter-think-tom-hanks-is-dead/

Gertz. Bill. 2020. Coronavirus May Have Originated In Lab Linked to China's Biowarfare Program. *Washington Times* 26 January. https://www.washingtontimes.com/news/2020/jan/26/coronavirus-link-to-china-biowarfare-program-possi/

Gessen, Masha. 2020. Life, Liberty, and the Pursuit of Spitting on Other People. *The New Yorker* 26 May. https://www.newyorker.com/news/our-columnists/life-liberty-and-the-pursuit-of-spitting-on-other-people

Gingeras, Ryan. 2019. How the Deep State Came to America: A History. *War on the Rocks* 4 February. https://warontherocks.com/2019/02/how-the-deep-state-came-to-america-a-history/

Gladwell, Malcolm. 2005. *Blink: The Power of Thinking Without Thinking.* New York: Little, Brown.

Goldstein, Diane E. 1993. Not Just a "Glorified Anthropologist": Medical Problem Solving Through Verbal and Material Art. *Folklore in Use* 1:15–24.

_____. 2001. Competing Logics and the Construction of Risk. In *Healing Logics: Culture and Medicine in Modern Health Belief Systems,* edited by Erika Brady, 129–142. Logan, UT: Utah State University Press.

_____. 2004. *Once Upon a Virus: AIDS Legends and Vernacular Risk Perception.* Logan, UT: Utah State University Press.

Government of Alberta. 2020. ABTraceTogether. *Alberta.ca.* https://www.alberta.ca/ab-trace-together.aspx

Government of Alberta (@youralberta.ca). 2020. Help prevent the spread of COVID-19. *Facebook,* 16 May. https://www.facebook.com/youralberta.ca/photos/a.239524369399056/4060 442947307160/?type=3

Gray-Fow, Michael J. G. 1998. Why the Christians? Nero and the Great Fire. *Latomus* 57.3: 595–616. https://www.jstor.org/stable/41538370

Green, Emma. 2019. Measles Can Be Contained. Anti-Semitism Cannot. *The Atlantic* 25 May. https://www.theatlantic.com/politics/archive/2019/05/orthodox-jews-face-anti-semitism-after-measles-outbreak/590311/

Grey Ellis, Emma. 2017. The Alt-Right Found Its Favorite Cartoonist—and Almost Ruined His Life. *Wired* 19 June. https://www.wired.com/story/ben-garrison-alt-right-cartoonist/

Gruzd, Anatoliy, and Philip Mai. 2020. Hospitals Around the World Are Being Targeted by Conspiracy Theorists." Covid19misinfo. 21 April. Ryerson University and Ted Rogers School of Management: Social Media Lab.

Gukas, Steve, dir. 2019. *93 Days.* Native FilmWorks.

Guterl, Fred, Naveed Jamali and Tom O'Connor. 2020. The Controversial Experiments and Wuhan Lab Suspected of Starting the Coronavirus Pandemic. *Newsweek* 27 April. https://www.newsweek.com/controversial-wuhan-lab-experiments-that-may-have-started-coronavirus-pandemic-1500503

Gutman, David, and Jim Brunner. 2019. Investigation into State GOP Lawmaker, Linked to Far-Right Extremists, to be Released. *Seattle Times* 20 December. https://www.seattletimes.com/seattle-news/politics/investigation-into-state-gop-lawmaker-linked-to-far-right-extremists-to-be-released/

Guy, Lindsey M. 2017. Review of Craig R. Koester, *Revelation: A New Translation with Introduction and Commentary. The Bible & Critical Theory* 13.1: 112–116.

Hajric, Vildana, and Claire Ballentine. 2020. Stocks Drop Most Since February 2008; Havens Gain: Markets Wrap. *Bloomberg* 24 February. https://www.bloomberg.com/news/articles/2020-02-23/aussie-drops-with-traders-cautious-on-virus-woes-markets-wrap

Halon, Yael. 2020. Dana Perino Calls Proposed $35M For Kennedy Center in House Coronavirus Bill "The New Bridge to Nowhere." *Fox News* 24 March. https://www.foxnews.com/media/dana-perino-democrats-coronavirus-bill-kennedy-center

Harriot, Michael. 2020. We Figured Out Why Coronavirus Is Killing Black People ... As If You Didn't Already Know the Answer. *The Root* 9 April. https://www.theroot.com/we-figured-out-why-coronavirus-is-killing-black-people-1842774532

Harriot, Michael, and Stephen A. Crockett. 2020. Maga vs. Hotep Conspiracy Theory Battle. *The Root* 17 April. https://www.theroot.com/maga-vs-hotep-the-coronavirus-conspiracy-theory-battl-1842907112

Harris, Margot. 2020. A Woman Inspired by Qanon Conspiracy Videos Was Arrested After Live-Streaming Her Trip to "Take Out" Joe Biden. *Insider* 1 May. https://www.insider.com/biden-qanon-supporter-arrested-attemp-live-streaming-trip-to-take-2020-5

Hartman-Caverly, Sarah. 2019. "TRUTH always wins" Dispatches from the Information War. In *Libraries Promoting Reflective Dialogue in a Time of Political Polarization,* edited by Andrea Baer, Ellysa Stern Cahoy and Robert Schroeder, 187–233. Chicago: Association of College and Research Libraries.

Hawkins, Devan. 2020. The Coronavirus Burden Is Falling Heavily on Black Americans. Why? *The Guardian* 16 April. https://www.theguardian.com/commentisfree/2020/apr/16/black-workers-coronavirus-covid-19.

Heath, Brad, Matt Wynn and Jessica Guynn. 2018. How a Lie About George Soros and the Migrant Caravan Multiplied Online. *USA Today* 31 October. https://www.usatoday.com/in-depth/news/nation/2018/10/31/george-soros-and-migrant-caravan-how-lie-multiplied-online/1824633002/

Heilweil, Rebecca. 2020. How the 5G Coronavirus Conspiracy Theory Went from Fringe to Mainstream. *Recode* by *Vox* 24 April. https://www.vox.com/recode/2020/4/24/21231085/coronavirus-5g-conspiracy-theory-covid-facebook-youtube

Heller, Jean. 2017 [1972]. AP WAS THERE: Black Men Untreated in Tuskegee Syphilis Study. *AP NEWS* 17 May. https://apnews.com/e9dd07eaa4e74052878a68132cd3803a

Hirsch, Afua. 2020. Why Are Africa's Coronavirus Successes Being Overlooked? *The Guard-*

ian 21 May. https://www.theguardian.com/commentisfree/2020/may/21/africa-coronavirus-successes-innovation-europe-us

Hofstadter, Richard. 1965. *The Paranoid Style in American Politics, and Other Essays*. New York: Alfred A. Knopf.

Hoft, Joe. 2020. Company Hired to Contract Trace Americans in Multiple States Has CEO Who Falsified Educational Backgrounds. *The Gateway Pundit* 6 June. https://www.thegatewaypundit.com/2020/06/company-hired-contact-trace-americans-multiple-states-ceo-falsified-educational-background/

Hogarth, Rana A. 2017. *Medicalizing Blackness: Making Racial Difference in the Atlantic World, 1780–1840*. Chapel Hill: University of North Carolina Press.

Holdorf, William J. 1987. Seat Belt Law an Assault on Freedom. *Chicago Tribune* 5 February. https://www.chicagotribune.com/news/ct-xpm-1987-02-05-8701090791-story.html

Hong, Caroline Kyungah. 2019. Comedy, Humor, and Asian American Representation. *Oxford Research Encyclopedia of Literature*. New York: Oxford University Press. http://dx.doi.org/10.1093/acrefore/9780190201098.013.809.

Horrox, Rosemary, ed. 1994. *The Black Death*. Manchester: Manchester University Press.

Hu, Jane C. 2018. Everything You Need to Know About 5G. *Quartz* 31 October. https://qz.com/1442559/everything-you-need-to-know-about-5g/

Huang, Chaolin, Yeming Wang, Xingwang Li, Lili Ren, Jianping Zhao, Yi Hu, Li Zhang, Guohui Fan, Jiuyang Xu, Xiaoying Gu, Zhenshun Cheng, Ting Yu, Jiaan Xia, Yuan Wei, Wenjuan Wu, Xuelei Xie, Wen Yin, Hui Li, Min Liu, Yan Xiao, Hong Gao, Li Guo, Jungang Xie, Guangfa Wang, Rongmeng Jiang, Zhancheng Gao, Qi Jin, Jianwei Wang, and Bin Cao. 2020. Clinical Features of Patients Infected With 2019 Novel Coronavirus In Wuhan, China. *Lancet* 395: 497–506. https://doi.org/10.1016/S0140-6736(20)30183-5

Huaxia. 2020. Confident Novel Coronavirus Outbreak Under Control by Late April: Health Expert. *Xinhua Net* 27 February. http://www.xinhuanet.com/english/2020-02/27/c_138824145.htm

Hubbard, Zachary K. 2020. Microsoft's Patent for Cryptocurrency System That Uses Body Activity Data, and Its March 26, 2020 Publication Date. *GematriaEffect.news* 19 April. https://gematriaeffect.news/microsofts-patent-for-cryptocurrency-system-that-uses-body-activity-data-and-its-march-26-2020-publication-date/

Hufford, David. 1982. Traditions of Disbelief. *New York Folklore Quarterly* 8/3–4:47–56.

Hume, Tim. 2020. Anti-vaxxers, Gun Nuts and QAnon: Germany's Bizarre Anti-Lockdown Protests Are Uniting the Fringe Left and Right. *Vice* 24 April. https://www.vice.com/en_ca/article/z3bpgx/anti-vaxxers-gun-nuts-and-q-anon-germanys-bizarre-anti-lockdown-protests-are-uniting-the-fringe-right-and-left

Humphreys, Margaret. 2002. No Safe Place: Disease and Panic in American History. *American Literary History* 14.4: 845–57. http://dx.doi.org/10.1093/alh/14.4.845

Hurst, Gayland W., and Robert L. Marsh. 1983. *Satanic Cult Awareness*. National Criminal Justice Reference Service. https://www.ncjrs.gov/pdffiles1/Photocopy/140554NCJRS.pdf

Hutter, Kristy. 2018. Three Percenters Are Canada's "Most Dangerous" Extremist Group, Say Some Experts. *CBC News* 10 May. https://www.cbc.ca/news/canada/three-percenters-canada-1.4647199

Itzkoff, Dave. 2020. Brad Pitt Plays Dr. Anthony Fauci in an At-Home Edition of "S.N.L." *New York Times* 26 April. https://www.nytimes.com/2020/04/26/arts/television/saturday-night-live-brad-pitt.html

Jackson, Jesse. 2020. A Continuing Terror, the Murder of Ahmaud Arbery. *Tribune Content Agency* 11 May. https://tribunecontentagency.com/article/a-continuing-terror-the-murder-of-ahmaud-arbery/

Jackson, Miles. 2015. A Conspiracy to Commit Genocide: Anti-Fertility Research in Apartheid's Chemical and Biological Weapons Programme. *Journal of International Criminal Justice* 13.5: 933–950. https://doi.org/10.1093/jicj/mqv060

Jackson, Sam. 2017. Conspiracy Theories in the Patriot/Militia Movement. Program on Extremism George Washington University. https://extremism.gwu.edu/sites/g/files/zaxdzs2191/f/downloads/Jackson%2C%20Conspiracy%20Theories%20Final.pdf

Jankowicz, Nina. 2020. Why We Need Information Distancing During the Coronavirus Crisis.

Newstatesman 3 April. https://www.newstatesman.com/science-tech/social-media/2020/04/why-we-need-informational-distancing-during-coronavirus-crisis

Jarrett, Mark, and Christine Sublett. 2019. The Anti-Vaxxer Movement and National Security. *The Infragard Journal* 2:1: 24–29.

Jarriel, Tom. 1985. *20/20*. The Devil Worshippers. Aired 16 May on *ABC News*.

Jessen, Nathan. 2019. Populism and Conspiracy: A Historical Synthesis of American Countersubversive Narratives. *American Journal of Economics and Sociology* 78.3: 675–175. doi https://doi.org/10.1111/ajes.12275

Johnson, George. 1983. *Architects of Fear: Conspiracy Theories and Paranoia in American Politics*. Los Angeles: Jeremy P. Tarcher.

Jolley, Daniel, and Karen M. Douglas. 2014a. The Effects of Anti-Vaccine Conspiracy Theories on Vaccination Intentions. *PloS ONE* 9.2: e89177. doi:10.1371/journal.pone.0089177

_____s. 2014b. The Social Consequences of Conspiracism: Exposure to Conspiracy Theories Decreases Intentions to Engage in Politics and to Reduce One's Carbon Footprint. *British Journal of Psychology* 105: 35–56. doi:10.1111/bjop.12018

Jones, Alex. 2020b. *InfoWars*. Episode aired 26 March. *PrisonPlanet TV*. http://tv.infowars.com/index/display/id/10499

Jones, Seth G. 2018. The Rise of Far-Right Extremism in the United States. *Center for Strategic and International Studies Briefs* 7 November. https://www.csis.org/analysis/rise-far-right-extremism-united-states

Jones, Seth G., Catrina Doxsee and Nicholas Harrington. 2020. The Escalating Terrorism Problem in the United States. *Center for Strategic and International Studies Briefs* 17 June. https://www.csis.org/analysis/escalating-terrorism-problem-united-states

Jones, Van. 2020. Black America Must Wake Up to This Viral Threat. *CNN* 7 April. https://www.cnn.com/2020/04/06/opinions/african-americans-covid-19-risk-jones/index.html

Joni, Saj-nicole. 2008. Never Waste a Crisis. *Forbes* 24 November. https://www.forbes.com/2008/11/24/global-crisis-management-lead-management-cx_snj_1124joni.html

Joseph, Andrew. 2017. Jaylen Brown Is Already Excited to Discuss Flat-Earth Theories with Kyrie Irving. *For The Win* (blog) 19 September. https://ftw.usatoday.com/2017/09/jaylen-brown-kyrie-irving-flat-earth-boston-celtics-nba

Journeyman Picture. 2020. Perspectives on the Pandemic | The (Undercover) Epicenter Nurse | Episode Nine. *YouTube* 9 June. https://youtu.be/UIDsKdeFOmQ

Joyce, Kathryn. 2017. The New War on Birth Control: How the Christian Right Is Coopting the Women's Rights Movement to Fight Contraceptives in Africa. *Pacific Standard* 17 August. https://psmag.com/magazine/new-war-on-birth-control

_____. 2020. The Long, Strange History of Bill Gates Population Control Conspiracy Theories. *Type Investigations* 12 May. https://www.typeinvestigations.org/investigation/2020/05/12/the-long-strange-history-of-bill-gates-population-control-conspiracy-theories/

Juan, Du. 2020. Wuhan Wet Market Closes Amid Pneumonia Outbreak. *ChinaDaily.Com.CN*, 1 January. https://www.chinadaily.com.cn/a/202001/01/WS5e0c6a49a310cf3e35581e30.html

JudyTsai. 2012. "Don't Use Your Cell Phone at the Gas Station [...]." *USC Digital Folklore Archives*. http://folklore.usc.edu/?p=15878

Kalčik, Susan. 1975. "...Like Ann's Gynecologist or the Time I Was Almost Raped": Personal Narratives in Women's Rap Groups. *Journal of American Folklore* 88.347: 3–11.

Kaler, Amy. 2009. Health Interventions and the Persistence of Rumour: The Circulation of Sterility Stories in African Public Health Campaigns. *Social Science & Medicine* 68.9: 1711–1719.

Karni, Annie, and Maggie Haberman. 2020. Trump Tests Negative for Coronavirus, His Doctor Says. *New York Times* 14 March. https://www.nytimes.com/2020/03/14/us/politics/trump-virus-test.html

Keil, Roger, and Harris Ali. 2018[2006]. Multiculturalism, Racism and Infectious Disease in the Global City: The Experience of the 2003 SARS Outbreak in Toronto. *TOPIA: Canadian Journal of Cultural Studies* 16: 23–49. https://utpjournals.press/doi/abs/10.3138/topia.16.23

Keith, Tamara. April 21, 2020. "Timeline: What Trump Has Said and Done About the Coronavirus." National Public Radio. https://www.npr.org/2020/04/21/837348551/timeline-what-trump-has-said-and-done-about-the-coronavirus

Kennedy, John M., Christopher D. Green and John Vervaeke. 1993. Metaphoric Thought and Devices in Pictures. *Metaphor and Symbol* 8:3: 243–255.

Kessel, Michelle, and Jessica Hopper. 2011. Victims Speak Out About North Carolina Sterilization Program, Which Targeted Women, Young Girls and Blacks. *NBC News* 7 November. http://rockcenter.nbcnews.com/_news/2011/11/07/8640744-victims-speak-out-about-north-carolina-sterilization-program-which-targeted-women-young-girls-and-blacks

Khalil, Seena. 2020. Donald Trump Calls COVID-19 "Kung flu" at Rally. *Al Jazeera NewsFeed* 29 June. https://www.aljazeera.com/programmes/newsfeed/2020/06/donald-trump-calls-covid-19-kung-flu-rally-200629091258959.html

Kim, Yoo Jung. 2020. Medical School Taught Me How to Talk to Conspiracy Theorists. *MedScape* 19 June. https://www.medscape.com/viewarticle/932592

Kinsella, Michael. 2011. *Legend-Tripping Online: Supernatural Folklore and the Search for Ong's Hat.* Jackson: University of Mississippi Press.

Kitta, Andrea. 2012. *Vaccinations and Public Concern in History: Legend, Rumor, and Risk Perception.* New York: Routledge.

_____. 2019. *The Kiss of Death: Contagion, Contamination, and Folklore.* Logan: Utah State University Press.

Klein, Betsy, and Jennifer Hansler. 2020. Trump Halts World Health Organization Funding Over Handling of Coronavirus Outbreak. *CNN* 15 April. https://www.cnn.com/2020/04/14/politics/donald-trump-world-health-organization-funding-coronavirus/index.html

Klein, Naomi. 2007. *The Shock Doctrine: The Rise of Disaster Capitalism.* Toronto: Random House of Canada.

Knight, Peter. 2003. Making Sense of Conspiracy Theories. In *Conspiracy Theories in American History: An Encyclopedia,* edited by Peter Knight, 15–25. Santa Barbara: ABC-CLIO.

Kofler, Natalie, and Françoise Baylis. 2020. Ten Reasons Why Immunity Passports Are a Bad Idea. *Nature* 581.7809: 379–81.

Kornfield, Meryl. 2020. Police Investigate Shooting Over a Face Mask in Michigan Store. *Washington Post* 4 May. https://www.washingtonpost.com/nation/2020/05/04/security-guards-death-might-have-been-because-he-wouldnt-let-woman-store-without-mask/

Koven, Mikel J. 2007. *Most Haunted* and the Convergence of Traditional Belief and Popular Television. *Folklore* 118:2: 183–202. DOI: 10.1080/00155870701337403

KrebsonSecurity 2020. Who's Behind the "Reopen" Domain Surge? 20 April. https://krebsonsecurity.com/2020/04/whos-behind-the-reopen-domain-surge/

Kukka, Chris. Massachusetts Enlists Volunteers for Its Contact Tracing Initiative to Curb COVID-19. *National Academy for State Health Policy* 11 May. https://www.nashp.org/massachusetts-enlists-volunteers-state-contact-tracing-model-to-curb-covid-19/

LaHaye, Tim, and Jerry B. Jenkins. 1995–2007. *Left Behind.* 16 vols. Carol Stream, IL: Tyndale House.

Lajka, Arijeta. 2020. Maps Do Not Show Link Between Coronavirus and 5G Wireless. *Associated Press* 8 April. https://apnews.com/afs:Content:8758210339

LaJune, April. 2019. Justin Trudeau Link to Epstein and the Pickton Pig Farm. *YouTube* 29 April. https://youtu.be/U6O4Uj2-r8I

Lamoureaux, Mack. 2020. Suspects of Canada Cell Tower Fires Are a Model and Failed Rapper. *Vice* 8 May. https://www.vice.com/en_ca/article/4aygzb/suspects-of-canada-cell-tower-fires-are-a-model-and-failed-rapper

Landes, Richard, and Steven T. Katz, eds. 2012. *The Paranoid Apocalypse: A Hundred-year Retrospective on the Protocols of the Elders of Zion.* New York: New York University Press.

Lee, Jon D. 2014. *An Epidemic of Rumors: How Stories Shape Our Perceptions of Disease.* Kogan, UT: Utah State University Press.

Lee, Julian. 2020. OPEC Underestimates China Virus. *Bloomberg* 15 February. https://www.bloomberg.com/opinion/articles/2020-02-16/opec-underestimates-china-virus-s-impact-on-oil-demand

Legum, Judd, and Tesnim Zekeria. 2020. The Dirty Secret Behind Ben Shapiro's Extraordinary Success on Facebook. *Popular Information* 25 June. https://popular.info/p/the-dirty-secret-behind-ben-shapiros

LeMarquand, Grant. 2000. New Testament Exegesis in (Modern) Africa. In *The Bible in Africa:*

Transactions, Trajectories, and Trends, edited by Gerald O. West and Musa W. Dube, 72–102. Leiden: Brill.

Lembcke, Jerry. 1998. *The Spitting Image: Myth, Memory, and the Legacy of Vietnam.* New York: New York University Press.

Lenepveu, V. [pseud.]. 1899. Caricature of Baron Alphonse de Rothschild as an Octopus with an Eyepatch. 2016.184.324. *United States Holocaust Memorial Museum Collection,* Gift of the Katz Family.

Levenson, Michael. 2020. Scale of China's Wuhan Shutdown Is Believed to Be Without Precedent. *New York Times* 22 January. https://www.nytimes.com/2020/01/22/world/asia/coronavirus-quarantines-history.html

Li Xiaosi (@li_xiaosi). 2020. Glad to hear the @_austrian airplane.... *Twitter,* 26 March. 3:20 p.m. https://twitter.com/li_xiaosi/status/1243233884130742272

Lillis, Mike, and Scott Wong. 2020. House Democrats Eyeing Much Broader Phase 3 Stimulus. *The Hill* 19 March. https://thehill.com/homenews/house/488543-house-democrats-eyeing-much-broader-phase-3-stimulus

Limbaugh, Rush. 2010. *Rush Limbaugh Show.* Episode aired 20 October, on *WABC.*

Lindahl, Carl. 2012. Legends of Hurricane Katrina: The Right to Be Wrong, Survivor-to-Survivor Storytelling, and Healing. *Journal of American Folklore* 125.496: 139–176. http://www.jstor.org/stable/10.5406/jamerfolk.125.496.0139

Lindelof, Damon, and Tom Perrotta. 2014–2017. *The Leftovers.* 28 episodes. Aired 29 June, 2014 to 4 June, 2017 on *HBO.*

Lindsey, Hal. 1970. *The Late Great Planet Earth.* Grand Rapids, MI: Zondervan

Lipka, Michael. 2019. 5 Facts About Religion in Canada. *Pew Research Center* 1 July. https://www.pewresearch.org/fact-tank/2019/07/01/5-facts-about-religion-in-canada/

Lipton, Eric, and Kenneth P. Vogel. 2020. Fine Print of Stimulus Bill Contains Special Deals for Industries. *New York Times* 25 March. https://www.nytimes.com/2020/03/25/us/politics/virus-fineprint-stimulus-bill.html?searchResultPosition=1

Longman, Nickita. 2018. End Forced Sterilizations of Indigenous Women in Canada. *Washington Post* 4 December. https://www.washingtonpost.com/opinions/2018/12/04/end-forced-sterilizations-indigenous-women-canada/

Loria, Kevin. 2018. Bill Gates Thinks a Coming Disease Could Kill 30 Million People Within 6 Months—and Says We Should Prepare for It as We Do for War. *Business Insider* 27 April. https://www.businessinsider.com/bill-gates-warns-the-next-pandemic-disease-is-coming-2018-4

Los Angeles Times. 1903. Medicos Meet. 3 June: 11. Archived at https://www.newspapers.com/clip/10421078/medicos-meet-radiophobia-1903/

Lui, Kevin. 2017. B.o.B. Starts GoFundMe Campaign to Prove the Earth Is Flat. *Time* 26 September. https://time.com/4956840/bob-rapper-flat-earth-gofundme/

MacFarquhar, Neil. 2020. Who's Enforcing Mask Rules? Often Retail Workers, and They're Getting Hurt. *New York Times* 15 May. https://www.nytimes.com/2020/05/15/us/coronavirus-masks-violence.html

MacKinnon, Bobbi-Jean. 2020. Doctor Linked to Campbellton COVID-19 Cluster Says He Made "An Error in Judgment." *CBC News* 2 June. https://www.cbc.ca/news/canada/new-brunswick/campbellton-doctor-covid-19-1.5594667

Magee, Ny. 2020. Idris Elba Slams Conspiracy That COVID-19 Doesn't Infect Black People. *TheGrio* (blog). 18 March. https://thegrio.com/2020/03/18/idris-elba-slams-conspiracy-theory/

Mandela, Barack. 2020. Ivanka Trump Is the New Queen Esther. *Times of Israel* 3 January. https://blogs.timesofisrael.com/ivanka-trump-is-the-new-queen-esther/

Mantyla, Kyle. 2020. Liz Crokin Claims Celebrities are Getting Coronavirus from Tainted "Adrenochrome Supply." *Right Wing Watch* 18 March. https://www.rightwingwatch.org/post/liz-crokin-claims-celebrities-are-getting-coronavirus-from-tainted-adrenochrome-supply/

Manuel-Logan, Ruth. 2012a. Black Conspiracy Theories 101: Church's Fried Chicken Will Make You Sterile? *NewsOne* (blog). 1 June. https://newsone.com/2018343/black-urban-legends-churchs-fried-chicken/

_____. 2012b. Black Conspiracy Theories 101: Tropical Fantasy Drinks Makes Black Men Sterile?! *NewsOne* (blog). 27 June. https://newsone.com/2022788/black-urban-legends-tropical-fantasy-soda/

_____. 2012c. Black Conspiracy Theories 101: HIV/AIDS Was Created to Extinguish Blacks. *NewsOne* (blog). 25 July. https://newsone.com/2026978/black-urban-legends-hiv-aids/.

Marshall, Alex. 2020. Marina Abramovic Just Wants Conspiracy Theorists to Let Her Be. *New York Times* 21 April. https://www.nytimes.com/2020/04/21/arts/design/marina-abramovic-satanist-conspiracy-theory.html

Martineau, Paris. 2017. The Storm Is the New Pizzagate—Only Worse. *Intelligencer* 19 December. https://nymag.com/intelligencer/2017/12/qanon-4chan-the-storm-conspiracy-explained.html

Mauro, Aaron. 2020. Coronavirus Contact Tracing Poses Serious Threats to Our Privacy. *The Conversation* 10 May. http://theconversation.com/coronavirus-contact-tracing-poses-serious-threats-to-our-privacy-137073

McEvoy, Louise. 2020. "Stevenage Medic's Anger Over Claims NHS Staff Are Deliberately Killing People During Coronavirus Crisis." *The Comet* 25 April. https://www.thecomet.net/news/facebook-group-suggests-nhs-workers-kill-patients-during-coronavirus-pandemic-1-6623487

McLean, Bethany. 2017. The Backstory Behind That "Fearless Girl" Statue on Wall Street. *The Atlantic* 13 March. https://www.theatlantic.com/business/archive/2017/03/fearless-girl-wall-street/519393/

McNeil, Donald G., Jr. 2019. Scientists Were Hunting for the Next Ebola. Now the U.S. Has Cut Off Their Funding. *New York Times* 25 October. https://www.nytimes.com/2019/10/25/health/predict-usaid-viruses.html

McNeil, Lynne A., and Elizabeth Tucker, eds. 2018. *Legend Tripping: A Contemporary Legend Casebook.* Logan: Utah State University Press.

Merlan, Anna. 2019. *Republic of Lies: American Conspiracy Theorists and Their Surprising Rise to Power.* New York: Metropolitan Books.

Michael, Katina, and M.G. Michael. 2009. *Innovative Automatic Identification and Location-Based Services: From Bar Codes to Chip Implants.* Hershey, PA: IGI Global. http://doi:10.4018/978-1-59904-795-9

_____. 2013. The Future Prospects of Embedded Microchips in Humans as Unique Identifiers: The Risks versus the Rewards. *Media, Culture & Society* 35.1: 78–86. doi:10.1177/0163443712464561.

Milbank, Dana. 2020. Could America's Pandemic Response Be Any More Medieval? *Washington Post* 30 June. https://www.washingtonpost.com/opinions/2020/06/30/could-americas-pandemic-response-be-any-more-medieval/

Millstein, Jeffrey. 2020. My Patient Survived COVID-19. Now She's Afflicted by Stigma. *The Philadelphia Inquirer* 3 June. https://www.inquirer.com/health/coronavirus/coronavirus-covid19-recovered-patient-stigma-20200602.html

Mintz, Frank P. 1985. *The Liberty Lobby and the American Right: Race, Conspiracy and Culture.* Westport, CT: Greenwood Press.

Misemer, Leah. 2019. A Historical Approach to Webcomics: Digital Authorship in the Early 2000s. *The Comics Grid: Journal of Comics Scholarship* 9.1:10, 1–21. DOI: https://doi.org/10.16995/cg.162

Mitra, Ritwika. 2020. "Communities Remain Hungry Amid Lockdown, Migrant Workers Worst Hit: Study" *The New Indian Express.* June 20. Accessed July 26, 2020.

Mock, Brentin. 2020. Why You Should Stop Joking That Black People Are Immune to Coronavirus. *Bloomberg CityLab* 14 March. https://www.bloomberg.com/news/articles/2020-03-14/no-black-people-aren-t-immune-to-covid-19.

Monmouth University. 2018. National: Public Troubled by "Deep State." *Monmouth University Poll* 19 March. https://www.monmouth.edu/polling-institute/documents/monmouthpoll_us_031918.pdf/

Morse, Hannah. 2020. Masks mandatory, Palm Beach County Commission Decides. *Palm Beach Post* 23 June. https://www.palmbeachpost.com/news/20200623/masks-mandatory-palm-beach-county-commission-decides

Mosher, Steven M. 2020. Don't Buy China's Story: The Coronavirus May Have Leaked from a Lab. *New York Post* 22 February. https://nypost.com/2020/02/22/dont-buy-chinas-story-the-coronavirus-may-have-leaked-from-a-lab/

Mould, Tom. 2016. The Welfare Legend Tradition in Online and Off-Line Contexts. *Journal of American Folklore* 129.514: 381–412. https://www.jstor.org/stable/10.5406/jamerfolk.129.514.0381

Myers, Steven Lee. 2020a. In China's Markets, a Thriving Lab for Viruses. *New York Times* 26 January [published online 25 January]. https://www.nytimes.com/2020/01/25/world/asia/china-markets-coronavirus-sars.html

_____. 2020b. China Spins Tale That the U.S. Army Started the Coronavirus Epidemic. *New York Times* 13 March. https://www.nytimes.com/2020/03/13/world/asia/coronavirus-china-conspiracy-theory.html

Nagle, Molly, and John Verhovek. 2020. Biden Releases Plan Focused on African-American Community, Racial Disparities in COVID-19's Impact. *ABC News* 4 May. https://abcnews.go.com/Politics/biden-releases-plan-focused-african-american-community-racial/story?id=70497573

National Association of Evangelicals. 2015. What Is an Evangelical? https://www.nae.net/what-is-an-evangelical/

Neergaard, Lauran, and Hannah Fingerhut. 2020. AP-NORC poll: Half of Americans Would Get a COVID-19 Vaccine. *Ap News* 27 May. https://apnews.com/dacdc8bc428dd4df6511bfa259cfec44

Nehamas, Nicholas, and Sarah Blaskey. 2020. The Price of Denial: Teenager Died After Attending Church Party as Florida Reopened. *Miami Herald* 10 July. https://www.miamiherald.com/news/coronavirus/article244027067.html

NewsOne. 2020. Farrakhan Warns Black People Against COVID-19 Vaccine and "Their Medications." *NewsOne* (blog). July 6, 2020. https://newsone.com/3971438/farrakhan-warns-black-people-covid-19-vaccine/ .

Newton, Leslie. 2012. Picturing Smartness: Cartoons in the *New Yorker*, *Vanity Fair*, and *Esquire* in the Age of Cultural Celebrities. *The Journal of Modern Periodical Studies* 3.1: 64–92.

Nguyen, Tina. 2020. How a Pair of Anti-Vaccine Activists Sparked a #Firefauci Furor. *Politico* 13 April. https://www.politico.com/news/2020/04/13/anti-vaccine-activists-fire-fauci-furor-185001

NIH (National Institutes of Health). 2019a. Electromagnetic Fields and Cancer. *National Cancer Institute at the National Institutes of Health* 3 January. https://www.cancer.gov/about-cancer/causes-prevention/risk/radiation/electromagnetic-fields-fact-sheet

_____. 2019b. Cell Phones and Cancer Risk. *National Cancer Institute at the National Institutes of Health* 9 January. https://www.cancer.gov/about-cancer/causes-prevention/risk/radiation/cell-phones-fact-sheet

Nix, Elizabeth. 2017. Tuskegee Experiment: The Infamous Syphilis Study. *History* 16 May. https://www.history.com/news/the-infamous-40-year-tuskegee-study

Noyes, Dorothy. 2018. Blaming the Polish Plumber, Blaming the French Voter: Bogeys and Attributions of Belief in Liberal Politics. *Journal of American Folklore* 131.522: 426–434. https://www.jstor.org/stable/10.5406/jamerfolk.131.522.0426

O'Donnell, Jayne. 2020. "Tuskegee Always Looms in Our Minds": Some Fear Black Americans, Hardest Hit by Coronavirus, May Not Get Vaccine. *USA Today* 19 April. https://www.usatoday.com/story/news/health/2020/04/19/coronavirus-vaccine-black-americans-prevention/5146777002/

Oelbaum, Jed. 2019. Ong's Hat: The Early Internet Conspiracy Game That Got Too Real. *Gizmodo* 21 February 21. https://gizmodo.com/ongs-hat-the-early-internet-conspiracy-game-that-got-t-1832229488

O'Hara, Andres. 2018. WTF is QAnon? "Pizzagate on Bath Salts" Gets National Attention at Tampa Trump Rally. *Gothamist* 1 August. https://gothamist.com/news/wtf-is-qanon-pizzagate-on-bath-salts-gets-national-attention-at-tampa-trump-rally

O'Kane. Caitlin. 2020. Televangelist Jim Bakker Sued for Selling Fake Coronavirus Cure. *CBS News* 12 March. https://www.cbsnews.com/news/jim-bakker-coronavirus-covid-19-fake-cure-televangelist-sued-by-missouri-symptoms-selling-treatment/

Oliver, J. Eric, and Thomas J. Wood. 2014. Conspiracy Theories and the Paranoid Style(s) of Mass Opinion: Conspiracy Theories and Mass Opinion. *American Journal of Political Science* 58.4: 952–66.

Olmstead, Kathryn S. 2019. *Real Enemies: Conspiracy Theories and American Democracy, World War I to 9/11.* 10th Anniversary Edition. New York: Oxford University Press.

Openshaw, Robyn. n.d. xZubi EMF Protection. *Green Smoothie Girl.* https://greensmoothiegirl.com/erinelizabeth/

@osamesama. 2008. Cell Phone Radiation Pops Popcorn, *YouTube* 30 August. https://youtu.be/pqIZDIxJgXw

Owen, Glenn. 2020. REVEALED: U.S. Government Gave $3.7million Grant to Wuhan Lab at Center of Coronavirus Leak Scrutiny That Was Performing Experiments on Bats from the Caves Where the Disease Is Believed to Have Originated. *Daily Mail* 11 April. https://www.dailymail.co.uk/news/article-8211291/U-S-government-gave-3-7million-grant-Wuhan-lab-experimented-coronavirus-source-bats.htmlgut

Owens, Candace (@realCandaceOwens). 2020. FACT: Bill and Melinda Gates, along with their partners. *Facebook,* 15 April. https://www.facebook.com/realCandaceOwens/posts/3655805241157317

Palma, Bethania. 2020. Did Chinese Doctors Confirm African People Are Genetically Resistant to Coronavirus? *Snopes.com* 17 February. https://www.snopes.com/fact-check/coronavirus-cameroonian-student/

Palmer, Richard. 2020. Coronavirus and the Mark of the Beast. *The Trumpet* 13 April. https://www.thetrumpet.com/22230-coronavirus-and-the-mark-of-the-beast

Pareles, Jon. 2020. Pop Music Faces the Coronavirus in Prime Time. *New York Times* 19 April. https://www.nytimes.com/2020/04/19/arts/music/lady-gaga-coronavirus-concert-one-world.html

Parham, Jason. 2015. Tupac Is Alive (and Probably Living in Cuba): A Conspiracy, Explained. *Black Bag* 31 March. http://blackbag.gawker.com/tupac-is-alive-and-probably-living-in-cuba-a-conspir-1693861660.

Patil, Anjuli. 2018. Why Groups Like the National Citizen Alliance Feel Comfortable Speaking Out. *CBC News* 28 May. https://www.cbc.ca/news/canada/nova-scotia/why-groups-like-the-national-citizens-alliance-feel-comfortable-speaking-out-1.4681406

PBS (Public Broadcasting Service). 2018. Black Genocide. *American Experience* 5 January. https://www.pbs.org/wgbh/americanexperience/features/pill-black-genocide/

Perakslis, Christine. 2013. Willingness to Adopt RFID Implants: Do Personality Factors Play a Role in the Acceptance of Uberveillance? *Uberveillance and the Social Implications of Microchip Implants: Emerging Technologies,* ed. M.G. Michael. 144–168. Hershey, PA: IGI Global. 10.4018/978-1-4666-4582-0.ch006

Perrotta, Tom. 2011. *The Leftovers.* New York: St. Martin's Press.

Pew Research Center. 2010. Public Sees a Future Full of Promise and Peril. *U.S. Politics & Policy* 22 June. https://www.people-press.org/2010/06/22/public-sees-a-future-full-of-promise-and-peril/

_____. 2018. Being Christian in Western Europe. *Religion & Public Life* 29 May. https://www.pewforum.org/2018/05/29/being-christian-in-western-europe/

Pew Research Forum. 2014. Religious Landscape Study. https://www.pewforum.org/religious-landscape-study/

Philipp. 2020. Corona-chan. *Know Your Meme.* https://knowyourmeme.com/memes/corona-chan

Philipp, Joshua. 2020. Tracking Down the Origins of the Wuhan Coronavirus. *Crossroads with Joshua Philipp.* 7 April. *YouTube.* https://youtu.be/Gdd7dtDaYmM

Phillips, Whitney, and Ryan M. Milner. 2020. *You Are Here: Field Guide for Navigating Polarized Speech, Conspiracy Theories, and Our Polluted Media Landscape.* Cambridge, MA: MIT Press. https://you-are-here.pubpub.org/

Phruksachart, Melissa. 2017. The Many Lives of Mr. Yunioshi: Yellowface and the Queer Buzz of *Breakfast at Tiffany's. Camera Obscura* 32.3 (96): 93–119. https://doi.org/10.1215/02705346-4205088

Pilgrim, Eva. 2018. Inside a Flat Earth Convention, Where Nearly Everyone Believes Earth Isn't Round. *Nightline* 27 June. https://www.youtube.com/watch?v=1gHbwT_R9t0

Plamondon, Raphaël. 2018. The Sustainability of Free Content: Learning from Webcomics. *Publishing in Action* 1: 119–125. https://ojs.scholarsportal.info/ottawa-school/index.php/PA/article/view/114

Plater, Roz. 2020. Why the African American Community Is Being Hit Hard by COVID-19. *Healthline* 14 April. https://www.healthline.com/health-news/covid-19-affecting-people-of-color

Plous, Scott. 1993. *The Psychology of Judgment and Decision Making.* New York: McGraw-Hill.

Potok, Mark. 2010. Rage on the Right. *Southern Poverty Law Center: Intelligence Report* 2 March. https://www.splcenter.org/fighting-hate/intelligence-report/2010/rage-right

Powell, Denise. 2020. Ahmaud Arbery's Murder Wasn't Shocking If You're a Black Runner. *Cosmopolitan* 9 May. https://www.cosmopolitan.com/politics/a32415907/ahmaud-arbery-murder-black-runner/.

Rahhal, Natalie. 2020. China Built a Lab to Study SARS and Ebola In Wuhan—And US Biosafety Experts Warned in 2017 That a Virus Could "Escape'" the Facility That's Become Key in Fighting the Outbreak. *Daily Mail* 23 January. https://www.dailymail.co.uk/health/article-7922379/Chinas-lab-studying-SARS-Ebola-Wuhan-outbreaks-center.html

Rahkonen, Carl. 2000. No Laughing Matter: The Viola Joke Cycle as Musicians' Folklore. *Western Folklore* 59.1: 49–63.

Randall, David K. 2019. Black Death at the Golden Gate: *The Race to Save America from the Bubonic Plague.* W. W. Norton & Company.

Ransom, Danielle. 2020. Keri Hilson's Coronavirus Conspiracy Theory About 5G Networks Has Black Twitter in Shambles. *BET* 16 March. https://www.bet.com/music/2020/03/16/keri-hilson-coronavirus-conspiracy-tweets-reactions.html

Rapaport, Daniel. 2017. Sammy Watkins Believes the Earth Is Flat. *Sports Illustrated.* 26 September. https://www.si.com/nfl/2017/09/20/sammy-watkins-los-angeles-rams-earth-flat

Raskin, Victor. 2008. On the Political Impotence of Humor. *Humor* 21.1: 26–30.

Ray, Daniel. 2020a. Personal interview with Wendy Welch. 24 April.

_____. 2020b. Personal interview with Wendy Welch. 13 May.

Ray, Rashawn. 2020. The Killing of Ahmaud Arbery Highlights the Danger of Jogging While Black. *Yahoo!News* 7 May. https://news.yahoo.com/killing-ahmaud-arbery-highlights-danger-203756569.html

Reagan, Ronald. 1986. Opening Statement at News Conference, Chicago, IL, 12 August. https://www.reaganfoundation.org/ronald-reagan/reagan-quotes-speeches/news-conference-1/

Rebecca Project. 2011. *Non-Consensual Research in Africa: The Outsourcing of Tuskegee.* Archived at https://web.archive.org/web/20180909133146/http:/rebeccaprojectjustice.org/images/stories/Fact%20Sheets/nonconsensualresearch20111120.pdf

_____. 2013. *Depo-Provera: Deadly Reproductive Violence Against Women.* http://rebecca projectjustice.org/wp-content/uploads/2019/12/depo-provera-deadly-reproductive-violence-rebecca-project-for-human-rights-2013-3.pdf

Reeves, Jay. 2020. In Clamor to Reopen, Many African Americans Feel Their Safety Is Ignored. *PBS NewsHour* 5 May. https://www.pbs.org/newshour/economy/in-clamor-to-reopen-many-african-americans-feel-their-safety-is-ignored.

Reid, Scott A. 2019. Conspiracy Theory. *Encyclopedia Britannica.* 2 January. https://www.britannica.com/topic/conspiracy-theory

Reuters. 2005. Spike Lee Targets Katrina for New Film. *Today* 12 October. http://www.today.com/popculture/spike-lee-targets-katrina-new-film-wbna9687336

Rich, Motoko, and Ben Dooley. 2020. Quarantined Cruise Passengers Have Many Questions. Japan Has Few Answers. *New York Times* 11 February. https://www.nytimes.com/2020/02/11/world/asia/japan-coronavirus-diamond-princess.html

Riedel, Stefan. 2005. Edward Jenner and the History of Smallpox and Vaccination. *Proceedings (Baylor University Medical Center)* 18.1: 21–5. doi:10.1080/08998280.2005.11928028

Rivera, Geraldo. 1988. *Geraldo Rivera Show.* Devil Worship: Exposing Satan's Underground. Aired 22 October, on *ABC.*

Rivers, Damian J. 2019. Political Cartoons as Creative Insurgency Delegitimization in the Culture of Convergence. *Discourses of (De)Legitimization: Participatory Culture in Digital Contexts,* edited by Andrew S. Ross and Rivers, 248–268. New York: Routledge.

Robb, Amanda. 2017. Anatomy of a Fake News Scandal. *Rolling Stone* 16 November. https://www.rollingstone.com/politics/politics-news/anatomy-of-a-fake-news-scandal-125877/

Robertson, David G., and Asbjørn Dyrendal. 2018. Conspiracy Theories and Religion: Superstition, Seekership, and Salvation. *Conspiracy Theories and the People Who Believe Them*, edited by Joseph E. Uscinski, 411–421. New York: Oxford University Press. doi: 10.1093/oso/9780190844073.003.0028.

Rogan, Josh, 2020. State Department Cables Warned of Safety Issues at Wuhan Lab Studying Bat Coronaviruses. *Washington Post* 14 April. https://www.washingtonpost.com/opinions/2020/04/14/state-department-cables-warned-safety-issues-wuhan-lab-studying-bat-coronaviruses/

Rogers, Katie. 2020. Protesters Dispersed With Tear Gas So Trump Could Pose at Church. *New York Times* 1 June. https://www.nytimes.com/2020/06/01/us/politics/trump-st-johns-church-bible.html

Rosenberg, Alyssa. 2019. I Understand the Temptation to Dismiss QAnon. Here's Why We Can't. *Washington* Post 7 August. https://www.washingtonpost.com/opinions/2019/08/07/qanon-isnt-just-conspiracy-theory-its-highly-effective-game/

Rosenthal, Jack. 2009. On Language: A Terrible Thing to Waste. *New York Times Magazine* 31 July. https://www.nytimes.com/2009/08/02/magazine/02FOB-onlanguage-t.html

Rosman, Rebecca. 2020. Racism Row as French Doctors Suggest Virus Vaccine Test in Africa. *Al Jazeera* 4 April. https://www.aljazeera.com/news/2020/04/racism-row-french-doctors-suggest-virus-vaccine-test-africa-200404054304466.html

Rozsa, Lori, Chelsea Janes, Rachel Weiner, and Joel Achenbach. 2020. The Battle Over Masks in a Pandemic: An All-American Story. *Washington Post* 19 June. https://www.washingtonpost.com/health/the-battle-over-masks-in-a-pandemic-an-all-american-story/2020/06/19/3ad25564-b245-11ea-8f56-63f38c990077_story.html

Samson, Andrea C., and Oswald Huber. 2007. The Interaction of Cartoonist's Gender and Formal Features of Cartoons. *Humor* 20. 1: 1–25

Samuels, Brett. 2018. Trump: I Wouldn't Be Surprised If Soros Were Paying the Migrant Caravan. *The Hill* 31 October. https://thehill.com/homenews/administration/414171-trump-i-wouldnt-be-surprised-if-soros-were-paying-for-migrant-caravan

Sansare, Kaustubh, V. Khanna and F Karjodkar. 2011. Early Victims of X-rays: A Tribute and Current Perception. *Dentomaxillofacial Radiology* 40:2: 123–125.

Santayana, George. 1906. *The Life of Reason, or, The Phases of Human Progress*. Five Volumes. London: Archibald Constable.

Savage, Maddy. 2018. Thousands of Swedes Are Inserting Microchips Under Their Skin. *NPR (National Public Radio)* 22 October. https://www.npr.org/2018/10/22/658808705/thousands-of-swedes-are-inserting-microchips-under-their-skin

Savage, Niara. 2020. Africa's First COVID-19 Vaccine Trials Have Begun in South Africa. *Atlanta Black Star* 30 June. https://atlantablackstar.com/2020/06/30/africas-first-covid-19-vaccine-trials-have-begun-in-south-africa/.

Schoen, Johanna. 2011. Reassessing Eugenic Sterilization: The Case of North Carolina. *A Century of Eugenics in America: From the Indiana Experiment to the Human Genome Era*, edited by Paul A Lombardo, 141–160. Bloomington: Indiana University Press.

Scott, Peter Dale. 1996. *Deep Politics and the Death of JFK*. Berkeley: University of California Press.
_____. 2007. *The Road to 9/11: Wealth, Empire, and the Future of America*. Berkeley: University of California Press.

Segal, Jakob, and Lili Segal. 1986. *AIDS: USA Home-Made Evil*. N.p.

Seppla [pseud. for Josef Plank]. 1938. Churchill as an Octopus. LC-USZ62–54514. Prints and Photographs Division, Library of Congress.

Servick, Kelly. 2020. COVID-19 Contact Tracing Apps Are Coming to a Phone Near You. How Will We Know Whether They Work? *Science* 21 May. https://www.sciencemag.org/news/2020/05/countries-around-world-are-rolling-out-contact-tracing-apps-contain-coronavirus-how

Serwer, Adam. 2020. The Coronavirus Was an Emergency Until Trump Found Out Who Was Dying. *The Atlantic* 8 May. https://www.theatlantic.com/ideas/archive/2020/05/americas-racial-contract-showing/611389/

Shafer, Ronald G. 2020. Spain Hated Being Linked to the Deadly 1918 Flu Pandemic. Trump's "Chinese Virus" Label Echoes That. *Washington Post* 23 March 23. https://www. washingtonpost.com/history/2020/03/23/spanish-flu-chinese-virus-trump/

Shahsavari, Shadi, Pavan Holur, Timothy R. Tangherlini, and Vwani Roychowdhury. 2020. Conspiracy in the Time of Corona: Automatic Detection of Covid-19 Conspiracy Theories in Social Media and the News. arXiv:2004.13783v1 [cs.CL]

Shelley, Cameron. 2001. Aspects of Visual Argument: A Study of the March of Progress. *Informal Logic* 21.2: 85–96. https://doi.org/10.22329/il.v21i2.2239

Shields, Leah. 2020. Jacksonville Research Center Needs Minority Participants for COVID-19 Vaccine Trials. *First Coast News* 26 June. https://www.firstcoastnews.com/article/news/ health/coronavirus/more-people-of-color-needed-for-jax-covid-19-vaccine-trials/77-0cf3040c-ff5f-4028-b890-e595af53ee17

Singh, Maanvi, Helen Davidson and Julian Borger. 2020. Trump Claims to Have Evidence Coronavirus Started in Chinese Lab but Offers No Details. *The Guardian* 30 April. https:// www.theguardian.com/us-news/2020/apr/30/donald-trump-coronavirus-chinese-lab-claim

Smith, Michelle, and Lawrence Pazder. 1980. *Michelle Remembers*. New York. St. Martins Press.

Stack, Liam. 2017. Who Is Mike Cernovich? A Guide. *New York Times* 5 April. https://www. nytimes.com/2017/04/05/us/politics/mike-cernovich-bio-who.html

@stevejacko. 2012. My Mobile Phone Cooked My Egg. *YouTube* 7 January. https://youtu.be/ l3ge9M54l7E

Stevenson, Alexandra, Nicholas Kulish and David Gelles. 2020. Frantic for Coronavirus Gear, Americans in Need Turn to China's Elite. *New York Times* 24 April. https://www.nytimes. com/2020/04/24/business/us-china-coronavirus-donations.html

Strasser T. 1989. "Health Passports": Changes and Trends. In *Travel Medicine*, edited by Robert Steffen, Hans Lobel, James Haworth and David J. Bradley, 528–530. Berlin: Springer.

Streicher, Lawrence H. 1967. On a Theory of Political Caricature. *Comparative Studies in Society and History* 9.4: 427–445.

Stutman, Shira, and Amy Spitalnick (@sixthandi). 2020. Hate of Pandemic Proportions. *Facebook* Livestream 20 May. https://www.facebook.com/sixthandi/videos/238219520608391/

Sullivan, Margaret. 2020. The Media Must Stop Live-Broadcasting Trump's Dangerous, Destructive Coronavirus Briefings. *Washington Post* 21 March. https://www.washingtonpost.com/ lifestyle/media/the-media-must-stop-live-broadcasting-trumps-dangerous-destructive-coronavirus-briefings/2020/03/21/b8a2a440-6b7c-11ea-11ea-9923-57073adce27c_story.html

Swire-Thompson, Briony and David Lazer. 2020. Public Health and Online Misinformation: Challenges and Recommendations. *Annual Review Public Health* 41:433–451.

Talev, Margaret. 2020. Axios-Ipsos Coronavirus Index: Protesters Fear the Spread. *Axios* 9 June. https://www.axios.com/axios-ipsos-coronavirus-index-week-12-protests-eed6e86b-f8a6-4e3f-9624-7c727dfa3397.html

Tangherlini, Timothy R. 2018. Toward a Generative Model of Legend: Pizzas, Bridges, Vaccines, and Witches. *Humanities* 7.1: 1–19.

Tangherlini, Timothy R., Shadi Shahsavari, Behnam Shahbazi, Ehsan Ebrahimzadeh, and Vwani Roychowdhury. 2020. An Automated Pipeline for the Discovery of Conspiracy and Conspiracy Theory Narrative Frameworks: Bridgegate, Pizzagate and Storytelling on the Web. *PLoS ONE* 15.6: e0233879. https://doi.org/10.1371/journal.pone.0233879

Taylor, Kevin. 2007. Boodog Roasting on an Open Fire. *High Country News* 24 December. Illustration by Ben Garrison. https://

@TCitizenExpress. 2020. [Patient 0 in Italy...]. *Twitter*, 25 March, 10:15 p.m. https://twitter. com/TCitizenExpress/status/1242975972221165568

Thomas, Helen Meriel. 2016. Six Musicians Conspiracy Theorists Believe Faked Their Own Death. *NME* 6 September. https://www.nme.com/blogs/nme-blogs/six-musicians-conspiracy-theorists-believe-faked-their-own-death-3524

Thomas, Stephen B., and Sandra Crouse Quinn. 1991. Public Health Then and Now: The Tuskegee Syphilis Study, 1932 to 1972: Implications for HIV Education and AIDS Risk Education Programs in the Black Community. *American Journal of Public Health* 81.11: 1498–1505.

Thompson, Hunter S. 1972. *Fear and Loathing in Las Vegas*. New York: Random House.

_____. 1973. *Fear and Loathing on the Campaign Trail '72*. San Francisco: Straight Arrow Press.

Threadcraft, Torry. 2020. YG Is the Latest Artist to Spread the 5G-Coronavirus Theory. *Okayplayer* March. https://www.okayplayer.com/culture/yg-5g-coronavirus.html

Tiffany, Kaitlyn. 2020. Something Is in the Air. *The Atlantic* 13 May. https://www.theatlantic.com/technology/archive/2020/05/great-5g-conspiracy/611317/

Trauner, Joan B. 1979. The Chinese as Medical Scapegoats 1870–1905. *California History* 57:1: 70–87.

Triggs, Robert. 2020. 5G Is Not Going to Microwave Your Brain: All the Myths, Debunked. *Android Authority* 7 April. https://www.androidauthority.com/5g-dangers-895776/

Tucker, Patrick. 2020. DHS Predicted a Summer of Violence, Radicalization, and Conspiracies. *Defense One* 25 June. https://www.defenseone.com/threats/2020/06/dhs-predicted-summer-violence-radicalization-and-conspiracies/166441/

Turner, Patricia A. 1993. *I Heard It through the Grapevine: Rumor in African-American Culture.* Berkeley: University of California Press.

Uscinski, Joseph E., and M. Joseph Parent. 2014. *American Conspiracy Theories.* New York: Oxford University Press.

van Prooijen, Jan-Willem, and Mark van Vugt. 2018. Conspiracy Theories: Evolved Functions and Psychological Mechanisms. *Perspectives on Psychological Science: A Journal of the Association for Psychological Science* 13.6: 770–788. doi:10.1177/1745691618774270

Vaughn, Robert. 1996 [1972]. *Only Victims: A Study of Show Business Blacklisting.* New York: Limelight.

Vedantam, Shankar. 2014. More Americans Than You Might Think Believe in Conspiracy Theories. *Morning Edition;* 4 June. https://www.npr.org/2014/06/04/318733298/more-americans-than-you-might-think-believe-in-conspiracy-theories

Verizon. 2019. What Is the Difference Between 3G, 4G and 5G? *Verizon (Personal Tech)* 18 November. https://www.verizon.com/about/our-company/5g/difference-between-3g-4g-5g

Victor, Jeffrey S. 1993. *Satanic Panic: The Creation of a Contemporary Legend.* Chicago, IL: Open Court.

Villarosa, Linda. 2020. "A Terrible Price": The Deadly Racial Disparities of Covid-19 in America. *New York Times Magazine* 29 April. https://www.nytimes.com/2020/04/29/magazine/racial-disparities-covid-19.html

Vincent, Danny. 2020. Coronavirus: A Cameroon Student on How He Recovered. *BBC News* 17 February. https://www.bbc.com/news/world-africa-51502711.

Virgil. 2016. The Deep State vs. Donald Trump. *Breitbart* 12 December. https://www.breitbart.com/politics/2016/12/12/virgil-the-deep-state-vs-donald-trump/

Vishneski, John S. 1988. What the Court Decided in Dred Scott v. Sandford. *The American Journal of Legal History* 32.4: 373–390. http://www.jstor.com/stable/845743

Vittert, Liberty. 2019. Are Conspiracy Beliefs on the Rise? *Live Science* 20 September. https://www.livescience.com/are-conspiracy-theory-beliefs-rising.html

Waisanen, Don J. 2011. Satirical Visions with Public Consequence?: Dennis Miller's Ranting Rhetorical Persona. *American Communication Journal* 13.1: 24–44.

Wakabayashi, Daisuke, Davey Alba and Marc Tracy. 2020. Bill Gates, at Odds with Trump on Virus, Becomes a Right-Wing Target. *New York Times* 17 April. https://www.nytimes.com/2020/04/17/technology/bill-gates-virus-conspiracy-theories.html

Wakefield, Jonny. 2019. Extremist Groups in Alberta Detailed in First-of-Its-Kind Report. *Edmonton Journal* 23 April. https://edmontonjournal.com/news/local-news/extremist-groups-in-alberta-detailed-in-first-of-its-kind-report

Wang, Chen, Peter W. Horby, Frederick G. Hayden and George F. Gao. 2020. A Novel Coronavirus Outbreak of Global Health Concern. *Lancet* 395: 470–473. https://doi.org/10.1016/S0140-6736(20)30185-9

Wason, Peter C. 1960. On the Failure to Eliminate Hypotheses in a Conceptual Task. *Quarterly Journal of Experimental Psychology* 12:3: 129–140. DOI: 10.1080/17470216008416717

Watson, Elijah C. 2020a. The 5G Coronavirus Conspiracy Theory Is False—That's Not Stopping Celebrities from Backing It. *Okayplayer* March. https://www.okayplayer.com/news/5g-coronavirus-conspiracy-theory.html.

_____. 2020b. Are Black People Immune to Coronavirus: How a Joke Turned into a Believable

Myth. *Okayplayer* April. https://www.okayplayer.com/news/are-black-people-immune-to-coronavirus.html.

Watt, Emily. 2020. 2020 World Watch List: 1 in 8 Christians Persecuted. *Open Doors New Zealand* 16 January. https://www.opendoors.org.nz/persecuted-christians/prayer-news/2020-world-watch-list-1-in-8-christians-persecuted/

Weiland, Noah, Emily Cochrane and Maggie Haberman. 2020. White House Asks Congress for Billions to Fight Coronavirus. *New York Times* 24 February. https://www.nytimes.com/2020/02/24/us/politics/trump-coronavirus-response.html

Weiss, Haley. 2018. Why You're Probably Getting a Microchip Implant Someday. *The Atlantic* 21 September. https://www.theatlantic.com/technology/archive/2018/09/how-i-learned-to-stop-worrying-and-love-the-microchip/570946/

Weiss, Sabrina. 2019. 5G Health Risks Are the Internet's New Favourite Conspiracy Theory. *Wired* [UK] 12 June. https://www.wired.co.uk/article/5g-health-risks-concerns

Welch, Wendy. 2020. *From the Front Lines of the Appalachian Addiction Crisis: Healthcare Providers Discuss Opioids, Meth and Recovery.* Jefferson, NC: McFarland.

Wells, H. G. 1940. *The New World Order.* London: Secker & Warburg

Wells, Veronica. 2014. Stay Woke! Crazy Conspiracy Theories Black Folk Believe. *Madame Noire* 25 February. https://madamenoire.com/404475/crazy-conspiracy-theories-black-folk-believe/.

Westcott, James. 2017. Marina Abramovic's Spirit Cooking. *MIT Press* (Blog). https://mitpress.mit.edu/blog/marina-abramovic%E2%80%99s-spirit-cooking

Weyn, Suzanne. 2004. *The Bar Code Tattoo.* New York: Scholastic Point Thriller.

_____. 2006. *The Bar Code Rebellion.* New York: Scholastic Point Thriller.

_____. 2012. *The Bar Code Prophecy.* New York: Scholastic.

White, Dawson. April 13, 2020. "Slashed Tires and Violence: Health Care Workers Face New Dangers Amid COVIC-19 Battle." Miami Herald. https://www.miamiherald.com/news/coronavirus/article241967281.html

The White House. 2020a. Statement from the Press Secretary Regarding the President's Coronavirus Task Force. 29 January. https://www.whitehouse.gov/briefings-statements/statement-press-secretary-regarding-presidents-coronavirus-task-force/

_____. 2020b. Proclamation on Suspension of Entry as Immigrants and Nonimmigrants of Persons Who Pose a Risk of Transmitting 2019 Novel Coronavirus. 31 January. https://www.whitehouse.gov/presidential-actions/proclamation-suspension-entry-immigrants-nonimmigrants-persons-pose-risk-transmitting-2019-novel-coronavirus/

WHO (World Health Organization). 2011. IARC Classifies Radiofrequency Electromagnetic Fields as Possibly Carcinogenic to Humans. *International Agency for Research on Cancer.* Press Release no. 208. https://www.iarc.fr/wp-content/uploads/2018/07/pr208_E.pdf

_____. 2015. World Health Organization Best Practices for the Naming of New Human Infectious Diseases. May. https://apps.who.int/iris/bitstream/handle/10665/163636/WHO_HSE_FOS_15.1_eng.pdf

_____. 2020. "Immunity Passports" in the Context of COVID-19. 24 April. https://www.who.int/news-room/commentaries/detail/immunity-passports-in-the-context-of-covid-19

Willrich, Michael. 2011. A Scar Nobly Got. *The Scientist* 30 June. https://www.the-scientist.com/reading-frames/a-scar-nobly-got-42261

Winfrey, Oprah. 1989. *The Oprah Winfrey Show.* Satanic Worship! Aired 11 May, on Harpo Productions [syndicated].

Wolchover, Natalie. 2017. Are Flat-Earthers Being Serious? *LiveScience* 30 May. https://www.livescience.com/24310-flat-earth-belief.html

Wong, Wilson. 2020. French Doctor Apologizes for Comments on Testing a COVID-19 Vaccine in Africa That Prompted Outrage on Social Media. *NBC News* 7 April. https://www.nbcnews.com/news/nbcblk/french-doctor-apologizes-comments-testing-covid-19-vaccine-africa-prompting-n1177991

Wood, Michael J., Karen M. Douglas and Robbie M. Sutton. 2012. Dead and Alive: Beliefs in Contradictory Conspiracy Theories. *Social Psychological and Personality Science* 3.6: 767–73. doi:10.1177/1948550611434786.

Wood, Roy., Jr. 2018. *The Daily Show.* CP Time: Government Conspiracies [segment]. Aired

20 July, on *Comedy Central*. http://www.cc.com/video-clips/qdgyoz/the-daily-show-with-trevor-noah-cp-time—government-conspiracy-theories.

World Bank. 2020. Fertility Rate, Total (Births Per Woman). *World Bank Open Data*. https://data.worldbank.org/indicator/sp.dyn.tfrt.in

Yingst, Alexandra (2020). "'I Really Need to Go Home': The Cruise Ship Employees Still Stuck at Sea." *Vice*. 20 May. https://www.vice.com/en_us/ *article/g5pb54/i-really-need-to-go-home-the-cruise-ship-employees-still-stuck-at-sea?*

Yocum, Margaret R. 1997. Family Folklore. *Folklore: An Encyclopedia of Beliefs, Customs, Tales, Music and Art*, edited Thomas A. Green, 278–284. Santa Barbara: ABC-CLEO.

@YTMostCensored. 2020. 5G Being Installed While Your Masters Tell You to Stay Home. *YouTube* 18 April. https://youtu.be/vqoi5eYDF60

Zadrozny, Brandy, and Ben Collins. 2018. How Three Conspiracy Theorists Took 'Q' and Sparked Qanon. *ABCNews* 14 August. https://www.nbcnews.com/tech/tech-news/how-three-conspiracy-theorists-took-q-sparked-qanon-n900531

Zambian Eye. 2020. African Blood Resists Corovirus. *Zambian Eye* 15 February. https://zambianeye.com/african-blood-resisit-corovirus/.

The Zambian Observer. 2020. Chinese Doctor Says African Skin Resists Coronavirus. *The Zambian Observer* 16 February. (Deleted from site). Archived at https://web.archive.org/web/20200314043101/https://www.zambianobserver.com/chinese-doctor-says-african-skin-resists-coronavirus/

Zhao, Lijian (@zlj517). 2020. CDC Was Caught on the Spot. *Twitter*, 12 March, 12:07 p.m. https://twitter.com/zlj517/status/1238111898828066823

Zingel, Avery. 2019. Indigenous Women Come Forward with Accounts of Forced Sterilization, Says Lawyer. *CBC News* 18 April. https://www.cbc.ca/news/canada/north/forced-sterilization-lawsuit-could-expand-1.5102981

Cartoons of Ben and Tina Garrison Discussed

Chinese Take Out. 25 January.
  Twitter: https://twitter.com/GrrrGraphics/status/1221173063292608512.
  Website: https://grrrgraphics.com/chinese-take-out.

Stock Market Catches a Cold. 25 February.
  Twitter: https://twitter.com/GrrrGraphics/status/1232321005084786688.
  Website: https://grrrgraphics.com/stock-market-catches-a-cold.

China in a Bull Shop. 28 February.
  Twitter: https://twitter.com/GrrrGraphics/status/1233417859541241856.
  Website: https://grrrgraphics.com/china-in-a-bull-shop.
  Retweeted 9 March: https://twitter.com/GrrrGraphics/status/1237015704395591681.

Deep State Cures. 2 or 3 March.
  Twitter: since deleted.
  Website: https://grrrgraphics.com/deep-state-cures

Black Swan. 9 March.
  Twitter: https://twitter.com/GrrrGraphics/status/1237034083722485760.
  Website: https://grrrgraphics.com/black-swan.

Make America Well Again. 12 March.
  Twitter: https://twitter.com/GrrrGraphics/status/1238123515619856390.
  Website: https://grrrgraphics.com/make-america-well-again.
  Retweeted 12 March: https://twitter.com/GrrrGraphics/status/1238258273314164736.
  13 March: https://twitter.com/GrrrGraphics/status/1238473627332272128.
  14 March: https://twitter.com/GrrrGraphics/status/1238977509409968128.
  Animated 19 March: https://twitter.com/GrrrGraphics/status/1240736070007848960.

The Blame Game. 14 March.
  Twitter: https://twitter.com/GrrrGraphics/status/1238839489113387009.
  Website: https://grrrgraphics.com/the-blame-game.

The Fear Parade. 16 March.
  Twitter: https://twitter.com/GrrrGraphics/status/1239565379334098945
  Website: https://grrrgraphics.com/the-fear-parade

Tina Toon: The Fear Channels. 17 March.
  Twitter: https://twitter.com/GrrrGraphics/status/1239939167183749123
  Website: https://grrrgraphics.com/the-fear-channels

Social Distancing. 18 March.
  Twitter: https://twitter.com/GrrrGraphics/status/1240282868082814979
  Website: https://grrrgraphics.com/social-distancing-with-joe-biden

Trump Ready to Help Americans. 19 March.
  Twitter: https://twitter.com/GrrrGraphics/status/1240694676539072512
  Website: https://grrrgraphics.com/trump-ready-to-help-americans

Tina Toon: Spare a Square? 20 March.
  Twitter: https://twitter.com/GrrrGraphics/status/1241025785844006913
  Website: https://grrrgraphics.com/spare-a-square

Beware the Deep State In a Crisis. 22 March.
  Twitter: https://twitter.com/GrrrGraphics/status/1241782661305098240
  Website: https://grrrgraphics.com/beware-the-deep-state-in-a-crisis

Tina Toon: The Visible Enemy. 23 March.
  Twitter: https://twitter.com/GrrrGraphics/status/1242114490964959232
  Website: https://grrrgraphics.com/the-visible-enemy

Pelosi Hates America. 25 March.
  Twitter: https://twitter.com/GrrrGraphics/status/1242892967049695232
  Website: https://grrrgraphics.com/pelosi-hates-america

The Plannedemic. 28 March.
  Twitter: https://twitter.com/GrrrGraphics/status/1243961164603609089
  Website: https://grrrgraphics.com/the-plannedemic

Tina Toon: Pelosi the Fiddler. 30 March.
  Twitter: https://twitter.com/GrrrGraphics/status/1244682323456454656
  Website: https://grrrgraphics.com/pelosi-the-fiddler

My Country. 1 April.
  Twitter: https://twitter.com/GrrrGraphics/status/1245417968315404288
  Website: https://grrrgraphics.com/my-country

Bill Gates Medical Fascist. 4 April.
  Twitter: https://twitter.com/GrrrGraphics/status/1246456156102385664
  Website: https://grrrgraphics.com/bill-gates-medical-fascist

Free Our Economy. 7 April.
  Twitter: https://twitter.com/GrrrGraphics/status/1247556619359023104
  Website: https://grrrgraphics.com/free-our-economy

Tina Toon: Face Mask Fashion Democrat Style. 8 April.
  Twitter: https://twitter.com/GrrrGraphics/status/1247900642854588422
  Website: https://grrrgraphics.com/face-mask-fashion-democrat-style

What Inflation? 10 April.
  Twitter: https://twitter.com/GrrrGraphics/status/1248640449675313155
  Website: https://grrrgraphics.com/what-inflation

Fire Fauci. 11 April.
  Twitter: https://twitter.com/GrrrGraphics/status/1249035186580250624
  Website: https://grrrgraphics.com/fire-fauci

Big Brother Bill. 13 April.
  Twitter: https://twitter.com/GrrrGraphics/status/1249705238816157696
  Website: https://grrrgraphics.com/big-brother-bill

Real Science Defenders. 14 April.
  Twitter: https://twitter.com/GrrrGraphics/status/1250099989046534145
  Website: https://grrrgraphics.com/real-science-defenders

Signs of the Times. 17 April.
  Twitter: https://twitter.com/GrrrGraphics/status/1251181082898083841
  Website: https://grrrgraphics.com/signs-of-the-times-2

Tina Toon: Horton Defunds the WHO. 20 April.
  Twitter: https://twitter.com/GrrrGraphics/status/1252249146431467520
  Website: https://grrrgraphics.com/horton-defunds-the-who

Oil Crash. 21 April.
  Twitter: https://twitter.com/GrrrGraphics/status/1252650430892396544
  Website: https://grrrgraphics.com/oil-crash

Give Me Safety AND Death. 22 April.
  Twitter: https://twitter.com/GrrrGraphics/status/1253165270421524480
  Website: https://grrrgraphics.com/give-me-safety-and-death

The Evolution of Bill Gates. 24 April.
  Twitter: https://twitter.com/GrrrGraphics/status/1253765524799975424
  Website: https://grrrgraphics.com/the-evolution-of-bill-gates

Goodbye Dear Leader. 27 April.
  Twitter: https://twitter.com/GrrrGraphics/status/1254804012940967936
  Website: https://grrrgraphics.com/goodbye-dear-leader

Fauci the Blue Demon. 28 April.
  Twitter: https://twitter.com/GrrrGraphics/status/1255231813884223491
  Website: https://grrrgraphics.com/fauci-the-blue-demon

Index

Numbers in *bold italics* indicate pages with illustrations

abortion 22, 89, 90, 113–114, 199
Abramovic, Marina 154, 200; *see also* Pizzagate
Adams, Jerome 93
adrenochrome 143, 158–159, 160, 206; *see also* QAnon
affirmative dismissal 214–215
Africa 73–*74*, 75, 81, 97–98, 100–103, 110, *111*, 113–114, 120, 174, 211
African-Americans *see* Black people
AIDS *see* HIV/AIDS
amplification 25, 98, 112–113, 150, 179, 204, 207
Antichrist 10, 112, 121, 123–125, 127, 129, 133
anti-lockdown 17, 24, 71, 91, 100, 135, 150, 152, 156, 172–173, 175–176, 197, 204–205
anti-semitism 12, 40, 56, 62–72, 86–87, 90–92, 94, 119, 125, 156, 163; puppet master 68–72, 114, 125; *see also* blood libel; scapegoats; Soros, George
anti-vaxxers 3, 7, 16, 17, 27, 51–52, 68, 95–116, *111*, 117, 189, 212; Smallpox 95–97, 140; *see also* vaccine
apocalypse/end times 16, 66, 88, 107, 117–118, 120–134, 138–139, 172
armageddon *see* apocalypse/end times
astroturfing 26, 98, 112–113, 135, 139, 204

baby boomers 56, 150, 160
Bannon, Steve 145
The Bar Code (book series) 128
bats 31–32, 34, 46, 66, 185, 186–187
Bezos, Jeff 67
Biden, Joe 160, 193
big pharma 46, 47, *48*, 52, 56, 103, 106, 110, 152, 178, 206
Bin Laden, Osama 18
Birth of a Nation (film) 90
The Black Death 59–68
"Black Lives Matter" movement 24–25, 94, 129; *see also* Floyd, George
Black people 9, 19, 50, 73–94, *82*, 99, 101, 102–103, 110–111, 113–114; 145, 169–*171*, 206; immunity 73–77, *74*, *76*; sterilization 85, 110–111; Tuskegee 83–85

blood libel 63–64, 163; *see also* anti-semitism; scapegoats
Bolsonaro, Jair 20
Boogaloo 7, 16, 72, 85, 88, 91
Bush, George H.W., Sr. 127
Bush, George W. 19, 83, 127

Canada 33, 87, 89–91, 110 ,111, 118, 137–138, 165, *171*, 173–174, 179; *see also* Trudeau, Justin
Centers for Disease Control (CDC) 50, 84, 114, 134, 172, 192, 194, 197
Central Intelligence Agency (CIA) 1, 11, *15*, 50, 81, 172, 18, 194
child sex trafficking *see* Pizzagate
China 2, 30–33, 35–42, *43*, *44*, 47 *48*, 49, 50, 52, 65, 66, 74, 165, 174, 185–191, 195, 199
Chinese stereotypes 31–33, 35, 186, *187*, 188
Christian Identity 86–88, 94
Christians 118–125, 128–130, 132–134, 138–139 *see also* Evangelicals
Clinton, Chelsea 135
Clinton, Hillary 14, 153, 154, 155–156, 197; *see also* Pizzagate
clustering bias 207
USNS *Comfort* 160–*161*
confirmation bias 22–25
contact tracing 134–141
Cotton, Tom 35–36
Cunial, Sara 21–22; *see also* Italy
cures 2, *74*, 102, 178; hydroxychloroquine 100, 198
Cusack, John *171*

deep state 12, 14, 19, 45, 46, 90, 103, 114, 143–147, 152, 155, 156, 163, 181, 182, 188, 191, 193–194, 196–197, 200; *see also* QAnon
DeGeneres, Ellen *157*
Department of Homeland Security 1, 91, 92
Diamond Princess 34
Diaz, Tracy 149; *see also* QAnon
digital tattoos 128, 130, 132, 140–141, 198, 199

elites 3, 12, 14, 26, *44*, 47, 49, 143, 146, 150, 156, 158–159, *161*, 163, 181, 199, 209, 211
end times *see* apocalypse/end times
Epstein, Jeffrey 153, 157
Evangelicals 117, 118–119, 121, 128, 131; *see also* Christians

Facebook *15*, 17, 24, 25, 53, 56, 85, 100, 104, 110, 150, 154, 160, 162, 165, 169; *see also* Zuckerberg, Mark
false flag 57, 109
Farrakhan, Louis 103
Fauci, Anthony 25, 36, 45–47, *48*, 52, 77, 103, 114, 151, 182, 197–199, 201
5G 11, 27, 38, 40, 47, 69, *74*, 108, 164–179, 182, *192*, 194, 196, 206; cellphones 167–*168*; COV-19 circuit 172–173; protection from 177–178
Floyd, George 3, 5, 24, 201; *see also* "Black Lives Matter" movement
4Chan 35, 33, *41*, *43*, *44*, 52, 55–56, 67, 68, 88, 149, 153, 154, *161*, 169, 180
Furber, Paul 149; *see also* QAnon
Freemasons 14, 40, 126

Garrison, Ben 7, 31, 180–203; "Chinese Take-out" *186*; "Fear Parade" *192*; "The Plannedemic" *195*
Garrison, Tina 192, 193, *195*, 196, 198, 199
Gates, Bill 9, 10, 16, 18–19, 21–22, 45, 47, *48*, 52, 103, 106–107, 112–116, *115*, 125, 130–*133*, 140, 172, 174, 188–189, 191–*192*, 194, *195*, 196–201, 214; *see also* Antichrist, mark of the beast; microchip; vaccine
Gates, Melinda 101, 103
great massacre *see* apocalypse/end times
great tribulation *see* apocalypse/end times

Hanks, Tom 157–158
Harrelson, Woody *171*
Hilson, Keri 169–170
HIV/AIDS 29, 32, 33, 51, 81–82, 100, 170; Fort Detrick 50
hoax 46, 50, 55–58, 67, 68, 136, 172, 175
Hollywood 143, 146, 154, 156, *157*, 158–159, 163, *171*, 206, 213; *see also* elites; Pizzagate
homophobia 32, 56, 88
hospitals 57, 109, 204
Hurren, Corey 162; *see also* QAnon
Hurricane Katrina *82*–83

Illuminati 27, 40, 126–127, 144, 199
immunity passport 109, 140–141
India 70, 102, 138–139
Instagram *15*, 75, 85, 162, 169–170, 182
Italy 21, 33, 60, 204; *see also* Cunial, Sara

Jacobson v. Massachusetts 96, 117, 139
Jones, Alex 14, 145–146, 154, 175

The Last Enemy (TV series) 128
The Late Great Planet Earth (book) 127, 130
Lee, Spike 82–83
The Leftovers (novel and TV series) 128
legend tripping *see* ostension
Lindell, Mike 196

mark of the beast 71, 117, 120, 123–125, 128–*134*, *133*, 139–142, 172, 197, 200–201, 214
masks 18, 23–25, 27, 129, 130, 198
McCarthy, Joseph 144
memes 14–*15*, *104*, 109, 149–150, 152, 204, 209, 215
Michelle Remembers (book) 150; *see also* Satanic panics
microchip 9, 40, 57, 108–109, 125, 128, 130–132, 134, 142, 194, 196, 214
Microsoft *see* Gates, Bill
Mikovits, Judy 25, 51, 103–*104*
militia movement 24, 45, 85–92, 94
Moreno, Eduardo 7, 160; *see also* QAnon
motivational interviewing 213–214
Muslims 16, 118–121, 128, 138–139; *see also* apocalypse/end times
myth 13

New World Order 16, 24, 27, 48, 68, 71, 90, 108–109, 125–129, 172
New York City 1, 70, 160, *161*, 204
Ngola, Jean-Robert 32
9/11 12, 19, 44, 91, 127, 145, 191
numerology *133*, *134*

Obama, Barack 12, 19, 20, 52, 71, 80, 91
One World Government 16, 17, 24, 45, 125–129,
Ong's Hat 57, 148–149, 212
organ theft 159, *161*
origin 49–52, 65–66, 107, 191; *see also* 5G; Wuhan
ostension 57, 136, 162, *176*–178

patient zero 32–34, 49
pedophiles *see* Pizzagate
Pelosi, Nancy 195, 196
Pizzagate 3, 25, 143–144, 146, 151–156, 160; Comet Ping Pong 154; *see also* QAnon
plagues: France 30; USA 33, 70, 73; *see also* The Black Death; SARS; Spanish Flu
Plandemic (YouTube video) 25, 51, 103–*104*
plandemic 172
prescription drugs 98
Prim, Jessica 160; *see also* USNS *Comfort*; QAnon

QAnon 7, 12, 17, 143–144, 146–152, *157*–158, *161*–163, 213; Satanists 151, 154–156, 159–160; *see also* deep state; Pizzagate; Satanic panics

racism 33, 35, 40, 44, 48, 65, 68, 75, 76–77, 79, *82*, 92–94, 100, 206; *see also* white power
Reddit 149, 153, 205
Revelation *see* apocalypse/end times
Riley, Teddy 170–*171*
Rockefellers *15*, 172
Rogers, Coleman 149; *see also* QAnon
Rothschilds 71, 172
Russia *41*–42, 50, 166

SARS-CoV (2003) 33, 38–39, 51, 185–186
Satanic panics 16, 126, 150–151
scapegoats 20–21, 28, 30, 48, 56, 60, 62–64, 66, 70, 94, 114
seat belt opposition 23, 24
second coming *see* apocalypse/end times
666 *see* mark of the beast
Soros, George 47, 67, 71, 107, 114, 125, 146–147, 197; *see also* anti-semitism
Spanish Flu (1918) 5, 31

Testing, Reaching, and Contacting Everyone (TRACE) Act/House Resolution 6666 134–135
totalitarianism 20, 27, 89, 90, 109, 135, 172
Trudeau, Justin 47, 71, 89–90, 114, 156–*157*, 162
Trump, Donald 12, 14, 20, 27, 31, 36, 45–46, 48, 52, 55, 71, 89–91, 99–100, 112, 125, 129–130, 145–146, 150–153, 156, 185, 188, 190–193, 196, 198; *see also* Antichrist; Deep State; QAnon
Trump, Ivanka 69
Turkey 145
Twitter 69, 75, 85, 91, 102, 112, 160, 170, *171*, 182

vaccine 19, 40, 47, 56, 69, 95, 101, 130–131, *133*, *134*, 138–141, 189, 194, 196–198, 200–201, 214; *see also* Gates, Bill; mark of the beast; microchip

West, Kanye 83
white power 67, 86–94,
Winfrey, Oprah 150, *157*
World Health Organization (WHO) 30, 45, 50, 98, 100, 107, 114, *115*, 166, 172, 190, 192, 197, 199, 201
Wuhan 30–31, 33, 34–35, 185; Huanan Seafood Market 185–186; lab theory 12, 34–36, 40–41, 45–47, *48*, 52, 191

YouTube 57, 103–*104*, 112, 135–137, 149, 150, 157, 162, 172

Zuckerberg, Mark *15*–16; *see also* Facebook

CPSIA information can be obtained
at www.ICGtesting.com
Printed in the USA
LVHW082023011221
704989LV00014B/451